D0377961

The Great Big Book of
Pencil
Puzzles

Selma and Jack Orleans

The Great Big Book of
Pencil
Puzzles

Selma and Jack Orleans

PERIGEE BOOK

Perigee Books
are published by
The Putnam Publishing Group
200 Madison Avenue
New York, New York 10016

Copyright © 1974, 1975 by Jacob S. and Selma R. Orleans
All rights reserved. This book, or parts thereof,
may not be reproduced in any form without permission.
Published simultaneously in Canada by General Publishing Co.
Limited, Toronto.

ISBN 0-399-50942-9

First Perigee printing, 1983
Four previous Grosset & Dunlap printings
Originally published as Pencil Puzzles 1, 2, and 3
Printed in the United States of America
                    18 19 20

contents book no. 1

contents book no. 2

contents book no.3

FOREWORD

THE GREAT BIG BOOK OF PENCIL PUZZLES is calculated to make the hours fly by as you guide a once-sharp pencil over the pages and fill in the hundreds of inviting puzzle blanks.

Included for your edification, but mostly enjoyment, are word scrambles, rhyming answers, multiple-choice quizzes, add-a-letter anagrams, vocabulary tests, mirror reflections, identi-quotes, equation puzzles, synonym and antonym tests and arithmetic problems, plus mini-puzzles, humorous stories, tongue twisters and much more. For added fun, many puzzles have been supplied with an Answers Correct rating system so that the solver can rate his abilities and judge where he STANDs. The categories are: Superbrain!, Terrific, Ability Shows, Not So Hot and Don't Ask.

If and when things get too rough, don't be too proud to consult a dictionary, Bartlett's Quotations, Roget's Thesaurus, an almanac or other source books. But remember, true knowledge comes from working out or *finding* the answers, not simply looking up the solutions. Speaking of the solutions, they are listed at the back of the book, starting on page 249. In some cases, where it was not feasible to include all of the possible correct answers, sample solutions only are provided.

Each book in the PENCIL PUZZLES series is meant to stimulate and challenge your mental abilities and provide hours of enjoyment, so good luck and happy solving.

WHAT DO YOU KNOW?

Select the correct one of the four possible answers for each item.

1. The first atom bomb was dropped in:
   1) July 1944   2) April 1945   3) August 1945   4) May 1946
2. Which of these were Vice Presidents who succeeded to the Presidency upon the death of the President?
   1) John Adams, Buchanan, Garfield   2) McKinley, Fillmore, Arthur
   3) Taylor, Jefferson, Coolidge   4) L. B. Johnson, Tyler, T. R. Roosevelt
3. The Library of Congress was founded in:
   1) 1878   2) 1854   3) 1815   4) 1800
4. Which was *not* one of the Confederate states?
   1) Texas   2) West Virginia   3) Tennessee   4) Virginia
5. The area of Iceland is about the same as that of:
   1) Florida   2) Virginia   3) Texas   4) California
6. How much did the U. S. pay for Alaska?
   1) $7,200,000   2) $15,600,000   3) $82,000,000   4) $122,500,000
7. Shakespeare was born in:
   1) 1506   2) 1721   3) 1564   4) 1812
8. The Prohibition (Eighteenth) Amendment became effective in:
   1) 1914   2) 1918   3) 1920   4) 1924
9. The famous poem at the entrance to the Statue of Liberty was composed by:
   1) Emma Lazarus   2) Walt Whitman   3) John Masefield
   4) Edna St. Vincent Millay
10. The state with the lowest rate of motor vehicle deaths is:
    1) Montana   2) Nevada   3) Massachusetts   4) Utah
11. The magazine with the largest circulation is:
    1) *Time*   2) *Reader's Digest*   3) *National Geographic*
    4) *Better Homes and Gardens*
12. Melbourne, Australia, is almost directly south of:
    1) Hong Kong   2) New Delhi   3) Honolulu   4) Tokyo
13. The nineteenth century began on:
    1) Jan. 1, 1800   2) Jan. 1, 1900   3) Jan. 1, 1801   4) Jan. 1, 1901
14. Which of these Presidents was assassinated?
    1) McKinley   2) Jackson   3) Harding   4) F. D. Roosevelt
15. Which language is spoken by the largest number of persons?
    1) Russian   2) Mandarin Chinese   3) English   4) Hindi

Answers are on page 250.

WHAT STATE ARE YOU IN?

The answer to each of the following clues is the *abbreviation* of the name of a state, possession or territory of the United States. For example, the answer to No. 1 is CAL — the nickname of former president Calvin Coolidge — which is also the abbreviation of California. (In a few instances, the clue is followed by the notation *sp*. In such cases the abbreviation and the item referred to are not spelled the same, although the pronunciation is the same.) Answers are on page 250.

1. nickname of a former president   _____

2. musical term   _____

3. exclamation   _____

4. girl's nickname   _____

5. another girl's nickname   _____

6. man's nickname (sp.)   _____

7. what miners dig for   _____

8. girl's name   _____

9. expression of sorrow   _____

10. nickname of a famous sports promoter   _____

11. proverbially, mightier than the sword (sp.)   _____

12. unfortunate state to be in   _____

13. good for the person who is in the unfortunate state   _____

14. half a score (sp.)   _____

15. progeny's sire   _____

16. religious ceremony   _____

	14 to 16 — S
	11 to 13 — T
	7 to 10 — A
Answers	*4 to 6 — N*
Correct	*1 to 3 — D*

TONGUE TANGLE

A tutor who tooted the flute tried to teach two young tooters to toot. Said the two to the tutor: "Is it harder to toot; or to tutor two tooters to toot?"

WORDS PLUS

From each word and the letter after it make a new word. You must make at least one change in the order of the letters of the original word. Answers are on page 250.

1. tapes   c   _____

2. taste   e   _____

3. crone   r   _____

4. lest   y   _____

5. base   u   _____

6. curse   a   _____

7. erase   c   _____

8. elope   p   _____

9. gaunt   h   _____

10. creeps   t   _____

11. marches   b   _____

12. rinse   g   _____

13. prone   s   _____

14. rope   a   _____

15. price   h   _____

16. meter   o   _____

17. dapple   i   _____

18. snore   a   _____

19. blame   r   _____

20. deign   n   _____

21. brine   d   _____

22. inmost   e   _____

23. inlet   s   _____

24. persons   e   _____

25. rituals   t   _____

26. claret   i   _____

27. ingrate   p   _____

28. trade   n   _____

29. scars   e   _____

30. greased   n   _____

	25 to 30 — S
	19 to 24 — T
	10 to 19 — A
Answers	5 to 9 — N
Correct	1 to 4 — D

TOOTHPICKS WILL DO!

You can work with the diagrams below, or you may prefer to use matches or toothpicks which you can move around. Answers are on page 250.

1. Remove 5 sticks and leave exactly 3 of the original squares. There must be no extra sticks left over.

2. Remove 3 sticks and leave just 4 of the original squares.

3. How many ways can you remove 4 sticks and leave just 4 of the original squares?

4. Move 3 sticks and leave 5 squares of the original size.

5. Remove 4 sticks and leave just 5 of the original squares.

6. Remove 5 sticks and leave just 6 squares, two in each row.

7. Remove 4 sticks and leave just 6 squares.

8. Move 2 sticks in such a way that you will have 6 squares of the original size.

9. How many ways can you move two sticks and still have 6 squares?

10. Move 3 sticks so that you will have 7 squares of the original size.

11. How many ways can you move 3 sticks so that you will still have 7 squares of the original size?

13

DO YOU KNOW YOUR "RINGS"?

For each description write one word ending in *ring*. For example, the right answer to the first one is *nearing*. Answers are on page 250.

A ring that:

1. approaches _____
2. makes beloved _____
3. causes dread _____
4. restores to view _____
5. is vulgar _____
6. flies high _____
7. fences _____
8. sweetens _____
9. plays a conspicuous part _____
10. talks incoherently _____
11. is faintly heard _____
12. smirks _____
13. grows gradually smaller _____
14. meddles _____
15. whines _____
16. delays going _____
17. comes inside _____
18. walks leisurely _____
19. harasses _____
20. tries to drive a bargain _____
21. serves _____
22. encourages _____
23. agrees _____
24. occupies space needlessly _____
25. burns without a flame _____

20 to 25 — S
15 to 19 — T
10 to 14 — A
Answers   5 to 9 — N
Correct   1 to 4 — D

SCRAMBLE

Make as many words as you can from the letters on each line, using all the letters each time. For example, from the letters *a e g l n* you can make the words *angel, angle,* and *glean.* Answers are on page 250.

1. a e g l n _____
2. e i l v _____
3. a p r s _____
4. u n g s _____
5. e i n s t _____
6. a e l s t _____
7. e i n s w _____
8. a e h l s _____
9. a g n o r _____
10. e f o r s t _____
11. e i l n s t _____
12. a b e l s t _____
13. a d e p r s _____
14. e g i n r s _____
15. a d e l s t _____
16. e h n o r t _____
17. a c i l o p t _____
18. a c e h s t _____
19. a g i n o r s t _____
20. a c d e i l m _____
21. a d d e m n _____
22. a e i n p r t _____
23. a b e e r t _____
24. a d e i r p _____
25. i n o o p s t _____

76 or more — S
60 to 75 — T
40 to 59 — A
Answers 21 to 39 — N
Correct   1 to 20 — D

SYNONYMS

For each word below give a synonym beginning with the letter *b*.

1. dark   _____

2. foundation   _____

3. impede   _____

4. inter   _____

5. annoy   _____

6. chatter   _____

7. whiten   _____

8. emblem   _____

9. frustrate   _____

10. equilibrium _____

11. vote   _____

12. expel   _____

13. insolvent   _____

14. savage   _____

15. sterile   _____

16. obstacle   _____

17. shy   _____

18. unpalatable _____

19. explode   _____

20. disseminate _____

21. margin   _____

22. protrude   _____

23. terseness   _____

24. confine   _____

25. trick   _____

26. gift   _____

27. quarrelsome _____

28. helpful   _____

29. genesis   _____

30. mix   _____

Answers are on page 250.

Answers are on page 250.

26 to 30 — S
20 to 25 — T
13 to 19 — A
Answers   6 to 12 — N
Correct   1 to 5 — D

WHAT NEXT?

The numbers in each line form a series. You are to write the next two numbers in the series. In the first series the next two numbers are 11 and 13. Answers are on page 250.

1. **1   3   5   7   9   __   __**
2. **32   16   8   4   2   __   __**
3. **3   6   12   21   33   __   __**
4. **0   1   4   9   16   __   __**
5. **85   60   45   30   15   __   __**
6. **1200   6   200   5   40   __   __**
7. **48   44   40   47   43   39   __   __**
8. **1   1   2   4   3   9   4   __   __**
9. **2   4   5   10   11   22   __   __**
10. **12   2   6   14   2   7   16   __   __**
11. **16   4   9   3   4   2   __   __**
12. **32   4   26   10   20   16   __   __**
13. **56   8   7   30   6   5   12   4   __   __**
14. **6   5   3   7   5   4   8   5   5   __   __**
15. **0   1   1   2   3   5   8   13   __   __**

	13 to 15 — S
	10 to 12 — T
	7 to 9 — A
Answers	4 to 6 — N
Correct	1 to 3 — D

PETER'S POSER

When Sherlock Holmes reached heaven, he was accorded a welcome suitable to his reputation. Saint Peter told him that everybody had looked forward to his arrival in the expectation of his demonstrating his remarkable powers of deduction. Holmes was pleased with all the attention that was shown him and said that he would be glad to oblige Saint Peter. Was there any problem in particular that they wanted him to solve? After a little thought Saint Peter suggested that a good test of Sherlock Holmes's genius would be whether he could pick out Adam and Eve from among all the souls in heaven. Holmes studied the matter very briefly and announced that he was certain he could identify Adam and Eve without any help from anyone. So Saint Peter and he set out and wandered about the celestial spheres among the many souls there. It didn't take Holmes long before he stopped Saint Peter, pointed to two souls and announced:

"There are Adam and Eve!"

Saint Peter and the many curious souls who accompanied the pair were astounded. When he was asked how he did it, Holmes replied:

"It was really very easy, you know,_____"

(If you can't fill in the rest of what Holmes said, look for the answer in the back of the book!)

Answer is on page 250.

17

SPOT THE STRANGER

Which word in each group does not belong with the other four?

1. emerald   green   olive   azure   lime
2. marigold   sweet pea   carnation   petunia   jonquil
3. inch   yard   meter   mile   foot
4. temper   discourtesy   impoliteness   rudeness   impudence
5. square   rhombus   rhomboid   triangle   rectangle
6. aphids   weevils   potato bugs   ants   cutworms
7. train   ship   bicycle   automobile   carriage
8. *La Bohème   Fidelio   La Gioconda   Lucia di Lammermoor   Rigoletto*
9. Labor Day   Memorial Day   Veterans Day   Election Day   New Year's Day
10. rabbit   mouse   beaver   lamb   squirrel
11. game   book   movies   radio   newspaper
12. seat   table   chair   bench   stool
13. magic   spell   charm   sorcery   astronomy
14. reduce   lessen   abridge   curtail   minimize
15. dream   phantasy   idea   vision   reverie
16. ant   roach   fly   mosquito   spider
17. slacks   pants   shorts   trousers   levis
18. constancy   obstinacy   stability   firmness   steadfastness
19. lyre   flute   piccolo   oboe   bassoon
20. turquoise   navy   lavender   indigo   sapphire
21. Manhattan   Cointreau   Bloody Mary   Martini   Screwdriver
22. *Cavalleria Rusticana   Madame Butterfly   Tosca   La Bohème   Manon Lescaut*
23. disgrace   humiliation   dishonor   ignominy   criticism
24. ostrich   chicken   kiwi   heron   emu
25. goat   kitten   colt   puppy   lamb

Answers are on page 251.

Answers Correct

21 to 25 — S
16 to 20 — T
10 to 15 — A
5 to 9 — N
1 to 4 — D

GEM

How many 6-letter words can you list, each containing four vowels?

_____   _____   _____

_____   _____   _____

_____   _____   _____

Answers are on page 251.

THROUGH THE LOOKING GLASS

For each figure below there are three mirror reflections, only one of which is correct. Pick the one that is the way the original figure would appear in a looking glass.
Answers are on page 251.

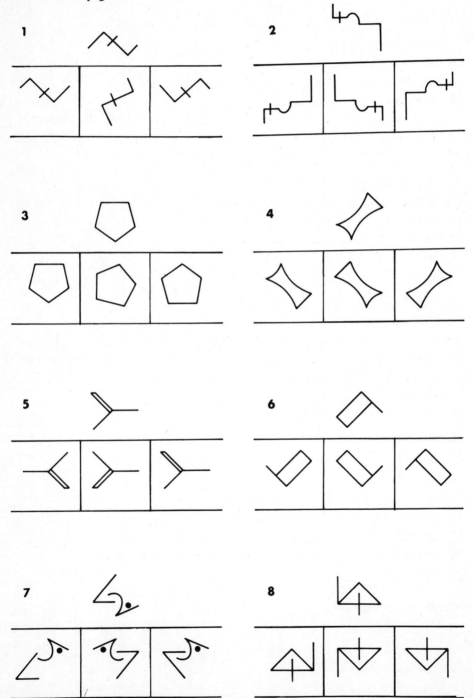

OPPOSITES ATTRACT

After each word below write its opposite. Each answer should begin with the letter *c*.

1. obey _____
2. warm _____
3. adept _____
4. desist _____
5. distrust _____
6. bless _____
7. deny _____
8. disagreement _____
9. order _____
10. soiled _____
11. dismiss _____
12. ruffled _____
13. agree _____
14. approval _____
15. oppose _____
16. unmannerly _____
17. quiet _____
18. continue _____
19. delicate _____
20. insincerity _____
21. destruction _____
22. unreliable _____
23. increase _____
24. optimist _____
25. disperse _____
26. loose _____
27. incongruous _____
28. discrete _____
29. parsimonious _____
30. unusual _____

Answers are on page 251.

Answers are on page 251.

	25 to 30 — S
	19 to 24 — T
	12 to 18 — A
Answers	6 to 11 — N
Correct	1 to 5 — D

DE UNO MULTUM

From each word below make as many words of at least four letters as you can. Only one form of a word is allowed — either *mean* or *meant*, but not both. Don't make words by adding the letter *s* to another word. You may not use proper nouns, foreign words, abbreviations, contractions or slang. Answers are on page 251.

DOMESTICATION

25 or more — S
19 to 24 — T
11 to 18 — A
Answers 6 to 10 — N
Correct 1 to 5 — D

MEASUREMENT

60 or more — S
50 to 59 — T
30 to 49 — A
Answers 23 to 34 — N
Correct 1 to 22 — D

TRANSPARENT

48 or more — S
36 to 47 — T
25 to 35 — A
Answers 16 to 24 — N
Correct 1 to 15 — D

NAMES OR WORDS?

After each clue below write an answer that is also a proper name (or nickname). The letter after each clue tells whether the name is masculine or feminine.

1. kind of collar, usually lace, worn about the shoulders by women (f) _____
2. plunder; harass; worry (m) _____
3. confidence; belief not based on proof (f) _____
4. place where rabbits breed or abound (m) _____
5. small domestic animal (f) _____
6. long cloak with a cape (m) _____
7. semiprecious iridescent stone (f) _____
8. candid; outspoken (m) _____
9. a nut (f) _____
10. mechanical contrivance for raising weights (m) _____
11. song (f) _____
12. large American bird with a red breast (f) _____
13. pity (f) _____
14. all right; OK; message received (m) _____
15. Irish girl (f) _____
16. college administrator (m) _____
17. nobleman (m) _____
18. another nobleman (m) _____
19. short crowbar; to pry open (m) _____
20. bestow; confer (m) _____
21. flower; fleur de lis (f) _____
22. kind of grass (m) _____
23. conqueror (m) _____
24. mechanism for spinning (f) _____
25. latter part of the day; early part of the night (f) _____

Answers are on page 252.

Answers are on page 252.

	22 to 25 — S
	18 to 21 — T
	10 to 17 — A
Answers	5 to 9 — N
Correct	1 to 4 — D

CREATE EQUALITY

Each line below has several numbers and arithmetic symbols like $+$, $-$, $\times$, $\div$, ( ). Every line also has an equal sign ($=$). You are to make an equation of the numbers and signs in each line, using all of them only once each. Here are three examples of how to do this.

3   4   7   =   + $\underline{3 \ + \ 4 \ = \ 7}$

3   6   8   10   =   + $\times$ $\underline{3 \ \times \ 6 \ = \ 10 \ + \ 8}$

3   4   4   9   22   = $-$ $-$ $\times$ ( ) $\underline{9 \ - \ 3 \ = \ 22 \ - \ (4 \ \times \ 4)}$

1. 2   3   3   8   =   + $-$ _____

2. 2   3   4   14   = $-$ $\times$ _____

3. 4   5   7   8   = $-$ $\div$ _____

4. 2   2   2   4   12   = $-$ $\times$ $\times$ ( )   _____

_____

5. 3   5   18   30   = $\div$ $\div$ _____

_____

6. 1   2   3   3   4   5   =   + $-$ $\times$ $\times$ ( )   ( )   _____

_____

7. 2   2   2   2   3   5   =   + $-$ $\times$ $\times$ ( )   ( )   _____

_____

8. 2   3   3   5   21   = $-$ $\times$ $\div$ ( )   _____

_____

9. 3   3   4   6   15   = $-$ $-$ $\div$ ( )   _____

_____

10. 2   2   2   3   3   5   =   +   +   + $\times$ _____

_____

Answers are on page 252.

LET'S PLAY HANKY PANKY!

After each expression write *two rhyming words* to which it refers. For example, an *obese rodent* is, in fact, a *fat rat*. Answers are on page 252.

1. obese rodent   _____
2. leading robber   _____
3. serious Indian   _____
4. chief road   _____
5. dull god of love   _____
6. valueless glue   _____
7. pure gustatory sensation _____
8. rational Scandinavian _____
9. prompt boy friend   _____
10. lively sewing gadget _____
11. Gallic female   _____
12. intense gleam   _____
13. more desirable missive _____
14. wide weapon   _____
15. stupid spiked animal _____
16. twofold globule   _____
17. more pleasingly pretty teacher _____
18. lively firewater   _____
19. memento-collecting Asian _____
20. colored Indian   _____
21. bigger arguer   _____
22. unobstructed insect   _____
23. big tow boat   _____
24. noisy mob   _____
25. comical animal   _____

	22 to 25 — S
	18 to 21 — T
	10 to 17 — A
Answers	5 to 9 — N
Correct	1 to 4 — D

WORDS! WORDS! WORDS!

From the four possibilities, select the correct meaning for each word at the left.

1. mien — attitude bearing conduct action
2. simulate — mimic reflect counterfeit feign
3. jovial — blithe hearty merry sunny
4. erudite — cognizant profound literary scholarly
5. bondage — confinement feudalism service slavery
6. unction — thrill anointing unguent lubricant
7. dogmatic — bigoted certain opinionated confident
8. emancipate — disband free release deliver
9. archaic — primitive obsolete antiquated old
10. nondescript — abnormal unnatural odd undefinable
11. knave — rogue shyster traitor trickster
12. hector — bully tease insult whip
13. gaunt — thin attenuated lean emaciated
14. warrant — authorization command firmness certainty
15. stalwart — lusty resolute hardy mighty
16. illicit — contraband arbitrary unlawful lawless
17. esoteric — unusual bookish profound erudite
18. theory — postulate hypothesis conjecture principle
19. mundane — worldly temporal empyrean carnal
20. custody — safekeeping bondage prison safety
21. gratuitous — unbiased exempt free independent
22. viscid — sticky slimy semiliquid thick
23. benign — tender mild indulgent kind
24. timbre — theme tone color melody euphony
25. perspicacity — shrewdness intelligence wisdom discernment

Answers Correct

22 to 25 — S
18 to 21 — T
10 to 17 — A
5 to 9 — N
1 to 4 — D

GEM

1. Name a word that contains three double letters. _____
2. Name a word that contains three double letters in a row — that is, with no other letters between them. _____

Answers are on page 252.

CAN YOU COUNT WHAT YOU CAN'T SEE?

Although you can't see all the blocks in each pile below, try to count them. Near each pile write the number of blocks in it. If there is a block missing from the outside of a pile and you can't tell what is behind or below it, assume that all the blocks in that row or column are missing. Answers are on page 252.

1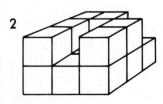

5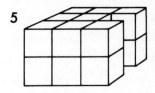

2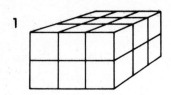

6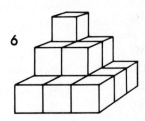

3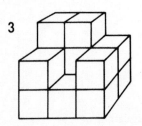

7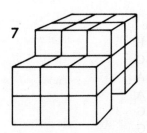

4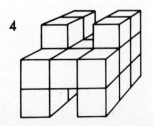

8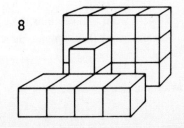

WHAT IS THE ANSWER?

1. Tom, Dick, and Harry were playing ball, and one of them threw the ball through a window of a neighboring house, breaking the window. The owner of the house questioned the boys. Each of them made three statements. Later, each admitted he had made one false statement. These are the statements they made:

   Harry: It was not my fault. I didn't even know the window was broken. I think the window was cracked before it was hit.

   Dick: I didn't break the window. Tom saw the ball break the window. When Tom had the ball last he threw it to Harry.

   Tom: I didn't throw the ball through the window. I didn't see the ball hit the window at all. When I had the ball last I threw it to Dick.

   Which one of the boys broke the window?

2. Dr. Alice Jones, Dr. Millie White, and Dr. Susie Smith were (*not* respectively) a dentist, a veterinary, and a physician. Alice Jones, Millie White, and Susie Smith were (*not* respectively) their nurses.
   a. The physician's office was farther uptown than the offices of the dentist and the veterinary.
   b. Millie White and Susie Smith roomed together.
   c. Dr. Smith and Alice Jones went to college together.
   d. The dentist's nurse was much younger than the dentist.
   e. Susie and Millie walked to work together every morning.
   f. Susie Smith was afraid of horses.
   g. Dr. Jones specialized in ear, nose, and throat cases.
   h. Alice Jones was the dentist's nurse.
   Who was the veterinary's nurse? What was the name of the dentist?

3. The following facts are known concerning the ancestry of Herbert Kent:
   a. His father's father was named Carl.
   b. Carl Nolan married Grace Done.
   c. Alice Done was the wife of Carl Kent.
   d. Alice Done had only one son, George.
   e. Grace Done was Mary Nolan's mother.
   f. George Kent was Mary Nolan's husband.
   What was the name of Herbert's grandfather on his mother's side?

Answers are on page 252.

27

WORDS PLUS

From each word and the letter after it make a new word, with at least one change in the order of the letters of the original word. Answers are on page 252.

1. game   i   _____
2. tear   f   _____
3. safe   l   _____
4. trees   c   _____
5. taper   e   _____
6. charts   c   _____
7. cancel   o   _____
8. preach   t   _____
9. scooped   m   _____
10. rote   w   _____
11. peers   h   _____
12. sling   a   _____
13. danced   i   _____
14. tried   c   _____
15. ogre   f   _____
16. tiny   u   _____
17. stirs   e   _____
18. brave   l   _____
19. pretense   r   _____
20. maple   s   _____
21. drive   a   _____
22. sail   a   _____
23. grieve   d   _____
24. tiding   y   _____
25. resign   y   _____
26. liars   o   _____
27. parson   o   _____
28. patterned   m   _____
29. charters   o   _____
30. tirades   s   _____

26 or more — S
20 to 25 — T
11 to 19 — A
Answers   5 to 10 — N
Correct   1 to   4 — D

STRANGE THINGS ABOUT WORDS

1. There are supposed to be just four words in the English language ending in *dous*. Can you name them?

   _____

2. Name a word with all five vowels in the order in which they appear in the alphabet.

   _____

3. Name an 8-letter word with all 5 vowels.

   _____

4. Name 10 other words with all 5 vowels.

   _____

5. What 5-letter word contains 3 e's?

   _____

6. Name a 6-letter word made up of two letters, each letter occurring three times.

   _____

7. Name a word with 6 i's in it.

   _____

8. Name a word with 5 a's.

   _____

9. Name a word with 5 e's.

   _____

10. Name a word with 4 o's.

    _____

11. Name a word with 4 u's.

    _____

12. Name a word with 4 a's.

    _____

13. What is the etymology of *good-bye*?

    _____

14. In how many ways can *ough* be pronounced? Give an illustration for each pronunciation.

    _____

15. What is the longest word that has only 1 vowel?

    _____

16. List as many 5-letter words as you can each containing 2 vowels and 3 consonants, all 3 consonants being the same letter.

    _____

17. What 5-letter words retain the same pronunciation after the removal of 4 of the letters?

    _____

18. List as many 5-letter words as you can each containing 4 vowels.

    _____

Answers are on page 252.

GEM

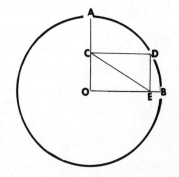

In the circle at the right the lines OA and OB are radii drawn at right angles to each other. The radius of the circle is fifteen feet long. The line CD is drawn from *any* point on OA and at right angles to OA, cutting the circumference at D. The line DE is drawn at right angles to OB.
How long is line CE?

Answer is on page 253.

ARE YOU A TOP SHOPPER?

Here is a list of foods with the price of each. How many of the questions about these foods can you answer? Answers are on page 253.

apples are 3 for 20¢   oranges are 60¢ a dozen
bananas are 5¢ each   melons are 30¢ each
carrots are 2 bunches for 25¢   pineapples are 3 for $1.00
grapes are 2 lbs. for 45¢   raspberries are 40¢ a box
               watermelons are $1.25 each

1. How many apples cost the same as a dozen oranges?
_____

2. How many melons cost the same as two dozen oranges?
_____

3. How many bunches of carrots cost the same as 3 pineapples?
_____

4. How many bananas cost as much as 2 melons?
_____

5. How many bunches of carrots cost the same as a watermelon?
_____

6. How many boxes of raspberries cost the same as two dozen oranges?
_____

7. How many pounds of grapes cost the same as 3 dozen oranges?
_____

8. How many apples cost the same as 8 bunches of carrots?
_____

9. How many melons cost the same as 3 boxes of raspberries?
_____

10. How many pounds of grapes cost the same as 3 pineapples?
_____

11. How many oranges cost the same as 2 watermelons?
_____

12. How many apples cost the same as a box of raspberries?
_____

                                    11 to 12 — S
                                    9 to 10 — T
                                    6 to 8 — A
                  Answers   3 to 5 — N
                  Correct   1 to 2 — D

ESTRANGED RELATIONS

What relation to you is your:

1. father's brother's uncle's sister? _____
2. grandmother's nephew's daughter? _____
3. aunt's mother's father's wife? _____
4. mother's aunt's grandson? _____
5. brother's son's sister's mother? _____
6. cousin's aunt's daughter's brother? _____
7. sister-in-law's father-in-law's grandson? _____
8. sister's father's stepson's mother? _____
9. uncle's father's only grandchild? _____
10. brother-in-law's wife's grandmother's husband? _____
11. uncle's father's mother's husband? _____
12. aunt's mother's granddaughter's only sibling? _____
13. granddaughter's brother's mother's mother-in-law? _____
14. niece's father's only brother? _____
15. aunt's husband's sister's daughter? _____

Answers are on page 253.

GEM

See if you can do this four-by-four crossword puzzle. Answers are on page 253.

Across

1. a strap
5. (slang) a blow
6. a time zone
7. a conveyor

Down

1. insects that hum
2. relaxation
3. building extensions
4. annoy

1	2	3	4
5			
6			
7			

SYNONYMS

For each word below give a synonym beginning with the letter *h*.
Answers are on page 253.

1. throng   _____
2. custom   _____
3. careless   _____
4. collect   _____
5. tender-hearted   _____
6. stop   _____
7. damp   _____
8. bargain   _____
9. pagan   _____
10. mirth   _____
11. proud   _____
12. valiant   _____
13. frank   _____
14. gaunt   _____
15. incurable   _____
16. psalm   _____
17. pester   _____
18. sanctity   _____
19. antagonistic   _____
20. beautiful   _____
21. austere   _____
22. pause   _____
23. delude   _____
24. meek   _____
25. random   _____
26. consecrate   _____
27. obstruct   _____
28. raise   _____
29. available   _____
30. submission   _____

	25 to 30 — S
	19 to 24 — T
	11 to 18 — A
Answers	5 to 10 — N
Correct	1 to 5 — D

DO YOU HAVE THE TIME?

Below is a list of different times of the day. Beside each time, write what the time would be if the minute hand and hour hand were interchanged. Do this mentally . . . no fair drawing clock faces! Answers are on page 253.

1. 3:01 _____

2. 6:07 _____

3. 4:22 _____

4. 3:42 _____

5. 9:08 _____

6. 2:35 _____

7. 5:32 _____

8. 8:23 _____

9. 12:06 _____

10. 8:47 _____

11. 12:51 _____

12. 7:18 _____

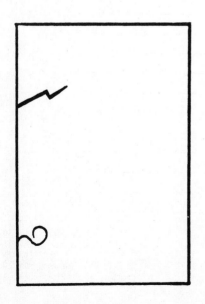

GEM

The famous French author Victor Hugo was known for his doodles. At the left is one of his better-known doodles. Can you tell what it is supposed to represent?

Answer is on page 253.

HOW GOOD ARE YOUR "IZE"?

For each clue below write one word ending in *ize*. The correct answer to the first one is *fraternize*. Answers are on page 253.

1. become friendly   _____
2. migrate and settle   _____
3. spray   _____
4. sear with a heated iron   _____
5. make greater   _____
6. make valid   _____
7. identify   _____
8. examine   _____
9. censure   _____
10. suffer   _____
11. oppose   _____
12. belittle   _____
13. exclude   _____
14. treat in a condescending manner   _____
15. liquidate   _____
16. make universal   _____
17. reconcile   _____
18. inoculate   _____
19. hypnotize   _____
20. describe   _____
21. acquaint   _____
22. granulate   _____
23. impoverish   _____
24. arrange in an order   _____
25. act with indecision   _____
26. empower   _____
27. punish   _____
28. change rapidly   _____
29. represent   _____
30. save   _____

	24 to 30 — S
	19 to 23 — T
	11 to 18 — A
Answers	6 to 10 — N
Correct	1 to 5 — D

SCRAMBLE

Make as many words as you can from the letters on each line, using *all* the letters each time. Answers are on page 253.

1. g m s u _____

2. a e m t _____

3. t l a s _____

4. e i m r _____

5. e f h l s _____

6. b d e e i l _____

7. a e p r s _____

8. e i m r s t _____

9. d e i r r _____

10. c e l r u _____

11. a e h p s _____

12. e e r s t t _____

13. a d e e s t _____

14. a d e g n r _____

15. a c e i l t t _____

16. e l m n o s _____

17. d e i r w _____

18. e n o s t _____

19. a e h r s _____

20. d e i n s t t _____

21. a c i n n o s t _____

22. o c l s t u _____

23. s e i g d n _____

24. a c e p s _____

25. a e g i l m n n t _____

60 or more — S
40 to 59 — T
26 to 39 — A
Answers   13 to 25 — N
Correct   1 to 12 — D

TOOTHPICKS WILL DO!

1. Remove 4 sticks and leave just 5 of the original squares.

2. Remove 2 sticks and leave just 6 of the original squares.

3. Move one stick so that you will still have 7 squares.

4. Move 2 sticks so that you will have 8 squares.

---

5. Remove 4 sticks and leave just 8 of the original squares.

6. How many ways can you remove 4 sticks and still leave just 8 squares?

7. Remove 3 sticks and leave just 9 squares.

8. Remove 3 sticks and leave 10 squares.

---

9. Remove 4 sticks and leave just 7 squares.

10. Remove 8 sticks and leave just 6 squares.

11. Remove 1 stick and leave 8 squares.

12. Remove 3 sticks and leave 7 squares.

Answers are on page 254.

SPOT THE STRANGER

Which word in each group does not belong with the other four?

1. France   Korea   Japan   China   Siberia
2. pinochle   Scrabble   bridge   canasta   casino
3. Huron   Suez   Panama   Kiel   Welland
4. gallant   brave   knightly   chivalrous   reckless
5. dictionary   encyclopedia   reader   atlas   almanac
6. nicotine   anaesthetic   drug   sedative   opiate
7. tale   narrative   picture   anecdote   account
8. kiosk   church   synagogue   mosque   temple
9. enraged   incensed   irate   furious   annoyed
10. bee   drone   wasp   termite   hornet
11. pine   maple   juniper   cypress   spruce
12. pillowcase   facial tissue   sheet   towel   tablecloth
13. carpet   rug   mat   lawn   linoleum
14. answer   response   reply   acknowledgment   contradiction
15. sword   scimitar   revolver   saber   cutlass
16. debarkation   advent   homecoming   arrival   destination
17. Beethoven   Raphael   Rembrandt   Michelangelo   Hals
18. *Aida   Rigoletto   Tosca   La Traviata   Il Trovatore*
19. apology   regret   penance   compromise   excuse
20. wind   current   breeze   zephyr   draft
21. linen   wool   cotton   nylon   silk
22. jet   ink   ebony   soot   charcoal
23. amethyst   opal   garnet   ruby   turquoise
24. solo   octet   sextet   quartet   trio
25. lemon   gold   canary   saffron   chartreuse

Answers are on page 254.

	20 to 25	— S
	16 to 19	— T
	10 to 15	— A
Answers	5 to 9	— N
Correct	1 to 4	— D

GEM

What two American coins, one of which is not a nickel, add up to 15¢?
Answer is on page 254.

WHAT'S MISSING?

John Heywood, who lived in England (1497–1580), published a book in 1546 "conteyning the number in effect of all the proverbes in the English tongue. . . ." The following are taken from an 1874 reprint. Can you fill in the missing words?

1. When the sunne shineth make ___ ___ ___.
2. The ___ ___ ___ ___ tarrieth for no man.
3. Better to ___ ___ ___ ___ than to take.
4. Two ___ ___ ___ ___ ___ are better than one.
5. When all candles bee out, all cats be ___ ___ ___ ___.
6. Neither fish, nor flesh, nor ___ ___ ___ ___ red herring.
7. Better ___ ___ ___ ___ than never.
8. A ___ ___ ___ ___ for your thoughts.
9. Many hands make ___ ___ ___ ___ ___ warke.
10. Haste maketh ___ ___ ___ ___ ___.
11. When the iron is hot, ___ ___ ___ ___ ___ ___.
12. No man ought to looke a given horse in the ___ ___ ___ ___ ___ ___.
13. ___ ___ ___ ___ ___ ___ ___ is impossible to a willing heart.
14. Better is to ___ ___ ___ then breake.
15. To tell ___ ___ ___ ___ ___ out of schoole.
16. Ill ___ ___ ___ ___ ___ groweth fast.
17. The ___ ___ ___ ___ ___ ___ ___ stone never gathereth mosse.
18. To ___ ___ ___ Peter and pay Poule.
19. ___ ___ ___ ___ was not built in one day.
20. Better is halfe a lofe than no ___ ___ ___ ___ ___.
21. One good turne asketh ___ ___ ___ ___ ___ ___ ___.
22. . . . in deede, a friend is never knowne till a man have ___ ___ ___ ___ ___ ___.
23. All thing is the woorse for the ___ ___ ___ ___ ___ ___ ___.
24. Small pitchers have wyde ___ ___ ___ ___ ___.
25. Would yee both eat your ___ ___ ___ ___ and have your cake?

Answers are on page 254.

20 to 25	— S
16 to 19	— T
10 to 15	— A
Answers 5 to 9	— N
Correct 1 to 4	— D

TONGUE TANGLE

Sis Fisk spooned fish sauce into the fish sauce dish.

OPPOSITES ATTRACT

After each word below write its opposite, beginning with the letter *a*.

1. continue   _____
2. loathing   _____
3. natural   _____
4. timid   _____
5. increase   _____
6. expend   _____
7. remote   _____
8. disperse   _____
9. rational   _____
10. discord   _____
11. certainty   _____
12. separate   _____
13. regular   _____
14. enlarge   _____
15. uncertainty   _____
16. yielding   _____
17. disunion   _____
18. cool   _____
19. disprove   _____
20. defend   _____
21. command   _____
22. real   _____
23. injure   _____
24. apathy   _____
25. unfinished   _____
26. dismiss   _____
27. disapprove   _____
28. derision   _____
29. dissimilar   _____
30. affinity   _____

Answers are on page 254.

	25 to 30	— S
	19 to 24	— T
	10 to 18	— A
Answers	5 to 9	— N
Correct	1 to 4	— D

THE STATES OF THE UNION

Near each state write its name. The shapes of the states are correct. The sizes are not necessarily in proportion. Answers are on page 254.

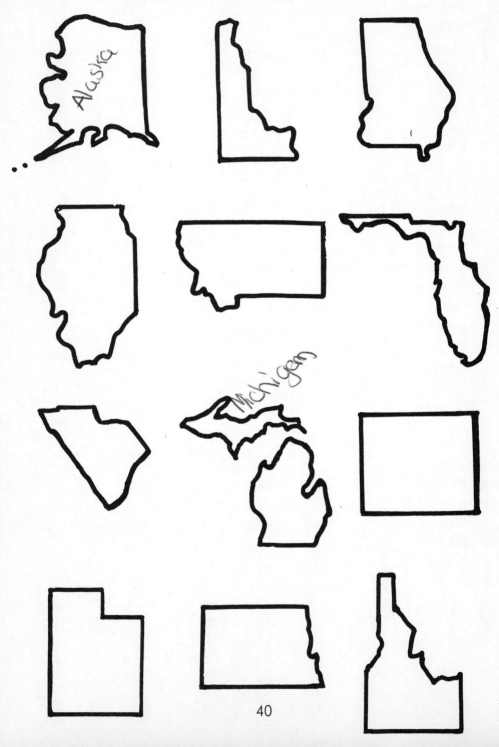

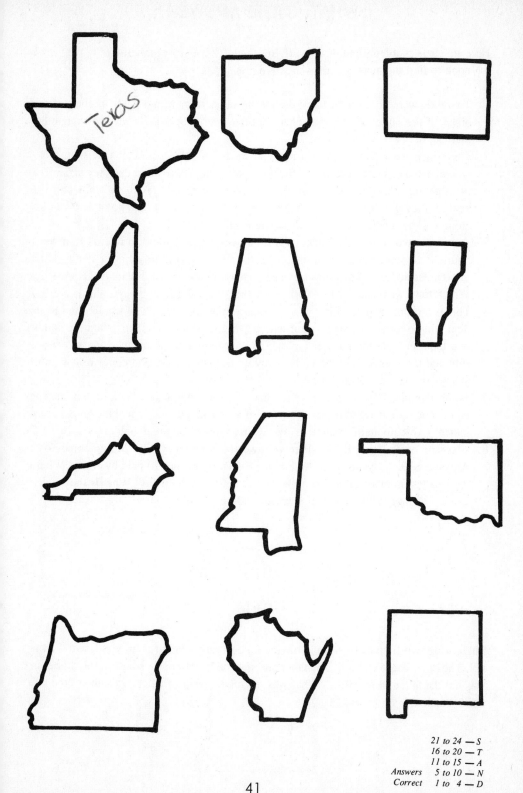

21 to 24 — S
16 to 20 — T
11 to 15 — A
Answers   5 to 10 — N
Correct   1 to 4 — D

WHAT IS THE ANSWER?

Here are some problems and puzzles. If you cannot solve any of them, turn to the back of the book to find the answer. Answers are on page 254.

1. Two girls were born on the same day of the same year, within a few minutes of each other, of the same father and mother. But they were not twins! Can you explain how that can be?
2. Three men were fishing from a rowboat in the middle of a lake. One man took a cigarette and offered cigarettes to the other two. They discovered that they had no way of lighting their cigarettes — no matches, nothing. Without moving their boat — they didn't go ashore, none of them was a boy scout, and no other boat came along — how could they get their cigarettes lit?
3. A train started from New York for Boston traveling at a uniform rate of 40 miles an hour. At the same moment a train left Boston for New York traveling at a uniform rate of 60 miles an hour. The trains traveled on parallel tracks and did not make any stops. Which train was nearer New York when they met, and how many miles nearer?
4. This is a problem in addition which you are to do *mentally*. The whole point to this item will be lost if you try to do it with paper and pencil. You are to add the number two thousand and the number eighty. To their sum add the number twenty. To that sum add the number twenty again. Now write your answer and compare it with the answer in the back of the book.
5. To do this puzzle you must have six matches (or toothpicks). With the six matches make four equilateral triangles. The side of each triangle must equal the length of one match. (An equilateral triangle is one whose three sides are equal.)
6. Algernon owes Percival $10. Percival owes Montmorency $20. Montmorency owes Aloysius $30. Aloysius owes Algernon $40. The debts are all paid by check. What is the smallest number of checks necessary to settle all the debts? What is the smallest amount of money that the checks could add up to?

GEM

There were two Indians in a canoe rowing up a stream. One of them was 6 feet 4 inches tall. The other was 6 feet tall. The taller one was the shorter one's son. But the shorter one was not the taller one's father. What was the relationship of the shorter one to the taller one? Answer is on page 255.

GROW-A-WORD

"Grow-a-Word" by adding a letter to the preceding word, as well as changing the sequence of its letters. For example: *is, sit, stir,* etc. The number of letters in each word is indicated by the number of dashes. Answers are on page 255.

1. a musical note   _ _
   illuminated   _ _ _
   fine sand   _ _ _ _
   picks up   _ _ _ _ _
   to suppress   _ _ _ _ _ _
   removes suspended impurities   _ _ _ _ _ _ _
   flutters   _ _ _ _ _ _ _ _

2. a Freudian term   _ _
   to pass away   _ _ _
   told an untruth   _ _ _ _
   covered with ceramic pieces   _ _ _ _ _
   to expand   _ _ _ _ _ _
   followed; dragged   _ _ _ _ _ _ _
   sold to consumers   _ _ _ _ _ _ _ _

3. a printing term   _ _
   openweave fabric   _ _ _
   directed to go   _ _ _ _
   a mug   _ _ _ _ _
   buries   _ _ _ _ _ _
   relaxing   _ _ _ _ _ _ _
   guiding a course   _ _ _ _ _ _ _ _
   units of ground forces   _ _ _ _ _ _ _ _ _

4. an adverb; a conjunction   _ _
   rested on lower part of body   _ _ _
   gone by   _ _ _ _
   leather belt   _ _ _ _ _
   meal   _ _ _ _ _ _
   mother and father   _ _ _ _ _ _ _
   decorative designs   _ _ _ _ _ _ _ _

WORDS! WORDS! WORDS!

From the four possibilities, select the one correct meaning for each word at the left. Answers are on page 255.

1. belittle   underestimate   mitigate   decry   disparage

2. garish   dazzling   colorful   glaring   shiny

3. kindred   similar   sympathetic   congenial   related

4. narcotic   stimulant   sedative   potion   dope

5. casualty   calamity   misfortune   affliction   disaster

6. sagacious   shrewd   penetrating   sensible   rational

7. quandary   doubt   crisis   emergency   dilemma

8. indict   accuse   arrest   try   judge

9. litigant   lawyer   contestant   libelant   suitor

10. obdurate   unfeeling   stubborn   firm   stern

11. talisman   fetish   amulet   spell   jinx

12. vacillate   oscillate   vibrate   undulate   waver

13. fabricate   frame   misrepresent   construct   imagine

14. raillery   ridicule   mockery   irony   banter

15. umbrage   anger   animosity   vexation   displeasure

16. defective   imperfect   unfinished   illogical   unsound

17. ignoble   vile   nasty   base   vulgar

18. mellow   sweet   delicate   ripe   seasoned

19. wanton   wayward   erratic   malicious   eccentric

20. abdicate   renounce   surrender   forego   abandon

21. palliate   relieve   mitigate   soften   smooth

22. jargon   slang   cant   tongue   gibberish

23. zephyr   breeze   draft   puff   wind

24. earnest   serious   purposeful   ardent   solemn

25. halcyon   moderate   friendly   calm   neutral

21 to 25 — S	
17 to 20 — T	
10 to 16 — A	
Answers 5 to 9 — N	
Correct 1 to 4 — D	

TONGUE TANGLE

Babysitter Barbara Benton bathed baby Bobby in the big bathtub because the bathinette was broken.

WHAT NEXT?

The numbers in each line form a series. You are to write the next two numbers in each series. Answers are on page 255.

1. **2   4   6   8   10** __ __
2. **0   1   3   6   10** __ __
3. **1   2   4   7   11** __ __
4. **32   29   26   23   20** __ __
5. **40   32   25   19   14** __ __
6. **10   12   16   22   30** __ __
7. **45   34   25   18   13** __ __
8. **6   6   9   9   12** __ __
9. **10   1   11   2   12** __ __
10. **4   5   7   10   14** __ __
11. **3   4   7   12   19** __ __
12. **4   4   5   6   6   8   8** __ __
13. **1   15   2   14   3   13** __ __
14. **3   21   4   20   6   18** __ __
15. **8   6   7   5   6   4** __ __

13 to 15 — S
10 to 12 — T
7 to 9 — A
Answers   4 to 6 — N
Correct   1 to 3 — D

AND THAT'S THE TRUTH!

During the Great Depression of the 1930s the government created the Citizens Conservation Corps where teenage boys worked and learned a way to earn a living. One day the Washington office of the CCC received a letter from a mother who wrote quite angrily that her son had been sent home from a CCC camp because he was suffering from nostalgia, and she wanted them to know that he did not have it before he left home!

RIGHT ON!

Examine each sequence both horizontally and vertically and figure out the pattern. Then fill in the vacant spaces correctly. Answers are on page 255.

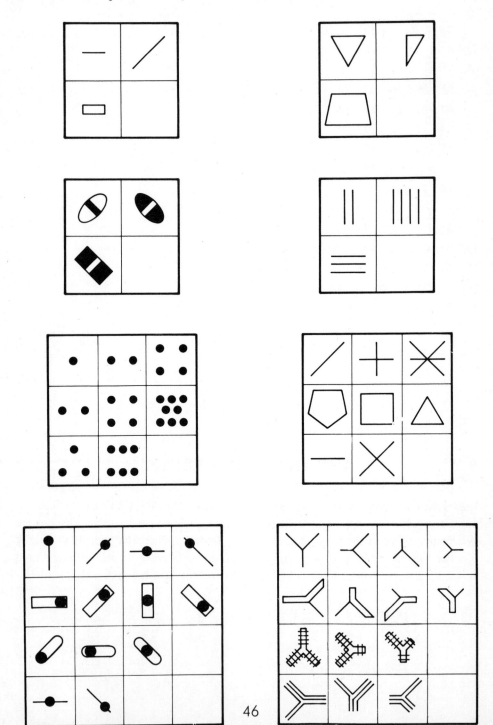

46

CREATE EQUALITY

Make an equation out of all the numbers and arithmetic signs in each line, using each number and sign only once. Answers are on page 255.

1. 2 3 5 10 = + −   _____

2. 2 3 4 11 = − ×   _____

3. 2 2 6 8 = − ÷   _____

4. 2 2 3 6 7 = + − ×   _____

5. 2 4 5 5 6 20 = + − × ÷ ( ) ( )   _____
_____

6. 1 3 4 5 5 7 = + + − ÷ ( ) ( )   _____
_____

7. 2 2 2 2 3 12 = + − × × ( ) ( )   _____

8. 2 2 3 4 6 8 = × × × ÷ ( )   _____

9. 2 3 3 10 15 = + + ÷ ( )   _____

10. 1 2 3 3 16 = − × ÷ ( ) ( )   _____
_____

11. 2 3 4 14 = + ÷   _____

12. 2 5 5 5 5 15 = + + − ÷ ( )   _____

13. 3 3 3 3 81 = × × ÷   _____

14. 2 2 3 4 5 = + × × ( )_____

15. 3 3 3 18 = + ÷ ( )   _____

16. 1 3 3 4 8 12 = + − × ÷ ( ) ( )   _____
_____

17. 2 3 3 3 5 8 = + − × × ( ) ( )   _____
_____

18. 2 2 3 6 18 = + − ÷ ( )   _____

19. 2 2 2 4 5 12 = + + × ÷ ( ) ( )   _____

20. 2 2 3 4 5 = + × × ( )   _____

47

CAN YOU COUNT WHAT YOU CAN'T SEE?

Near each pile of blocks below write the number of blocks in it. If there is a block missing from the outside of the pile and you can't tell what is behind or below it, assume that all the blocks in that row or column are missing. Answers are on page 255.

1
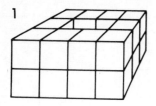

5
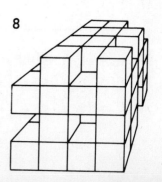

2
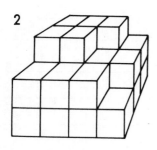

6
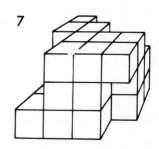

3
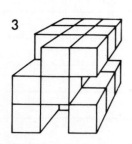

7
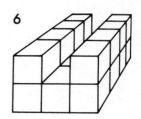

4
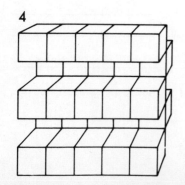

8
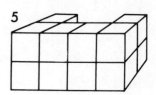

LET'S PLAY HANKY PANKY!

After each expression write the *two rhyming words* to which it refers. Answers are on page 255.

1. joyful parent _____
2. talkative feline _____
3. happy passenger ship _____
4. lawful dog _____
5. expensive hour _____
6. glass weapon _____
7. angry employer _____
8. actual repast _____
9. pleasant evil action _____
10. smallest dinner _____
11. spoiled fiber _____
12. beautiful urban community _____
13. red-faced pal _____
14. odoriferous bread spread _____
15. pleasant servant _____
16. cowardly blackbird _____
17. less fast grasscutter _____
18. larger visitor _____
19. uncommon specialty shop _____
20. empty area _____
21. happier dog _____
22. important bet _____
23. slender missile _____
24. concealed refuse heap (Br.) _____
25. lone facial depression _____

22 to 25 — S
18 to 21 — T
10 to 17 — A
Answers   5 to 9 — N
Correct   1 to 4 — D

49

DE UNO MULTUM

From each word below make as many words of at least four letters as you can. Only one form of a word is allowed — either *mean* or *meant*, but not both. Don't make words by adding the letter *s* to another word. You may not use proper nouns, foreign words, abbreviations, contractions or slang. Answers are on page 255.

SUBJECTIVE

22 or more — S
17 to 21 — T
10 to 16 — A
Answers 6 to 9 — N
Correct 1 to 5 — D

ENDEARMENT

45 or more — S
33 to 44 — T
20 to 32 — A
Answers 11 to 19 — N
Correct 1 to 10 — D

TIMELINESS

55 or more — S
45 to 54 — T
29 to 44 — A
Answers 16 to 28 — N
Correct 1 to 15 — D

WHAT DO YOU KNOW?

Select the correct one of the four possible answers for each item.

1. New York City is directly north of:
   1) Mexico City . 2) Bogota, Colombia 3) Buenos Aires   4) Rio de Janiero
2. Napoleon was defeated at Waterloo in:
   1) 1793 2) 1789 3) 1812 4) 1815
3. The "gate" for the Dempsey-Tunney fight was about:
   1) $200,000 2) $500,000 3) $1,000,000 4) $2,500,000
4. Which were Vice Presidents who first became Presidents upon the death of the President?
   1) McKinley, T. Roosevelt, Burr 2) Clay, Harding, Harrison
   3) Fillmore, Coolidge, Truman   4) Arthur, Grant, Madison
5. After being in last place, the N. Y. Giants won the National League pennant during the last game of the year by means of a home run in the ninth inning in:
   1) 1946 2) 1949 3) 1951 4) 1953
6. The State of Israel was created in:
   1) 1918 2) 1929 3) 1945 4) 1948
7. The Sacco-Vanzetti Case had to do with:
   1) a murder 2) citizenship 3) kidnapping 4) Communist Party membership
8. The Communist Revolution in Russia took place in:
   1) 1914 2) 1917 3) 1919 4) 1929
9. Stock market losses in the crash of 1929 totaled:
   1) $500,000,000 2) $5,000,000,000 3) $15,000,000,000 4) $100,000,000,000
10. The largest city on the West Coast of the United States is:
    1) San Francisco 2) Seattle 3) Portland 4) Los Angeles
11. London is at about the same latitude as:
    1) Labrador 2) New York 3) Los Angeles 4) Anchorage, Alaska
12. The first astronauts landed on the moon in:
    1) 1969 2) 1971 3) 1963 4) 1967
13. About how many colleges (including junior colleges) are there in the United States?
    1) 500 2) 800 3) 1200 4) 2000
14. Which of these countries has the largest population?
    1) Spain 2) United Kingdom 3) France 4) Italy
15. Antiseptic surgery owes its greatest debt to:
    1) Pasteur 2) Long 3) Lister 4) Jenner

Answers are on page 256.

SPOT THE STRANGER

Which picture in each group does not belong with the other four?

Answers are on page 256.

OPPOSITES ATTRACT

After each word below write its opposite, beginning with the letter *s*.

1. insecurity _____
2. unholy _____
3. weak _____
4. welcome _____
5. happy _____
6. glad _____
7. easygoing _____
8. irregularity _____
9. rough _____
10. inappropriate _____
11. join _____
12. ruddy _____
13. friend _____
14. industrious _____
15. rigid _____
16. ruffled _____
17. loquacious _____
18. unwise _____
19. hypocritical _____
20. flat _____
21. wanderer _____
22. antonym _____
23. moving _____
24. inexpert _____
25. port _____
26. gaseous _____
27. dry _____
28. civilized _____
29. useless _____
30. dull _____

Answers are on page 256.

Answers are on page 256.

25 to 30 — S
19 to 24 — T
12 to 18 — A
Answers   6 to 11 — N
Correct   1 to 5 — D

53

WHAT IS "MENT"?

For each clue below write one word ending in *ment*. The answer to the first one is *attachment*. Answers are on page 256.

1. it adheres _____
2. an incentive _____
3. dispute _____
4. spice _____
5. a piece of something _____
6. a place to live _____
7. something to be done _____
8. that is achieved _____
9. from bill to law _____
10. alleviates pain _____
11. food _____
12. that is demanded _____
13. getting involved _____
14. what many youth today don't like _____
15. being uninvolved _____
16. illness _____
17. foundation _____
18. memorial structure _____
19. dregs _____
20. system _____
21. emotion _____
22. being sent away _____
23. obligation _____
24. penalty _____
25. mental disorder _____
26. act of controlling _____
27. location _____
28. classification _____
29. praise _____
30. act of adapting _____

24 to 30 — S
20 to 24 — T
11 to 19 — A
Answers   *6 to 10 — N*
Correct   *1 to 5 — D*

ON THE SQUARE

Each square below is made up of the pieces to the right of it. Draw the appropriate lines in the squares to show how the pieces fit. Answers are on page 256.

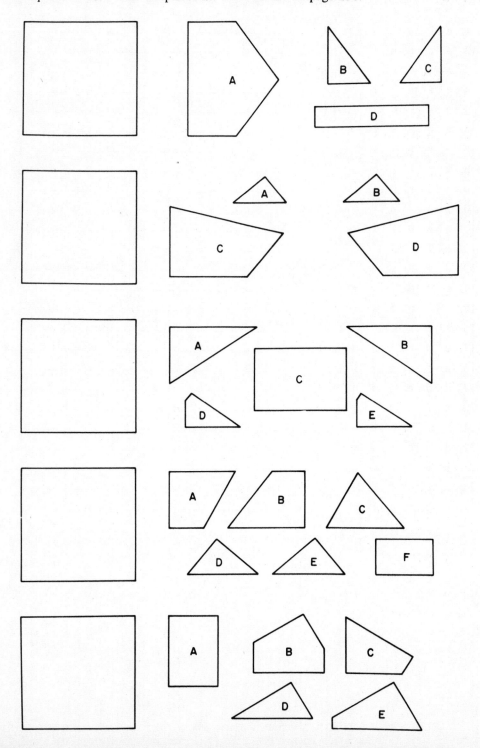

SCRAMBLE

Make as many words as you can from the letters on each line, using *all* the letters each time. Answers are on page 256.

1. e   i   m   t   _____
2. a   c   e   h   _____
3. a   h   t   w   _____
4. e   i   m   r   t   _____
5. a   e   r   s   t   _____
6. a   e   p   s   t   _____
7. a   b   e   l   s   _____
8. a   p   r   s   t   _____
9. a   e   l   s   v   _____
10. a   c   d   e   r   _____
11. a   e   k   r   s   t   _____
12. e   i   r   s   t   v   _____
13. e   o   r   s   w   _____
14. a   c   d   e   n   r   _____
15. a   e   p   r   s   s   _____
16. c   e   i   k   r   s   t   _____
17. c   d   e   i   n   o   r   t   u   _____
18. a   d   e   g   r   t   y   _____
19. a   d   e   g   i   n   r   t   _____
20. a   d   e   e   n   r   _____
21. i   n   o   p   s   t   _____
22. a   d   e   h   r   t   _____
23. b   e   f   i   r   _____
24. a   c   e   l   l   r   _____
25. d   e   f   g   i   t   _____

	60 or more — S
	46 to 59 — T
	29 to 45 — A
Answers	16 to 28 — N
Correct	1 to 15 — D

TOOTHPICKS WILL DO!

1. Move 1 stick and have 8 squares.

2. Move 3 sticks and have 10 squares.

3. Move 2 sticks and have 9 squares.

4. Remove 2 sticks and have 7 squares.

---

5. Move 4 sticks and have 16 squares.

6. Move 3 sticks and have 14 squares.

7. Remove 2 sticks and have 12 squares.

8. Remove 2 sticks and have 13 squares.

---

9. Move 2 sticks and have 10 squares.

10. Move 4 sticks and have 10 squares.

11. Remove 3 sticks and have 8 squares.

12. Move 1 stick and have 9 squares.

13. Move 3 sticks and have 10 squares.

14. How many ways can you move 3 sticks and still have 10 squares?

Answers are on page 257.

THE STATES OF THE UNION

Near each state write its name. The shapes of the states are correct. The sizes are not necessarily in proportion. Answers are on page 257.

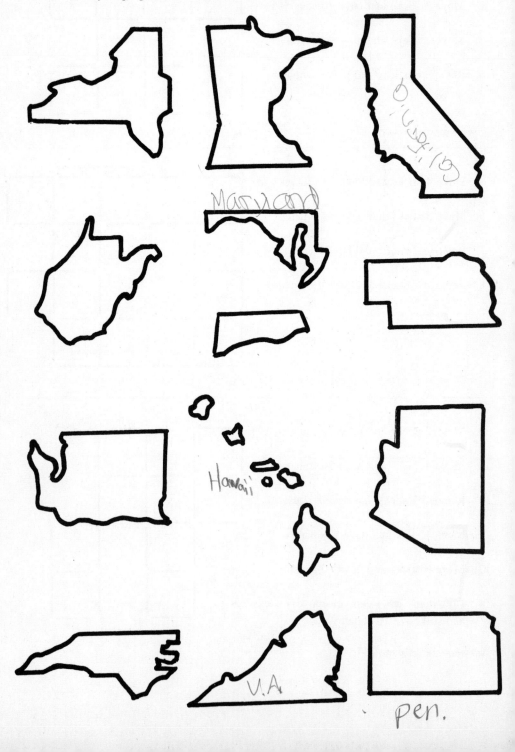

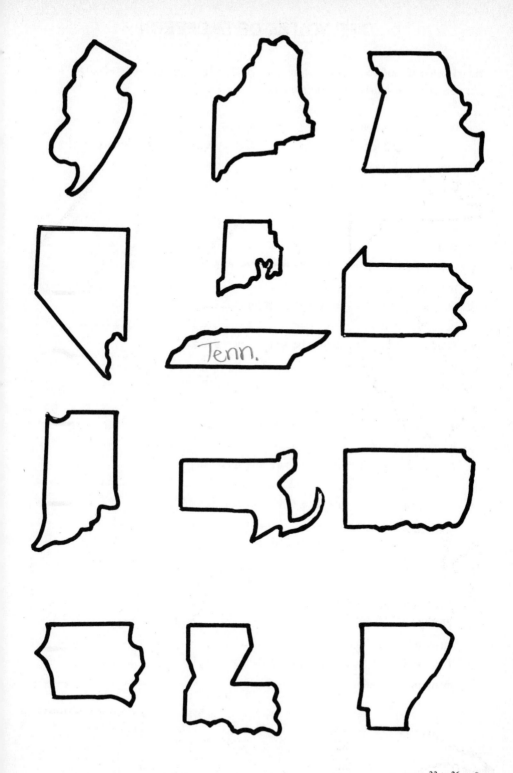

Tenn.

59

ARE YOU A TOP SHOPPER?

Here is a list of foods with the price of each. How many of the questions about these foods can you answer? Answers are on page 257.

butter is 80¢ a pound
margarine is 20¢ a pound
sour cream is 60¢ a pint
cottage cheese is 35¢ a pint

yogurt is 30¢ a pint
Jack cheese is $1.05 a pound
Swiss cheese is $1.50 a pound
milk is 30¢ a quart

1. Three pounds of margarine cost the same as how many pints of yogurt? _____

2. One pound of Swiss cheese costs as much as how many pints of yogurt? _____

3. How many quarts of milk can you get for the price of 3 pounds of butter? _____

4. How many pints of cottage cheese cost the same as 2 pounds of Jack cheese? _____

5. How many pints of sour cream can you buy for the same price as 6 pints of cottage cheese? _____

6. Two pints of sour cream cost the same as how many pounds of butter? _____

7. Four quarts of milk cost the same as how many pounds of margarine? _____

8. Two pounds of Jack cheese cost the same as how many pounds of Swiss cheese? _____

9. Two pints of yogurt cost the same as how many pounds of butter? _____

10. How many quarts of milk can you buy for the price of two pounds of Jack cheese? _____

11. Two pints of cottage cheese cost the same as how many pounds of margarine? _____

12. Two pounds of Swiss cheese cost the same as how many pints of sour cream? _____

	11 to 12 — S
	9 to 10 — T
	6 to 8 — A
Answers	*3 to 5 — N*
Correct	*1 to 2 — D*

60

WORDS PLUS

From each word and the letter after it make a new word, with at least one change in the order of the letters of the original word. Answers are on page 257.

1. grind u _____
2. streams t _____
3. steer c _____
4. twine r _____
5. sheer p _____
6. piece r _____
7. down u _____
8. shot g _____
9. turf i _____
10. leaden c _____
11. music b _____
12. under f _____
13. elide y _____
14. enter u _____
15. action n _____
16. linger y _____
17. ended i _____
18. ingrate l _____
19. carrot e _____
20. infer g _____
21. vaster h _____
22. mash c _____
23. erase l _____
24. nutted s _____
25. waned g _____
26. hinged a _____
27. juices t _____
28. treating e _____
29. empire s _____
30. steaming l _____

25 to 30 — S
19 to 24 — T
10 to 18 — A
Answers   5 to 9 — N
Correct   1 to 4 — D

61

WHAT DO YOU SEE?

Do not use a straight edge or ruler to answer any of these questions until after you have decided on the answer. Answers are on page 257.

1. Which are farther apart, *a* and *b* or *c* and *d*?

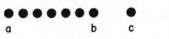

2. Are you above the steps or below them? (Don't decide until you have looked at them for some time.)

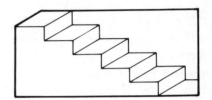

3. Which is longer, line AB or line AC?

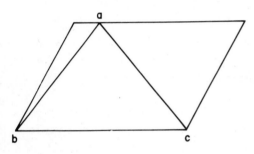

6. Which of the three lines at the right is a continuation of the line at the left?

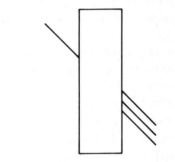

4. Follow these instructions carefully and you will see something most unusual and interesting. Hold your hands out straight in front of you with your hands closed, except for your index fingers, which should barely touch each other. Look at the wall or some object right in front of you with your eyes *just above* your fingers. Slowly move your hands apart. What do you see?

7. Which cylinder is the shortest in the drawing below?

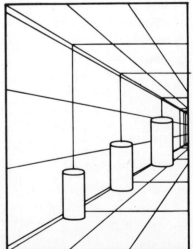

5. Are the two areas below the same width?

DO YOU HAVE THE TIME?

Since it takes the earth 24 hours to rotate on its axis, the surface of the earth is divided into 24 time zones. Each time zone is about 1000 miles wide at the equator. The United States is about 3000 miles wide. There are four time zones in this country, which is more than 3000 miles north of the equator. The eastern time zone starts in the Atlantic Ocean and ends somewhere in Indiana; the central time zone goes as far as western Nebraska; the mountain zone reaches to Nevada; the Pacific zone ends in the Pacific Ocean. The time of day in these zones is known, respectively, as eastern standard, central standard, mountain standard, and Pacific standard.

When it is 6 o'clock in the morning along the East Coast, as the sun rises, it is 5 o'clock in the central zone, since the sun won't get there till an hour later. It is then 4 o'clock in the mountain zone, and 3 o'clock in the Pacific zone. The time-of-day situation is complicated further by the fact that during the summer some places are on daylight saving time, which is one hour earlier than standard time. See how well you can answer the following questions.

1. Mr. Brand lives in Denver. He was visiting in Philadelphia. He had an appointment for 1:00 in the afternoon. Philadelphia was not on standard time; Denver was. What time was it in Denver when he had his appointment in Philadelphia?

2. Mr. Olson took a plane from Kansas City to New York. An elderly lady had the seat next to him. After the plane started she asked: "What time are we supposed to land in New York?" Mr. Olson in turn asked: "Do you want to know the New York time or the St. Louis time?" After some thought the old lady settled for St. Louis time. The plane was supposed to arrive in New York at 6:30 P.M., according to the time table. The time given in the time table is always according to the time in the city to which it refers. Both St. Louis and New York City were on daylight saving time. What should Mr. Olson have told the old lady?

3. On the last Saturday night in April, in places which go on daylight saving time, the people set their watches ahead one hour. Mr. Bright changed his watch to daylight saving time before going to bed. When he woke up his watch read 10 o'clock. What time would his watch have read if he had not changed it to daylight saving time before going to bed?

4. A plane left Los Angeles at 11 A.M. Pacific standard time. When Mr. Bright got off the plane in New York City the clock at the airport read 8 o'clock. That was the same evening, and the time was eastern standard time. How long did the trip actually take?

Answers are on page 257.

ESTRANGED RELATIONS

What relation to you is your:

1. uncle's father? _____
2. nephew's sister's son? _____
3. aunt's mother's only grandchild? _____
4. brother-in-law's sister's son? _____
5. aunt's daughter's adopted child? _____
6. mother's aunt's daughter's daughter? _____
7. father's mother's son by a second marriage? _____
8. brother's wife's mother's son? _____
9. grandmother's sister's daughter's son? _____
10. cousin's father's father? _____
11. husband's sister's daughter's son? _____
12. grandnephew's mother's father? _____
13. sister's husband's sister? _____
14. grandnephew's sister's grandmother? _____
15. sister's mother's father? _____

Answers are on page 257.

RHYME TIME

A farmer named Mergatroid Beam
Had a cow which was simply a dream
Mergy's hands were so cold
That without being told
Old bossy gave out with ice cream

WHAT NEXT?

The numbers in each line form a series. You are to write the next two numbers in each series. Answers are on page 257.

1. **4 8 16 28** __ __
2. **2 4 15 4 8 30 6** __ __
3. **2 4 3 9 4** __ __
4. **8 9 12 15 16 19 22** __ __
5. **8 64 7 49 6 36** __ __
6. **12 24 11 22 10** __ __
7. **1 2 4 8** __ __
8. **1 8 27 64** __ __
9. **12 15 9 16 7 18** __ __
10. **1 1 4 8 9 27** __ __
11. **72 72 36 24 18** __ __
12. **30 31 35 44 60** __ __
13. **1/2 2/3 3/4 4/5** __ __
14. **60 30 20 15** __ __
15. **2 3 6 3 4 12 4** __ __

13 to 15 — S
10 to 12 — T
7 to 9 — A
Answers   *4 to 6 — N*
Correct   *1 to 3 — D*

GEM

Who wrote this statement, and when?

"Our earth is degenerate in these latter days . . . children no longer obey their parents."

Answer is on page 257.

WORDS! WORDS! WORDS!

From the four possibilities, select the one correct meaning for each word at the left. Answers are on page 257.

1. patrician   magnate   aristocrat   prince   squire

2. nonchalance   disdain   coolness   apathy   indifference

3. indolent   passive   stagnant   lazy   inactive

4. hazard   risk   exposure   jeopardy   accident

5. debase   adulterate   weaken   humble   depress

6. sentient   quick   emotional   keen   sensitive

7. fidelity   uniformity   loyalty   equality   probity

8. lucid   translucent   obvious   distinct   clear

9. transcend   outweigh   exceed   outrank   outdo

10. alacrity   activity   energy   readiness   briskness

11. harbinger   forerunner   bellwether   warning   omen

12. explicit   open   manifest   definite   positive

13. cynical   haughty   sneering   arrogant   sarcastic

14. jejune   anemic   dull   boring   subnormal

15. bombastic   swollen   high-flown   turgid   explosive

16. supine   inert   torpid   inclined   sluggish

17. gullible   childish   simple   credulous   trustful

18. validate   regulate   honor   test   confirm

19. felicitous   congruous   elegant   appropriate   neat

20. stricture   criticism   obloquy   compression   narrowing

21. circumvent   baffle   entrap   deceive   elude

22. penury   want   scarcity   destitution   need

23. emanate   exude   issue   appear   proceed

24. recreant   faithless   dishonest   unmanly   cowardly

25. tentative   makeshift   experimental   fortuitous   empirical

22 to 25 — S
18 to 21 — T
10 to 17 — A
Answers   5 to 7 — N
Correct   1 to 4 — D

THROUGH THE LOOKING GLASS

For each figure below there are three mirror reflections, only one of which is correct. Pick the one that is the way the original figure would appear in a looking glass. Answers are on page 257.

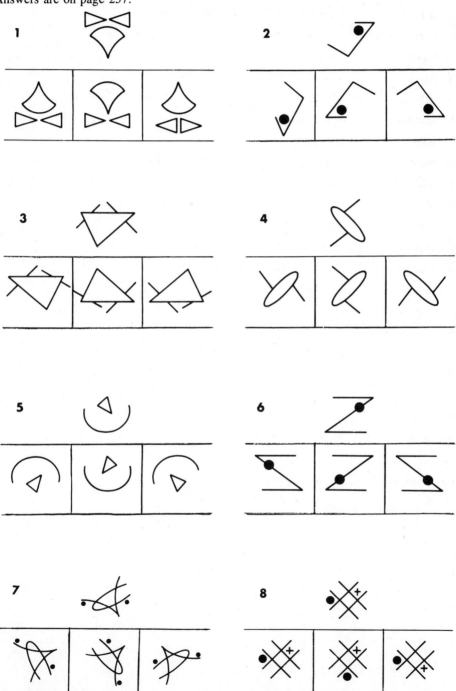

SYNONYMS

For each word below write a synonym beginning with the letter *w*.

1. stagger   _____
2. twist   _____
3. blink   _____
4. sinewy   _____
5. court   _____
6. grapple   _____
7. valuation   _____
8. contorted   _____
9. swathe   _____
10. cascade   _____
11. fatigue   _____
12. interlace   _____
13. gloss over   _____
14. notion   _____
15. pier   _____
16. cry   _____
17. flinch   _____
18. brandish   _____
19. iniquity   _____
20. intelligence   _____
21. surprise   _____
22. shabby   _____
23. fury   _____
24. spin   _____
25. arduous   _____

Answers are on page 258.

22 to 25 — S
18 to 21 — T
10 to 17 — A
Answers   5 to 9 — N
Correct   1 to 4 — D

WHAT IS THE ANSWER?

1. Place the point of a pencil at any spot on one of the lines in this diagram. Then trace the diagram without removing the point of the pencil from the paper and without retracing any of the lines.

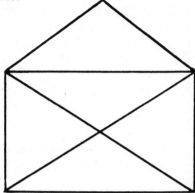

2. A man who considered himself "smart" (a wise guy) addressed a letter to a friend in the following manner. The letter was delivered! The mailman was apparently able to decipher the address. Can you?

HILL
———
MASS.

3. A man went into his room to get a pair of socks. He knew that he had twenty socks in the top drawer of his chest, ten of them black and ten white. When he flipped the electric light switch, nothing happened — the bulb had blown out. He didn't want to bother going downstairs or to another room for a bulb; so he reached into the drawer in the dark to take out some socks. He found that they had not been put together in pairs. What is the smallest number of socks he would have to take out in order to be sure of having at least one pair of socks of the same color — it doesn't matter whether they are both white or both black?

4. Three Swedish explorers met three Hungarian travelers in the middle of a jungle and decided to join forces against the wilderness. A few hours later, they came to a broad river. Between them, the men had only one small boat which could carry two people. Only two of the men knew how to row — one Hungarian and one Swede. The Hungarians, however, were a bit suspicious of their fellow travelers and decided among themselves not to let any of their party be outnumbered by the others. Yet, they all made it across the river. How did they manage it? (A good way to solve the problem is to use three nickels for the Hungarians and three pennies for the Swedes, turning the rowers face up and the non-rowers face down.)

5. A man started at a certain point on the face of the earth and walked 200 miles due south. Then he turned and walked 200 miles due west. Then he turned and walked 200 miles due north and found himself back at the spot where he had started from. Assuming that the earth is a perfect sphere, at what point did he start? (Note: there is one fairly obvious answer, but there are also many other not-so-obvious answers.)

Answers are on page 258.

DE UNO MULTUM

From each word below make as many words of at least four letters as you can. Only one form of a word is allowed — either *mean* or *meant*, but not both. Don't make words by adding the letter *s* to another word. You may not use proper nouns, foreign words, abbreviations, contractions or slang. Answers are on page 258.

WATERGATE

	115 or more — S
	91 to 114 — T
	46 to 90 — A
Answers	26 to 45 — N
Correct	1 to 25 — D

CELESTIAL

	72 or more — S
	56 to 71 — T
	33 to 55 — A
Answers	20 to 32 — N
Correct	1 to 19 — D

SATURNINE

	70 or more — S
	50 to 69 — T
	31 to 49 — A
Answers	19 to 30 — N
Correct	1 to 18 — D

RIGHT ON!

Examine each sequence both horizontally and vertically and figure out the pattern. Then fill in the vacant spaces correctly. Answers are on page 259.

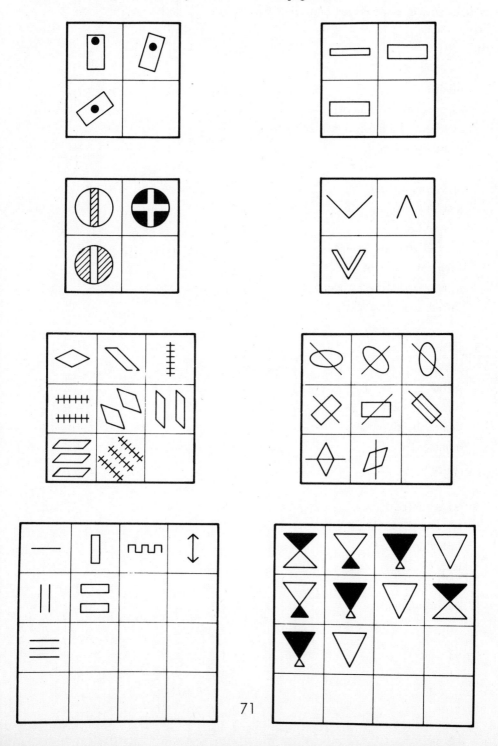

GROW-A-WORD

"Grow-a-Word" by adding a letter to the preceding word, as well as changing the sequence of its letters. The number of letters in each word is indicated by the number of dashes after it. Answers are on page 259.

1. exist   — — —
   speed contest   — — — —
   bright   — — — — —
   more openwork material   — — — — — —
   keyboard of a musical instrument — — — — — — —
   courtly gentleman   — — — — — — — —

2. specifying a point   — —
   a color   — — —
   talk wildly   — — — —
   a set of attached vehicles   — — — — —
   keep possession of   — — — — — —
   solution used to color wood   — — — — — — —
   forced; tried very hard   — — — — — — — —

3. father   — —
   strike   — — —
   a fruit   — — — —
   a hanging cloth   — — — — —
   dealt leniently with   — — — — — —
   commended   — — — — — — —
   heaven   — — — — — — — —

4. what miners dig for   — — —
   what you bind things with   — — — —
   heavy drinker   — — — — —
   tell   — — — — — —
   apportion   — — — — — — —
   one who plunders   — — — — — — — —

WORDS! WORDS! WORDS!

From the four possibilities, select the one correct meaning for each word at the left.

1.	prelude	herald preface preamble harbinger
2.	forlorn	hopeless dejected wretched deserted
3.	rancid	bad unclean nasty rank
4.	amorphous	unshapely malformed formless misshapen
5.	mottled	blotched marbled pied varied
6.	vapid	dull insipid feeble dry
7.	ghastly	wan ugly frightful deathlike
8.	crass	dense raw dull coarse
9.	nugatory	worthless irrelevant mediocre impotent
10.	refractory	firm stubborn tenacious sullen
11.	scurrilous	uncivil abusive rude impolite
12.	dissident	differing dissonant discordant improper
13.	luscious	piquant tasty delicious rich
14.	heinous	vicious lawless odious immoral
15.	whimsical	grotesque freakish ridiculous odd
16.	strident	grating hoarse gutteral coarse
17.	banter	sarcasm raillery horseplay ridicule
18.	expound	edify preach instruct interpret
19.	fervent	ardent earnest trenchant fiery
20.	mettle	dash confidence spirit brawn
21.	recondite	occult abstruse tortuous furtive
22.	lethargy	stupor dullness numbness drowsiness
23.	infringe	transgress purloin invade intrude
24.	peremptory	binding conclusive tyrannical imperative
25.	scrupulous	careful prudent precise cautious

Answers are on page 259.

Answers are on page 259.

	22 to 25	— S
	18 to 21	— T
	10 to 17	— A
Answers	5 to 7	— N
Correct	1 to 4	— D

OPPOSITES ATTRACT

After each word below write an opposite beginning with the letter *g*.

1. harsh _____
2. take leave _____
3. loss _____
4. play safe _____
5. reticent _____
6. stingy _____
7. sullen, gloomy _____
8. sudden _____
9. generosity _____
10. host _____
11. be modest _____
12. awkward _____
13. individual _____
14. tiny _____
15. thankless _____
16. artificial _____
17. disperse _____
18. forthrightness _____
19. displease _____
20. brightness _____
21. jovial _____
22. simplicity _____
23. joy _____
24. unimpressive _____
25. specific _____
26. suspicious _____
27. ending _____
28. cheerful _____
29. homeliness _____
30. clear _____

Answers are on page 259.

25 *to* 30 — S
19 *to* 24 — T
10 *to* 18 — A
Answers 5 *to* 9 — N
Correct 1 *to* 4 — D

WHAT DO YOU KNOW?

Select the correct one of the four possible answers for each item.

1. Which of these rivers is the longest?
   1) Congo   2) Niger   3) Volga   4) Amazon
2. The man who invented the friction match was:
   1) Swedish   2) American   3) English   4) German
3. Which of these was a Vice President who completed his term as Vice President and later was elected to the Presidency?
   1) Burr   2) Truman   3) John Adams   4) Harding
4. The Titanic was sunk by an iceberg in 1912 with a loss of how many lives?
   1) 246   2) 659   3) 1042   4) 1517
5. The first successful steamboat trip was made in the United States in:
   1) 1776   2) 1807   3) 1842   4) 1863
6. Which was *not* a signer of the Declaration of Independence?
   1) Franklin   2) Button Gwinett   3) Washington   4) John Adams
7. About how many miles is it from Earth to the moon?
   1) 240,000   2) 1 million   3) 2,400,000   4) 2 million
8. The U. S. has about how many miles of surfaced highways?
   1) 3,000,000   2) 1,400,000   3) 5,200,000   4) 7,750,000
9. The man who discovered penicillin was:
   1) British   2) French   3) American   4) Russian
10. The highest peak in the world is Mount:
    1) Aconcagua   2) Everest   3) McKinley   4) Kilimanjaro
11. The largest of the following islands is:
    1) Madagascar   2) New Guinea   3) Borneo   4) Greenland
12. The first solo flight from the U. S. to Europe was made in:
    1) 1919   2) 1927   3) 1931   4) 1935   this was right... I messed-up
13. When a clock in London reads 5 P.M., a clock in New York would read:
    1) Midnight   2) 3 P.M.   3) 9 P.M.   4) Noon
14. The North Pole was first reached in:
    1) 1896   2) 1903   3) 1909   4) 1919
15. The largest city in the world is:
    1) Tokyo   2) New York   3) London   4) Paris

Answers are on page 259.

ON THE SQUARE

In each square below draw lines showing how it is made up of the pieces to the right of it. Answers are on page 259.

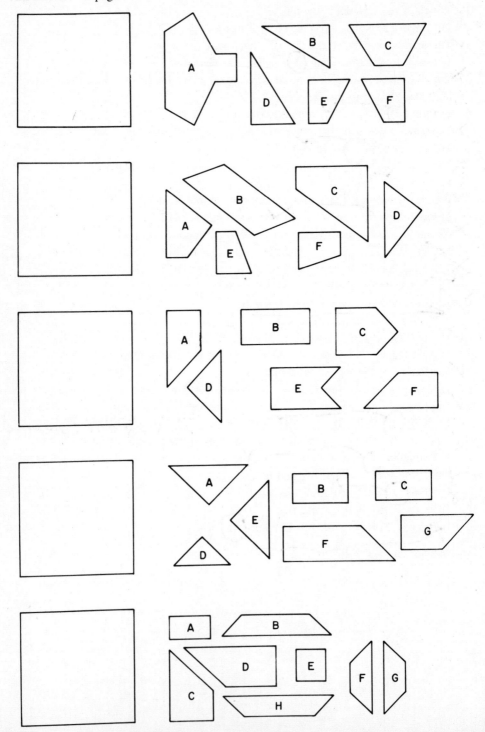

WHAT ARE THE "RATES"?

For each clue below write one word ending in *rate*. The answer to the first one is *narrate*.

1. tell a story
2. make a hole through
3. free
4. become detached
5. grow worse
6. confirm
7. stubborn
8. convalesce
9. revive
10. pierce
11. magnify
12. ponder
13. mangle, tear
14. crumble
15. thoughtful
16. apportion
17. overestimate
18. thwart
19. install
20. quicken
21. honor
22. function
23. buccaneer
24. reasonable
25. associate

Answers are on page 259.

Answers are on page 259.

Answers Correct	
24 to 30	— S
20 to 24	— T
11 to 19	— A
6 to 10	— N
1 to 5	— D

WHAT'S MISSING?

Can you fill in the missing words in the following sayings?

1. Too many cooks _ _ _ _ _ the broth.
2. Once _ _ _ _ _ twice shy.
3. Butter wouldn't _ _ _ _ _ in her mouth.
4. _ _ _ _ _ goes before a fall.
5. The _ _ _ _ the merrier.
6. It's an _ _ _ _ wind that blows no good.
7. In one _ _ _ and out the other.
8. Where there's a _ _ _ _ _ there's a way.
9. All's well that ends _ _ _ _ _.
10. To put the _ _ _ _ _ before the horse.
11. _ _ _ _ may force a man to cast beyond the moon.
12. Who is worse shod than the _ _ _ _ _ _ _ _ _ _ _ _ _ wife?
13. Cut my coat according to my _ _ _ _ _ _.
14. To hold with the hare and run with the _ _ _ _ _ _.
15. _ _ _ _ _ _ _ should not be choosers.
16. You have too many _ _ _ _ _ _ _ _ to your bow.
17. A _ _ _ _ _ 's bolt is soon shot.
18. There is no _ _ _ _ _ without some smoke.
19. A _ _ _ _ may look at a king.
20. I know on which side my bread is _ _ _ _ _ _ _ _ _ _.
21. Love me, love my _ _ _ _.
22. When I give you an _ _ _ _ _, you take an ell.
23. One _ _ _ _ _ _ _ _ does not a summer make.
24. Look before you _ _ _ _ _.
25. A new broom sweeps _ _ _ _ _ _.

Answers are on page 259.

20 to 25 — S
16 to 19 — T
10 to 15 — A
Answers   5 to 9 — N
Correct   1 to 4 — D

TONGUE TANGLE

Shelley sold small shabby silver shears.

SPOT THE STRANGER

Which word in each group does not belong with the other four?

1. Giants   Cardinals   Dodgers   Indians   Pirates
2. England   France   Holland   Italy   Greece
3. orange   lemon   grapefruit   apple   kumquat
4. gladiolus   tulip   iris   rose   nasturtium
5. book   movie   newspaper   magazine   brochure
6. Brazil   Argentina   Chile   Bolivia   Equador
7. basketball   tennis   baseball   football   lacrosse
8. Norway   Denmark   Spain   Belgium   Holland
9. headlight   lamp   carburetor   flashlight   sun
10. classify   systematize   list   tabulate   index
11. Cadillac   Chevrolet   Ford   Maxwell   Plymouth
12. pot   pan   kettle   cup   skillet
13. swimming   broad jump   lacrosse   pole vault   bowling
14. red   blue   yellow   green   chartreuse
15. ounce   gram   degree   minute   temperature
16. console   desk   shelf   table   chaise longue
17. carrots   peas   beans   broccoli   artichoke
18. Portugal   Finland   Spain   Greece   Poland
19. cousin   son   daughter   father   mother
20. New Zealand   India   Hawaii   Madagascar   Cuba
21. courage   politeness   gentility   refinement   courtesy
22. scarlet   rose   ruby   vermillion   orange
23. chess   checkers   gin rummy   Monopoly   Scrabble
24. horse   raccoon   pig   sheep   cow
25. acquittal   reprieve   pardon   release   indictment

Answers are on page 259.

Answers Correct

20 to 25 — S
16 to 19 — T
10 to 15 — A
5 to 9 — N
1 to 4 — D

RHYME TIME

There once was a colonel from Kenya
Who was told that he had schizophrenia.
It wasn't the big word
That bothered the old bird;
But which of his egos was senior!

SCRAMBLE

Make as many words as you can from the letters on each line, using all the letters each time. Answers are on page 260.

1. i t d e _____
2. b e r t u _____
3. e e r s t _____
4. b e l s t u _____
5. e d o s _____
6. a c e r s t _____
7. a c h n s t _____
8. a c l p s _____
9. a c n o o r _____
10. e i p r s t _____
11. c e r t u _____
12. a b d e e r t _____
13. c e o p s _____
14. a c e h l s t _____
15. a e l r y _____
16. a d d e l s w _____
17. d e e i m r t _____
18. d e i l o p s _____
19. a e e g l n r _____
20. c e h i k n t _____
21. e o p r s t u _____
22. a e e h r t w _____
23. c e n o r s t u _____
24. a e g i l n r t _____
25. a c g h i n p t _____

60 or more — S
46 to 59 — T
29 to 45 — A
Answers   16 to 28 — N
Correct   1 to 15 — D

CAN YOU COUNT WHAT YOU CAN'T SEE?

Near each pile of blocks below, write the number of blocks in it. If there is a block missing from the outside of a pile and you can't tell what is behind or below it, assume that all the blocks in that row or column are missing. Answers are on page 260.

1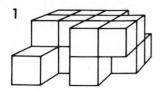

5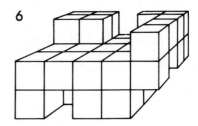

2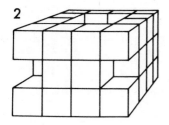

6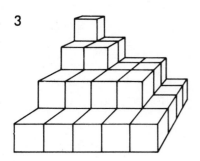

3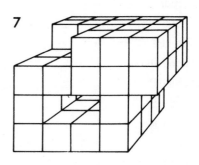

7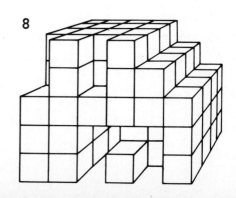

4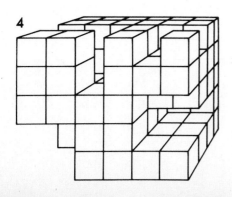

8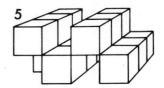

WORDS PLUS

From each word and the letter after it make a new word, with at least one change in the order of the letters of the original word. Answers are on page 260.

1. indeed   f   _____
2. notice   s   _____
3. gained   h   _____
4. direct   k   _____
5. palest   o   _____
6. racing   o   _____
7. ornate   s   _____
8. enlist   c   _____
9. infest   f   _____
10. cantered   n   _____
11. recited   l   _____
12. indorse   c   _____
13. stream   m   _____
14. neglects   i   _____
15. burn   a   _____
16. trail   e   _____
17. crude   e   _____
18. tiled   a   _____
19. amidst   u   _____
20. conduits   e   _____
21. dilates   y   _____
22. teasing   v   _____
23. derange   l   _____
24. lagoon   d   _____
25. heart   w   _____
26. smearing   u   _____
27. screams   a   _____
28. nicotine   p   _____
29. ratable   y   _____
30. broaches   l   _____

25 to 30 — S
19 to 24 — T
10 to 18 — A
Answers   5 to 9 — N
Correct   1 to 4 — D

OPPOSITES ATTRACT

After each word below write its opposite, beginning with the letter *a*.

1. scarce _____
2. below _____
3. concrete _____
4. relative _____
5. reject _____
6. like _____
7. incompetent _____
8. create _____
9. praise _____
10. gradual _____
11. retard _____
12. deliberate _____
13. betrayer _____
14. sluggish _____
15. remove _____
16. opponent _____
17. unreal _____
18. depart _____
19. modern _____
20. near _____
21. deny _____
22. young _____
23. request _____
24. insufficient _____
25. exact _____
26. fail _____
27. consequent _____
28. institute _____
29. dull _____
30. lethargy _____

Answers are on page 260.

25 to 30 — S
18 to 24 — T
10 to 17 — A
Answers 5 to 9 — N
Correct 1 to 4 — D

83

WHAT DO YOU SEE?

Do not use a straight edge or ruler to answer any of these questions until you have decided on the answer. Answers are on page 260.

1. Is the figure at the center of the circles made of straight lines?

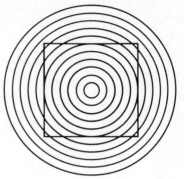

2. Look at the picture below. Are sides *a* and *c* in front of *b* and *d*, or behind them? Keep looking at the glass until something happens. What happens?

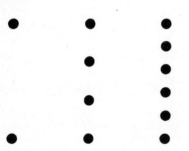

5. Which is longer, line AB or line AC?

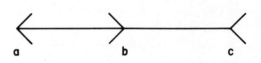

3. How do the distances compare between the top and bottom dots in each column?

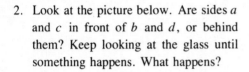

6. Which of the two circles in the squares below is the lighter one?

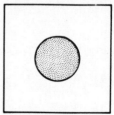

4. Look at the figure below until something happens. What happens?

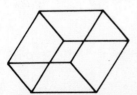

84

DE UNO MULTUM

From each word below make as many words of at least four letters as you can. Only one form of a word is allowed — either *mean* or *meant*, but not both. Don't make words by adding the letter *s* to another word. You may not use proper nouns, foreign words, abbreviations, contractions or slang. Answers are on page 260.

INTRODUCE

E.T., duct, ride ~~⨯⨯⨯⨯⨯⨯~~

	62 or more — S
	50 to 61 — T
	31 to 49 — A
Answers	16 to 30 — N
Correct	1 to 15 — D

EXCEPTION

	23 or more — S
	18 to 22 — T
	11 to 17 — A
Answers	7 to 10 — N
Correct	1 to 6 — D

FOREIGNERS

	35 or more — S
	29 to 34 — T
	20 to 28 — A
Answers	11 to 19 — N
Correct	1 to 10 — D

85

SYNONYMS

For each word give a synonym beginning with the letter *s*.

1. rascal   _____
2. demure   _____
3. wages   _____
4. elder   _____
5. isolation   _____
6. imitation   _____
7. strainer   _____
8. crimson   _____
9. tremble   _____
10. holy   _____
11. choke   _____
12. balance   _____
13. feign   _____
14. prophet   _____
15. wise   _____
16. jeer   _____
17. smash   _____
18. boil   _____
19. winding   _____
20. protection   _____
21. inadequate   _____
22. ruler   _____
23. likeness   _____
24. detective   _____
25. pale   _____
26. denote   _____
27. decay   _____
28. redemption   _____
29. tarry   _____
30. abusive   _____

Answers are on page 260.

	25 to 30 — S
	19 to 24 — T
	11 to 18 — A
Answers	5 to 10 — N
Correct	1 to 4 — D

OH SAY CAN YOU SING?

During World War I it was customary to begin all public presentations — plays, movies, concerts, as well as baseball games — with the singing of "The Star-Spangled Banner." One citizen was so upset over the difficulty many persons had singing our national anthem that he wrote an anonymous letter to a New York City newspaper (since defunct) complaining about what he regarded as a disgraceful situation. With his letter he sent this parody on the way people sing our national anthem — to be sung to the tune of "The Star-Spangled Banner."

WHAT OFTEN HAPPENS

Oh say can you sing from the start to the end
What so proudly you stand for when orchestras play it,

When the whole congregation in voices that blend
Strike up the grand hymn and then torture and slay it.

How they bellow and shout when they're first starting out!
But the dawn's early light finds them floundering about.

It's "The Star-Spangled Banner" that they're trying hard to sing,
But they don't know the words of the precious old thing.

Hark! The twilight's last gleaming has some of them stopped.
But the valiant survivors press onward serenely

To the ramparts we watched where some others are dropped,
And the loss of the leaders is manifest keenly.

The rockets' red glare gives the bravest a scare.
There are few left to face the bombs bursting in air.

'Tis a thin line of heroes that manage to save
The last of the verse and the home of the brave.

(Anonymous)

THE COMPLAINT OF THE WIFE OF A PSYCHOANALYST

I never get mad, I get hostile;
I never feel sad, I'm depressed;
If I sew or I knit, and enjoy it one bit,
I'm not handy—I'm merely obsessed.

I never regret, I feel guilty;
And if I should vacuum the hall,
Wash the woodwork and such, and not mind it too much,
Am I tidy? Compulsive, that's all.

If I can't choose a hat I have conflicts,
With ambivalent feelings toward net.
I never get worried or nervous or hurried—
Anxiety, that's what I get.

If I'm happy, I must be euphoric;
If I go to the Stork Club or Ritz
And have a good time making puns or a rhyme,
I'm manic, or maybe a schiz.

If I tell you you're right, I'm submissive,
Repressing aggressiveness, too!
And when I disagree, I'm defensive, you see,
And projecting my symptoms on you.

I love you, but that's just transference,
With Electra rearing her head;
My breathing asthmatic is psychosomatic,
A fear of exclaiming, "Drop dead!"

I'm not lonely, I'm simply dependent;
My dog has no fleas, just a tic—
So if I act hateful, never mind—just be grateful
I'm not really a stinker—I'm sick!

Author Unknown

LEFT, RIGHT! LEFT, RIGHT!

Do you know left from right? Write R for right, and L for left.

Answers are on page 261.

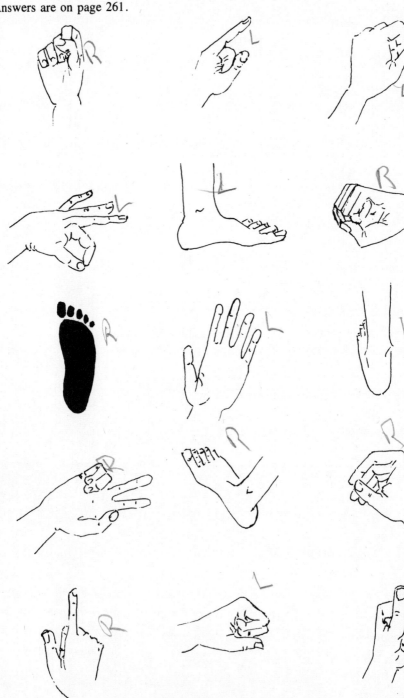

WORDS! WORDS! WORDS!

From the four possibilities, select the one correct meaning for each word at the left.

1. libertine   deceiver rake courtesan voluptuary
2. dissent   protest discord variance disagreement
3. condiment   seasoning stimulant appetizer chutney
4. fop   dasher swinger dandy poser
5. philanthropist patriot liberal humanitarian altruist
6. shortcoming   neglect defect omission deficit
7. motive   reason incentive excuse occasion
8. sobriety   steadiness abstention calmness temperance
9. relegate   consign transpose banish promote
10. impiety   ungodliness profanity sacrilege sin
11. equivocal   obscure ambiguous perplexing mysterious
12. retaliation   reprisal punishment retort accusation
13. oscillation   beat throb vibration fluctuation
14. caution   vigilance advice forethought discretion
15. filament   hair fiber capillary string
16. posterity   family descendants lineage breed
17. keepsake   memory symbol souvenir token
18. servile   oily enslaved pliant obsequious
19. harmony   consent congruity symmetry agreement
20. latent   potential unknown invisible concealed
21. deprecate   protest belittle disapprove remonstrate
22. veracity   honesty sincerity truth candor
23. tenacity   persistence cohesion strength firmness
24. sedulous   vigorous lively diligent agile
25. ululation   crying howling twittering yapping

Answers are on page 261.

22 to 25 — S
18 to 21 — T
10 to 17 — A
Answers   5 to 9 — N
Correct   1 to 4 — D

GEM

Who is the shortest man mentioned in the Bible?
Answer is on page 261.

WORDS PLUS

From each word below and the letter after it make a new word. You must make at least one change in the order of the letters of the original word. Answers are on page 261.

1. dare   b   _____
2. trips   i   _____
3. last   e   _____
4. rite   h   _____
5. trim   e   _____
6. hurt   t   _____
7. tail   v   _____
8. liar   t   _____
9. grade   r   _____
10. site   x   _____
11. lead   y   _____
12. pride   o   _____
13. healer   t   _____
14. nail   e   _____
15. field   r   _____
16. roped   w   _____
17. this   g   _____
18. grin   e   _____
19. inset   n   _____
20. relay   p   _____
21. apple   a   _____
22. green   y   _____
23. crape   h   _____
24. stern   i   _____
25. strainer   p   _____
26. direct   v   _____
27. scene   r   _____
28. encase   b   _____
29. tensions   a   _____
30. pettish   e   _____

28 to 30 — S
23 to 27 — T
10 to 22 — A
Answers   5 to 9 — N
Correct   1 to 4 — D

DO YOU KNOW YOUR "RINGS"?

For each description write one word ending in *ring*. The answer to the first one is *wandering*. Answers are on page 261.

A ring that:

1. roams _____
2. meditates _____
3. is uncertain _____
4. keeps ships from drifting _____
5. ties an animal _____
6. gets better _____
7. talks hesitatingly _____
8. flaps rapidly _____
9. reduces in intensity _____
10. spreads on bread _____
11. gathers in a bunch _____
12. dilutes _____
13. hesitates _____
14. collects _____
15. yields to the whims of _____
16. gives refuge _____
17. moves heavily _____
18. commands _____
19. thins out _____
20. annoys _____
21. trembles _____
22. makes a loud noise _____
23. refrains from using _____
24. gazes fixedly _____
25. fusses around _____

	20 to 25 — S
	15 to 19 — T
	10 to 14 — A
Answers	5 to 9 — N
Correct	1 to 4 — D

PUT IT ALL TOGETHER

Each design is made up of the numbered blocks shown near the top of the page. Each block may be used repeatedly. On each design write the numbers of the blocks used.

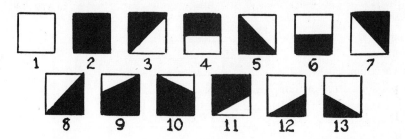

Answers are on page 261.

HIDDEN PRESIDENTS

The names of 20 presidents are hidden among the letters below. Starting with any letter you may read up, down, left, right, or at an angle. The name can be entirely in one straight line, or it can change in one or more directions. How many can you find? Answers are on page 261.

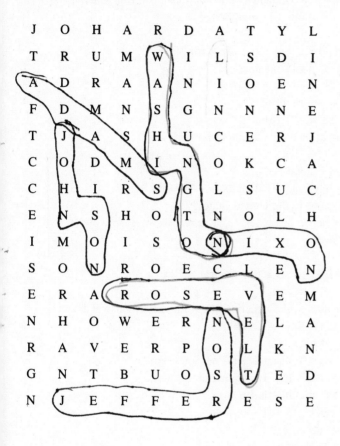

```
J   O   H   A   R   D   A   T   Y   L
T   R   U   M   W   I   L   S   D   I
A   D   R   A   A   N   I   O   E   N
F   D   M   N   S   G   N   N   N   E
T   J   A   S   H   U   C   E   R   J
C   O   D   M   I   N   O   K   C   A
C   H   I   R   S   G   L   S   U   C
E   N   S   H   O   T   N   O   L   H
I   M   O   I   S   O   N   I   X   O
S   O   N   R   O   E   C   L   E   N
E   R   A   R   O   S   E   V   E   M
N   H   O   W   E   R   N   E   L   A
R   A   V   E   R   P   O   L   K   N
G   N   T   B   U   O   S   T   E   D
N   J   E   F   F   E   R   E   S   E
```

20 — S
17 to 19 — T
12 to 16 — A
Answers   6 to 11 — N
Correct   1 to 5 — D

WHAT DO YOU KNOW?

Select the correct one of the four possible answers to each item.

1. The former name of Ethiopia was:
   1) Afghanistan   2) Congo   3) Abyssinia   4) Pakistan
2. To get from Australia to New Zealand you would have to travel generally:
   1) west   2) northeast   3) south   4) southeast
3. Most gold is mined in:
   1) the U. S.   2) South Africa   3) Asia   4) Australia
4. About what percent of the air is oxygen?
   1) 10   2) 20   3) 40   4) 75
5. The defeat at the Alamo occurred in:
   1) 1798   2) 1812   3) 1836   4) 1861
6. When Alexander the Great died he was about how old?
   1) 80   2) 65   3) 50   4) 35
7. The highest mountain in Europe is:
   1) the Matterhorn   2) Jungfrau   3) Weisshorn   4) Mont Blanc
8. How low is the lowest point in the United States?
   1) sea level   2) 50 feet below sea level   3) 130 feet below sea level
   4) 275 feet below sea level
9. Afghanistan is in:
   1) Southwest Asia   2) Eastern Asia   3) Central Africa
   4) Northeast Africa
10. The number of battle deaths in the American Revolutionary War was about:
    1) 4500   2) 10,500   3) 15,000   4) 21,000
11. Raold Amundsen is noted for:
    1) discovery of antibiotics   2) discovery of the South Pole
    3) first flight over the North Pole   4) exploration of Africa
12. Anesthetics such as ether and chloroform were first used about:
    1) 1760   2) 1805   3) 1845   4) 1875
13. Which planet is farthest from the sun?
    1) Uranus   2) Jupiter   3) Neptune   4) Pluto
14. Which of these is *not* one of the Seven Wonders of the Ancient World?
    1) Pyramids of Egypt   2) Labyrinth of Crete   3) Colossus of Rhodes
    4) Hanging Gardens of Babylon
15. The Republican Party participated in a national election for the first time:
    1) before 1800   2) about 1820   3) before the Civil War
    4) after the Civil War

Answers are on page 261.

GROW-A-WORD

"Grow-a-Word" by adding a letter to the preceding word, as well as changing the sequence of its letters. For example: *is, sit, stir,* etc. The number of letters in each word is indicated by the number of dashes.

1. anger   _ _ _
   a layer; a row   _ _ _ _
   threefold   _ _ _ _ _
   combustible material   _ _ _ _ _ _
   reproduced from type   _ _ _ _ _ _ _
   fearless   _ _ _ _ _ _ _ _
2. a conjunction; in case that   _ _
   an exclamation; for shame!   _ _ _
   of common occurrence   _ _ _ _
   an aviator   _ _ _ _ _
   a thing of small value   _ _ _ _ _ _
   prolific   _ _ _ _ _ _ _
3. a dessert   _ _ _ _
   ready to gather   _ _ _ _ _
   steeple   _ _ _ _ _ _
   liveliness   _ _ _ _ _ _ _
   interval of relief   _ _ _ _ _ _ _ _
   status   _ _ _ _ _ _ _ _ _
4. to a degree   _ _
   juice of a woody plant   _ _ _
   a vaulted recess in a church   _ _ _ _
   a brown pigment   _ _ _ _ _
   commendation   _ _ _ _ _ _
   walk idly   _ _ _ _ _ _ _
   one who lives on another   _ _ _ _ _ _ _ _

Answers are on page 261.

GEM

Place the point of a pencil on the dot at the center of the circle at the right. Now, without lifting the pencil from the paper, how can you trace the circle with the pencil?

Answer is on page 261.

DO YOU HAVE THE TIME?

Below is a list of different times of the day. Beside each time, write what the time would be if the minute hand and hour hand were interchanged. Do this mentally . . . no fair drawing clock faces! Answers are on page 261.

1. 7:03 _____

2. 12:26 _____

3. 5:27 _____

4. 8:13 _____

5. 2:01 _____

6. 9:28 _____

7. 5:07 _____

8. 6:31 _____

9. 11:48 _____

10. 3:16 _____

11. 1:51 _____

12. 10:19 _____

GEM

Can you do this crossword puzzle? The answers are the same for both Horizontal and Vertical. Answers are on page 261.

1. a vital organ
2. silly
3. boast
4. boredom ,
5. join again

1	2	3	4	5
2				
3				
4				
5				

IS THIS GREEK TO YOU?

Below is a list of gods, Greek and Roman. Write the letter G after the name of each Greek god, and an R after each Roman god. Then look in the right-hand column and write the letter of the domain of each god.

1. Neptune ____ ____
2. Hera ____ ____
3. Hestia ____ ____
4. Zeus ____ ____
5. Mars ____ ____
6. Hades ____ ____
7. Poseidon ____ ____
8. Vesta ____ ____
9. Athena ____ ____
10. Venus ____ ____
11. Juno ____ ____
12. Apollo ____ ____
13. Jupiter ____ ____
14. Mercury ____ ____
15. Artemis ____ ____
16. Pluto ____ ____
17. Aphrodite ____ ____
18. Vulcan ____ ____
19. Ares ____ ____
20. Hephaestes ____ ____
21. Minerva ____ ____
22. Diana ____ ____
23. Hermes ____ ____

a. the skies
b. the seas
c. the underworld
d. civilized life
e. light
f. the hunt
g. love and beauty
h. messenger of the gods
i. war
j. fire
k. hearth and home
l. marriage

38 to 46 — S
30 to 37 — T
20 to 29 — A
Answers 12 to 19 — N
Correct 1 to 11 — D

SCALE WISE

A numismatist was showing a friend his coin collection. He was especially proud of the latest additions to his collection — nine valuable coins that looked exactly alike. They also weighed the same except for one that weighed slightly more than any of the others and was therefore worth more than any of them. As he talked about that one coin, which he had been keeping in a separate container, it slipped from his hand and fell among the others.

"Now look at that," he said "I'll have to weigh all these coins two at a time on my balance scale to find the heavier coin. That could mean as many as 36 weighings."

"No," his friend disagreed, "I can find it for you in two weighings."

How can the heavier coin be detected in just two weighings on the balance scale?

SCRAMBLE

Make as many words as you can from the letters on each line, using all the letters each time. For instance, by scrambling the letters *b e r t u* you can make *brute, rebut* and *tuber*.

1. b e r t u _____
2. a i l r _____
3. a e m n _____
4. a m e d _____
5. e i n l _____
6. a b d r _____
7. a e k l _____
8. i s d a _____
9. a e f r s _____
10. a d e r t _____
11. e i s v w _____
12. a c k l s _____
13. o b e l w _____
14. a d e l p _____
15. a d e e l r _____
16. a c e n r t _____
17. d s a d e r _____
18. d e i r s t _____
19. c e i n s t _____
20. e b g n i _____
21. a e l p n _____
22. e d u o r t _____
23. a e h r s t t _____
24. c d e o p r r u _____
25. e i l l r s t _____

Answers are on page 262.

Answers are on page 262.

	63 or more — S
	56 to 62 — T
	36 to 55 — A
Answers	19 to 35 — N
Correct	1 to 18 — D

TONGUE TANGLE

Mrs. Shine's son shuns sunshine.

TOOTHPICKS WILL DO!

You can work with the diagrams below, or you may prefer to use matchsticks or toothpicks, which you can move around freely. Answers are on page 262.

1. Move two sticks so that you will have eight squares of the original size.
2. Move one stick and still have seven squares of the original size.
3. Move two sticks and still have seven squares of the original size.
4. How many ways can you remove two sticks and still have six of the original squares?

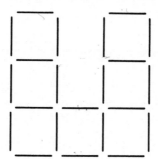

5. Move three sticks so that you will have nine squares of the original size.
6. Move two sticks so that you will have eight squares.
7. How many ways can you move two sticks and still have eight squares?
8. Move three sticks so that you will have eight squares.

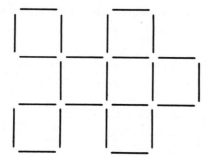

9. Remove one stick and leave just four of the original squares.
10. Move three sticks so that you will have six squares.
11. Move three sticks so that you will have five squares.
12. Move one stick so that you will still have five squares.

OPPOSITES ATTRACT

After each word below write one that means the opposite. But each answer must begin with the letter *d*. Answers are on page 262.

1. safety   _____
2. crawl   _____
3. honesty   _____
4. wild   _____
5. bright   _____
6. respect   _____
7. fragile   _____
8. vacillate   _____
9. collect   _____
10. alive   _____
11. coarse   _____
12. join   _____
13. uncertain   _____
14. apathetic   _____
15. credit   _____
16. cowardly   _____
17. conceal   _____
18. shallow   _____
19. gay   _____
20. obey   _____
21. rush   _____
22. continue   _____
23. uniformity   _____
24. reassure   _____
25. perfect   _____
26. hobo   _____
27. certain   _____
28. assert   _____
29. enlarge   _____
30. rise   _____

	25 to 30 — S
	19 to 24 — T
	12 to 18 — A
Answers	6 to 11 — N
Correct	1 to 5 — D

WHO SAID THAT?

In the first column are quotations, and in the second a list of possible sources for them. In front of each quotation write the letter of its source. Answers are on page 262.

_____ 1. Do not do to others what you do not wish done to you.

_____ 2. We are not amused.

_____ 3. I would rather be right than be President.

_____ 4. Peace for our time . . . peace with honor.

_____ 5. To give the devil his due.

_____ 6. Every dog has his day.

_____ 7. We have nothing to fear but fear itself.

_____ 8. Then spare the rod and spoil the child.

_____ 9. A finger in every pie.

_____10. Am I my brother's keeper?

_____11. Comparisons are odious.

_____12. Man doth not live by bread alone.

_____13. Lord, what fools these mortals be.

_____14. Get thee behind me Satan.

_____15. How are the mighty fallen!

_____16. Uneasy lies the head that wears a crown.

_____17. I shall return!

_____18. With malice toward none, with charity for all . . . .

_____19. No man can serve two masters.

_____20. Eye for eye, tooth for tooth.

a. Confucius
b. F. D. Roosevelt
c. Shakespeare
d. Queen Victoria
e. Old Testament
f. Sophocles
g. Neville Chamberlain
h. Samuel Butler
i. New Testament
j. Henry Clay
k. Cervantes
l. Lincoln
m. Douglas McArthur

Answers Correct
16 to 20 — S
12 to 15 — T
8 to 11 — A
4 to 7 — N
1 to 3 — D

GEM

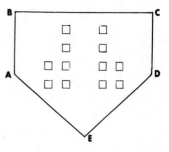

A man had a piece of land near the seashore, shaped like the figure at the right. On it were 12 cabins, as shown. He received an offer to buy the land provided it could be cut into 6 pieces all of the same size and shape with 2 cabins on each piece. The owner found he could do it with four lines. Can you?

Answer is on page 262.

ON THE SQUARE

In each square below, draw lines showing how it is made up of the pieces to the right of it. Answers are on page 262.

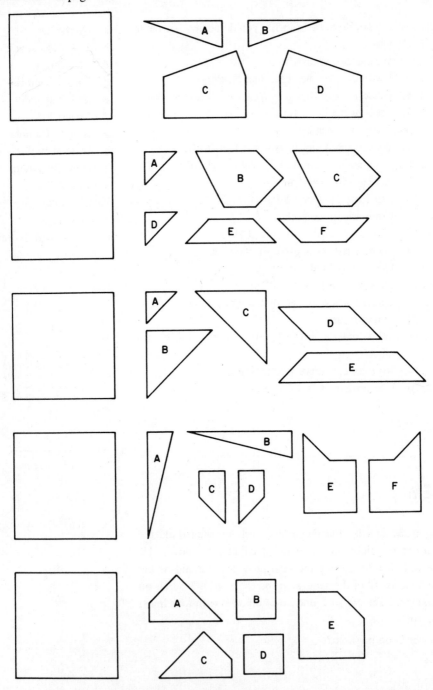

NAMES OR WORDS?

After each clue below write an answer that is also a proper name (or nickname). The letter after each description tells whether the name is masculine or feminine.

1. reigning beauty (f) _____
2. the unit of inheritance (m) _____
3. to deprive of something by unlawful force (m) _____
4. the plants of a particular region (f) _____
5. power of choosing one's own actions; a legal document (m) _____
6. French gold coin (m) _____
7. precious stone; deep red (f) _____
8. evergreen cultivated for its fruit (f) _____
9. woman of antiquity possessing powers of prophecy (f) _____
10. the expression of what is beautiful or appealing (m) _____
11. the uncut loop of the pile of a fabric (f, m) _____
12. four-base hit (in baseball) (m) _____
13. stout twilled cotton fabric (f, m) _____
14. live-bearing fish; a sort of toggle bolt (f) _____
15. little pie (f) _____
16. plant of the mint family (m) _____
17. highly colored variety of quartz (m) _____
18. clear transparent glass (f) _____
19. child's toy baby (f) _____
20. bluish-purple color; a flower (f) _____
21. skein of yarn (m) _____
22. bird; the American flycatcher; the pewit (f) _____
23. hard, smooth, highly lustrous concretion; used in jewelry (f) _____
24. non-noble freeholder in the Middle Ages (m) _____
25. evergreen; emblem of love; sacred to Venus (f) _____

Answers are on page 263.

20 to 25 — S
16 to 19 — T
9 to 15 — A
Answers   5 to 8 — N
Correct   1 to 4 — D

LET'S PLAY HANKY PANKY!

After each expression write the *two rhyming words* to which it refers. For example, for *speedy thoroughfare* you would write *fleet street*. Answers are on page 263.

1. speedy thoroughfare   _____
2. cunning Indian   _____
3. colored vegetable   _____
4. single icecream container   _____
5. ponderous tax   _____
6. more satisfactory communication   _____
7. inexpensive spiced vegetable   _____
8. better steamship   _____
9. second male sibling   _____
10. small ridiculous picture   _____
11. translucent lachrymal product   _____
12. halting female   _____
13. delayed server   _____
14. cowardly male   _____
15. bleached blonde   _____
16. filet mignon   _____
17. clean diaper   _____
18. indolent flower   _____
19. frenzied trick   _____
20. happier performer   _____
21. large volcanic depression   _____
22. wealthier baseball player   _____
23. steady piece of furniture   _____
24. desolate mountain top   _____
25. one thrill   _____

	22 to 25 — S
	18 to 21 — T
	11 to 17 — A
Answers	5 to 10 — N
Correct	1 to 4 — D

HOW ODD?

You occasionally may play a game in which the beginner is decided by throwing a pair of dice to see who throws the largest number. Or you may play a game in which the number of spaces you move is determined by the numbers appearing on a throw of dice. See if you can tell what the chances are, or what odds would be fair, in each of the following situations. Answers are on page 263.

1. On a single throw of a pair of dice, what are the chances of throwing:

   a) a 2?_____   e) a 6?_____   i) a 10?_____

   b) a 3?_____   f) a 7?_____   j) an 11?_____

   c) a 4?_____   g) an 8?_____   k) a 12?_____

   d) a 5?_____   h) a 9?_____

2. What are the odds in favor of throwing each of the above numbers?

   a) _____   e) _____   i) _____

   b) _____   f) _____   j) _____

   c) _____   g) _____   k) _____

   d) _____   h) _____

3. You throw a pair of dice and get a 5. What are the chances that your opponent will throw the same number or a smaller number?

4. You throw a pair of dice and get a 6. What are the chances of your throwing a 6 again? a number more than 6?

5. What are the chances of throwing a 7 or an 11 on a single throw of a pair of dice?

6. On a second throw of a pair of dice, what are your chances of beating what you got on your first throw, if on your first throw you got:

   a) a 3?_____   d) a 6?_____   g) a 9?_____

   b) a 4?_____   e) a 7?_____   h) a 10?_____

   c) a 5?_____   f) an 8?_____

7. On a second throw of a pair of dice, what are your chances of getting the same number as you got on your first throw if on the first throw you got:

   a) a 3?_____   c) a 5?_____   f) a 9?_____

   b) a 4?_____   d) a 6?_____   g) a 10?_____

                        e) an 8?_____

WORDS! WORDS! WORDS!

From the four possibilities, select the one correct meaning for each word at the left.

 1. jubilant   triumphant   laughing   rejoicing   happy
 2. loquacious   chattering   fluent   eloquent   talkative
 3. upbraid   revile   condemn   reproach   reject
 4. haggard   gaunt   ugly   fatigued   thin
 5. effervesce   ferment   bubble   foam   sparkle
 6. quirk   dodge   peculiarity   evasion   subterfuge
 7. chronic   constant   regular   repeated   unceasing
 8. wry   distorted   oblique   irregular   gnarled
 9. irrelevant   unessential   unrelated   incidental   inconsistent
10. malefactor   scourge   destroyer   criminal   jailbird
11. sonorous   powerful   vehement   resonant   loud
12. genesis   evolution   origin   formation   bible
13. ephemeral   fugitive   elusive   transitory   passing
14. yeoman   beefeater   attendant   aide   petty officer
15. purvey   prepare   conserve   procure   furnish
16. dauntless   spirited   gallant   intrepid   fearful
17. robust   hardy   solid   unyielding   tough
18. instigate   motivate   induce   incite   urge
19. votary   adherent   devotee   saint   admirer
20. feasible   desirable   expedient   appropriate   workable
21. bourgeois   mean   vulgar   everyday   ordinary
22. ostracize   expatriate   exclude   segregate   eliminate
23. tantalize   disappoint   torture   baffle   tease
24. ascetic   austere   regretful   abstemious   fasting
25. nubile   mature   marriageable   betrothed   wedded

Answers are on page 263.

Answers Correct

22 to 25 — S
18 to 21 — T
10 to 17 — A
5 to 9 — N
1 to 4 — D

GEM

Who wrote this statement, and when?

    "The children now have luxury. They have bad manners, contempt for authority. They show disrespect for elders, and have to chatter in place of exercise. They no longer rise when elders enter the room. They contradict their parents, chatter before company and tyrannize over their teachers."

Answer is on page 263.

THROUGH THE LOOKING GLASS

For each figure below there are three mirror reflections, only one of which is correct. Pick the one that is the way the original figure would appear in a looking glass.

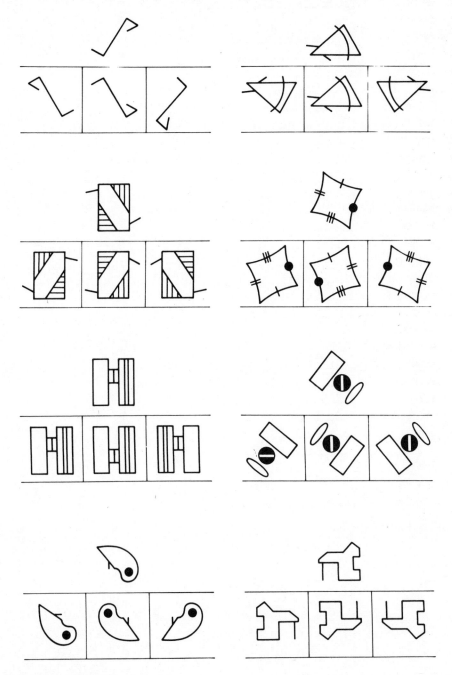

Answers are on page 263.

SYNONYMS

For each word below give a synonym beginning with the letter *r*.

1. actual _____
2. discard _____
3. ask _____
4. sane _____
5. far _____
6. look _____
7. riffraff _____
8. mad _____
9. uproar _____
10. piquant _____
11. sparkling _____
12. spread _____
13. mania _____
14. plunder _____
15. clothing _____
16. hoist _____
17. saunter _____
18. haphazard _____
19. span _____
20. plausible _____
21. tumbledown _____
22. puzzle _____
23. crack _____
24. stiff _____
25. sentimental _____
26. spin _____
27. pitiless _____
28. gossip _____
29. path _____
30. irregular _____

Answers are on page 263.

	26 to 30 — S
	20 to 25 — T
	13 to 19 — A
Answers	6 to 12 — N
Correct	1 to 5 — D

SPOT THE STRANGER

Which word in each group does not belong with the other four?

1. swimming   tennis   boxing   soccer   wrestling
2. Dodge   Pierce Arrow   Buick   Chrysler   Chevrolet
3. Taft   Washington   Cleveland   Wilson   Jackson
4. zebra   gazelle   leopard   ocelot   giraffe
5. loyal   honest   rich   courageous   kind
6. Equator   International Date Line   Arctic Circle
   Antarctica   Greenwich Meridian
7. sundial   clock   chronometer   watch   timetable
8. Truman   Tyler   Coolidge   Arthur   Wilson
9. fluorescent   incandescent   candle   moon   gas
10. Shell   Exxon   Union   Phillips   Westinghouse
11. marigold   calendula   forsythia   daffodil   iris
12. pot   pan   roaster   barbecue   skillet
13. Lincoln   Mercedes   Chrysler   Cadillac   Oldsmobile
14. four   nine   sixteen   twenty-five   thirty
15. doublet   coat   shawl   jacket   sweater
16. halfpenny   shilling   nickel   pound   guinea
17. play   recess   break   respite   intermission
18. subtract   reduce   diet   dilute   weaken
19. recognize   acknowledge   identify   know   remember
20. ceiling   floor   window   anteroom   wall
21. stool   chair   table   sofa   floor
22. bas relief   oil painting   etching   water color   drawing
23. needlepoint   knitting   crewel   embroidery   tapestry
24. currency   coin   check   cash   specie
25. lion   tiger   cougar   leopard   coyote

Answers are on page 263.

21 to 25 — S
16 to 20 — T
10 to 15 — A
Answers   5 to 9 — N
Correct   1 to 4 — D

RHYME TIME

Carbon paper put in backwards
Causes second sheets to lack words

ALL MIXED UP

Hidden in the column below are the names of animals and birds. How many of them can you unscramble? Answers are on page 263.

1. i o b n s   _____
2. a g i l l o r   _____
3. a b d e g r   _____
4. e k m n o y   _____
5. a a g k n o o r   _____
6. s e o r t y   _____
7. a d e g i p r r t   _____
8. a d e l o p r   _____
9. a c g o r u   _____
10. a c c e k o p   _____
11. d e e e i n r r   _____
12. a e e g l l z   _____
13. a e m m o r s t   _____
14. a a e h n p s t   _____
15. a o o b b n   _____
16. a e e l n o p t   _____
17. a c e e h i m n p z _____
18. a b c i o r u   _____
19. e g i n o p   _____
20. c e h i n o o r r s _____
21. d e g h n o r u y   _____
22. a e g g h i i l n n t _____
23. e o o c l t   _____
24. a h i m o o p p p s t u _____
25. a e e h l n p t   _____

23 to 25 — S
19 to 22 — T
11 to 18 — A
Answers   5 to 10 — N
Correct   1 to 4 — D

OH BOY!

A farm boy wrote home after he had been in the army only a few weeks: "Dear Ma: Army life is wonderful. They let you sleep 'til quarter to six every morning, even in the summer!"

DE UNO MULTUM

From each word below make as many words of at least four letters as you can. Only one form of a word is allowed — either *mean* or *meant*, but not both. Don't make words by adding the letter *s* to another word. You may not use proper nouns, foreign words, abbreviations, contractions or slang. Answers are on page 264.

SECRETIVE

34 or more — S
29 to 33 — T
19 to 28 — A
Answers   11 to 18 — N
Correct   1 to 10 — D

MODERNIZES

43 or more — S
38 to 42 — T
25 to 37 — A
Answers   13 to 24 — N
Correct   1 to 12 — D

ENUMERATE

33 or more — S
29 to 32 — T
21 to 28 — A
Answers   11 to 20 — N
Correct   1 to 10 — D

RIGHT ON!

Examine each sequence both horizontally and vertically, figure out the pattern, and fill in the vacant spaces correctly. Answers are on page 264.

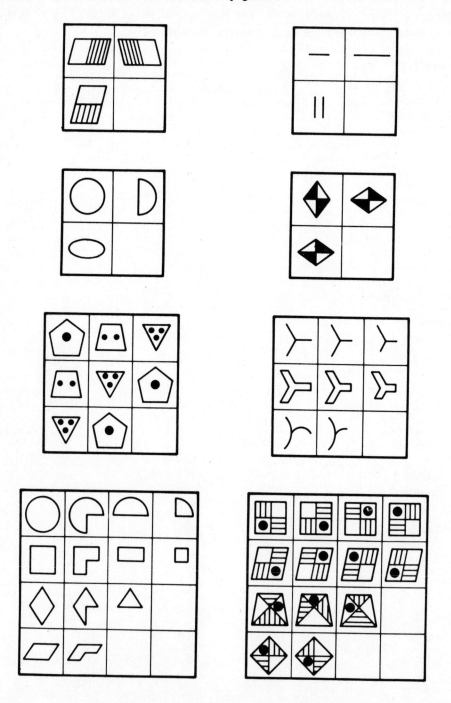

WORDS PLUS

From each word and the letter after it make a new word, with at least one change in the order of the letters in the original word. Answers are on page 264.

1. fringe   o   _____
2. garble   a   _____
3. metering   a   _____
4. retreads   u   _____
5. centered   i   _____
6. maintain   e   _____
7. reading   a   _____
8. falter   u   _____
9. brighten   a   _____
10. mattress   e   _____
11. mailed   m   _____
12. diners   i   _____
13. caressed   e   _____
14. lassoing   e   _____
15. neared   y   _____
16. coasting   l   _____
17. ruminate   i   _____
18. impels   g   _____
19. caring   o   _____
20. relations   a   _____
21. canister   a   _____
22. whomever   l   _____
23. turnings   e   _____
24. harden   u   _____
25. lading   u   _____
26. oracle   h   _____
27. bracelet   a   _____
28. trounces   i   _____
29. ultimate   s   _____
30. adherent   e   _____

	26 to 30 — S
	17 to 25 — T
	9 to 16 — A
Answers	4 to 8 — N
Correct	1 to 3 — D

After the name of each country write the letter of it from the map on page 116. Then find the capital of that country in the column at the right and write its number in the second space. Answers are on page 264.

1.	Albania	—— ——	1.	Amsterdam
2.	Austria	—— ——	2.	Athens
3.	Belgium	—— ——	3.	Belgrade
4.	Bulgaria	—— ——	4.	Bern
5.	Czechoslovakia	—— ——	5.	Bonn
6.	Denmark	—— ——	6.	Brussels
7.	East Germany	—— ——	7.	Bucharest
8.	England	—— ——	8.	Budapest
9.	Finland	—— ——	9.	Copenhagen
10.	France	—— ——	10.	Dublin
11.	Greece	—— ——	11.	East Berlin
12.	Hungary	—— ——	12.	Edinburgh
13.	Ireland	—— ——	13.	Helsinki
14.	Italy	—— ——	14.	Lisbon
15.	Luxembourg	—— ——	15.	London
16.	Netherlands	—— ——	16.	Luxembourg
17.	Norway	—— ——	17.	Madrid
18.	Poland	—— ——	18.	Moscow
19.	Portugal	—— ——	19.	Oslo
20.	Romania	—— ——	20.	Paris
21.	Russia	—— ——	21.	Prague
22.	Scotland	—— ——	22.	Rome
23.	Spain	—— ——	23.	Sofia
24.	Sweden	—— ——	24.	Stockholm
25.	Switzerland	—— ——	25.	Tirana
26.	Wales	—— ——	26.	Vienna
27.	West Germany	—— ——	27.	Warsaw
28.	Yugoslavia	—— ——		

	50 to 56 — S
	42 to 49 — T
	31 to 41 — A
Answers	19 to 30 — N
Correct	1 to 18 — D

CAN YOU GUESS THESE "AGES"?

After each clue write one word ending in *age*. The answer to number 1 is *manage*.

1. administer _____
2. close union _____
3. food for cattle _____
4. extensive slaughter _____
5. transportation _____
6. ancestry _____
7. wagon _____
8. legacy _____
9. flight _____
10. bombardment _____
11. wrong _____
12. resentment _____
13. mail _____
14. ordinary _____
15. refuse _____
16. barbarian _____
17. parcel _____
18. benefit _____
19. concept _____
20. mooring, _____
21. drink _____
22. bravery _____
23. face _____
24. feathers _____
25. trip _____

Answers are on page 264.

	20 to 25	— S
	15 to 19	— T
	10 to 14	— A
Answers	5 to 9	— N
Correct	1 to 4	— D

TONGUE TANGLE

Theodore Thatch thanked Thaddeus Thistle for the theme of the thesis, "The Thespians of Thessaly."

OPPOSITES ATTRACT

After each word below write its opposite, beginning with the letter *m*.

1. sane   _____
2. reduce   _____
3. benefit   _____
4. ample   _____
5. superiority   _____
6. intemperate   _____
7. small   _____
8. rejoice   _____
9. separate   _____
10. generous   _____
11. lesser   _____
12. effeminate   _____
13. deathless   _____
14. least   _____
15. unhappy   _____
16. destroy   _____
17. arrogant   _____
18. inconspicuous   _____
19. uncover   _____
20. unripe   _____
21. succeed   _____
22. ancient   _____
23. blessing   _____
24. weakness   _____
25. disperse   _____
26. few   _____
27. ruthless   _____
28. unworldly   _____
29. master   _____
30. real   _____

Answers are on page 265.

	25 to 30 — S	
	19 to 24 — T	
	12 to 18 — A	
Answers	6 to 11 — N	
Correct	1 to 5 — D	

GROW-A-WORD

"Grow-a-Word" by adding a letter to the preceding word, as well as changing the sequence of its letters. The number of letters in each word is indicated by the number of dashes. Answers are on page 265.

1. a pronoun   — —
   bind   — — —
   a ceremonial act   — — — —
   between; bury   — — — — —
   hold onto   — — — — — —
   a tract of land   — — — — — — —
   situated in front   — — — — — — — —
2. old piece of cloth   — — —
   what cogs are on   — — — —
   wrath   — — — — —
   male goose   — — — — — —
   apprehending meaning of symbols   — — — — — — —
   a flower   — — — — — — — —
3. a favorite American dessert   — — — —
   mature   — — — — —
   landing places for ships   — — — — — —
   a silly smile   — — — — — — —
   express assurance   — — — — — — — —
   makes more desirable   — — — — — — — — —
   extemporize   — — — — — — — — — —
4. note of the musical scale   — —
   a beverage   — — —
   fabric made of openwork threads   — — — —
   a balance   — — — — —
   situations   — — — — — —
   one who sells at higher than official rates — — — — — — —
   instruments for fine measurements   — — — — — — — —

HOW ABOUT A DATE?

After each event listed below write the letter of the time period during which it occurred. (Hint: Some time periods are used more than once, others not at all.)

1. Sulfa drugs first came into use in _____
2. Marco Polo visited China in _____
3. Fidel Castro assumed power in Cuba in _____
4. The first U.S. space flight was made in _____
5. The Egyptian pyramids were begun in _____
6. Romulus founded Rome in _____
7. The Edict of Milan legalized Christianity in Rome in _____
8. The Chicago fire occurred in _____
9. Julius Caesar was assassinated in _____
10. Pompeii was destroyed by Vesuvius in _____
11. The great fire of London occurred in _____
12. Franklin proved lightning is electricity in _____
13. Gutenberg completed the first printed Bible in _____
14. The Gregorian calendar was adopted by Great Britain and its colonies in _____
15. The first human heart transplant was done in _____
16. The first talking movie was shown in _____
17. Bell invented the telephone in _____
18. The Wright brothers invented an airplane with a motor in _____
19. The Turks captured Constantinople in _____
20. The Taj Mahal was completed in _____

a. 3000–2500 B.C.
b. 2000–1500 B.C.
c. 1000–501 B.C.
d. 500–1 B.C.
e. 1–199 A.D.
f. 200–499 A.D.
g. 500–999 A.D.
h. 1000–1499 A.D.
i. 1500–1599 A.D.
j. 1600–1699 A.D.
k. 1700–1749 A.D.
l. 1750–1799 A.D.
m. 1800–1824 A.D.
n. 1825–1849 A.D.
o. 1850–1874 A.D.
p. 1875–1899 A.D.
q. 1900–1924 A.D.
r. 1925–1949 A.D.
s. 1950–1974 A.D.

Answers are on page 265.

Answers Correct
17 to 20 — S
13 to 16 — T
8 to 12 — A
4 to 7 — N
1 to 3 — D

TIC OR TRIST

Someone who was asked to tell the difference between a psychotic, a neurotic and a psychiatrist explained that the neurotic builds castles in the air, the psychotic lives in the castles, and the psychiatrist? He's the one who collects the rent.

CAN YOU COUNT WHAT YOU CAN'T SEE?

Although you can't see all the blocks in each pile below, try to count them. Near each pile write the number of blocks in it. If there is a block missing from the outside of the pile and you can't tell what is behind or below it, assume that all the blocks in that row or column are missing. Answers are on page 265.

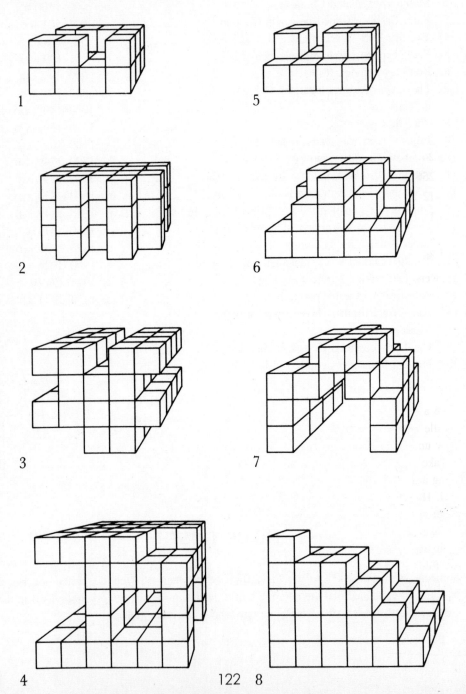

1

5

2

6

3

7

4

8

WHAT NEXT?

The numbers in each line below form a series. Write the next two numbers in each series.

1. **2 5 10 17 26** ____ ____
2. **4 7 13 22 34** ____ ____
3. **2 4 5 3 9 10 4** ____ ____
4. **120 60 40 30** ____ ____
5. **11/12 10/11 9/10 8/9** ____ ____
6. **4 3 12 5 4 20 6** ____ ____
7. **8 7 11 9 7 12 10 7** ____ ____
8. **216 125 64 27** ____ ____
9. **1 2 9 28 65** ____ ____
10. **24 23 21 28 27 25 32** ____ ____
11. **256 17 169 14 100 11 49** ____ ____
12. **12 10 8 11 9 9 10 8 10** ____ ____
13. **1 5 11 19 29** ____ ____
14. **2 4 8 3 9 27 4** ____ ____
15. **36 216 25 125 16** ____ ____

Answers are on page 265.

13 to 15 — S
10 to 12 — T
7 to 9 — A
Answers   4 to 6 — N
Correct   1 to 3 — D

PAPER WORK

Take a sheet of paper and fold it in two. Then cut (or tear) a small piece from the middle of the fold. How many holes will there be if you unfold the paper? _____ Now unfold the paper and see if you are right.

Take a second sheet and fold it once. Then fold it again in fourths (the second fold being at right angles to the first fold). Now cut a hole from the middle of the second fold. How many holes will you find when you unfold the paper? _____ Unfold the paper and see if you are right.

Take a third sheet of paper and fold it once; then a second time as before. Fold it again at right angles to the middle of the second fold. Cut a hole in the middle of the last fold. How many holes will there be in the paper when you unfold it? _____ Once more unfold the paper and see if you are right.

Take a fourth sheet of paper. Suppose you were to fold it six times and cut a hole in the middle of the last fold. How many holes would there be in the paper when you unfold it? _____

Answers are on page 265.

PUT IT ALL TOGETHER

Each of the figures below was made by cutting up a square, and rearranging the parts. Draw lines in each figure to show the separate parts and than arrange them in the blank square at the right. Answers are on page 265.

SCRAMBLE

Make as many words as you can from the letters on each line, using all the letters each time. Answers are on page 265.

1. a b g r _____
2. a b e k r _____
3. c i n o s _____
4. e e l r v _____
5. b s t u _____
6. a b e r s t _____
7. a b d e l m _____
8. a c e n r v _____
9. c c o r s u _____
10. c p s u _____
11. a c p r s _____
12. a d e i l t _____
13. e f i n s t _____
14. a d e s t _____
15. a d e i p r s _____
16. a e g r r t _____
17. b e l o r s t _____
18. d o r w y _____
19. c d e i n r s _____
20. c e n o r t u _____
21. d e i o p s t _____
22. d e g i n l u _____
23. d e e g h i n _____
24. e e l r s t t _____
25. a g i n p r s _____

65 or more — S
50 to 64 — T
28 to 49 — A
Answers   16 to 27 — N
Correct   1 to 15 — D

SYNONYMS

For each word below give a synonym beginning with the letter c.

1. profession   ————————————
2. disguise   ————————————
3. frankness   ————————————
4. mortification   ————————————
5. alter   ————————————
6. quote   ————————————
7. talon   ————————————
8. associate   ————————————
9. disaster   ————————————
10. applaud   ————————————
11. praise   ————————————
12. wheedle   ————————————
13. outcome   ————————————
14. collide   ————————————
15. felony   ————————————
16. sarcastic   ————————————
17. stingy   ————————————
18. subtlety   ————————————
19. reckon   ————————————
20. calculate   ————————————
21. uproar   ————————————
22. serenity   ————————————
23. attribute   ————————————
24. systematize   ————————————
25. egoism   ————————————

Answers are on page 265.

22 to 25 — S
18 to 21 — T
10 to 17 — A
Answers   5 to 9 — N
Correct   1 to 4 — D

TONGUE TANGLE

Click quick (repeat five times rapidly)

126

SOUND FAMILIAR?

Write the name of the product to which each of these slogans refers.

1. So good you hate to put it down. _____
2. The breakfast of champions. _____
3. I can't believe I ate the whole thing! _____
4. Daddy! Daddy! Only one! _____
5. It always lifts you up. _____
6. Building a better way to see the USA. _____
7. Makes you feel cleaner than soap. _____
8. Brings you face to face. _____
9. It cools, refreshes and soothes (the face). _____
10. Lifts the dirt right off the wall. _____
11. Take care of yourself. Take _____. _____
12. Covers all sorts of things. _____
13. If your friends could see you now! _____
14. The kind doctors recommend most. _____
15. You can't make it better; you can make it different. _____
16. For your peace of mind. _____
17. Fly the friendly skies of _____. _____
18. Tastes as good as it looks. _____
19. It's the little things that make us big. _____
20. They have to do a better job. _____
21. Try it. You'll like it! _____
22. It will help suppress the cough *you* can't suppress. _____
23. Sooner or later you'll own _____. _____
24. If you've got the time, we've got the beer. _____
25. It never lets you down. _____

Answers are on page 266.

RHYME TIME

A young woman supporter of lib
Was known as cuttingly glib
When faced with old Adam
She'd reply with sarcasm
"Don't you know that old story's a rib?"

127

SPOT THE STRANGER

Which word in each group does not belong with the other four?

1. oak   elm   maple   mahogany   pine
2. broadsword   dagger   poniard   stiletto   dirk
3. trumpet   cornet   lute   trombone   bugle
4. scarlet   vermillion   crimson   orange   rose
5. gram   centimeter   liter   yard   stere
6. hawk   pheasant   owl   eagle   osprey
7. morning   forenoon   A.M.   morn   aurora
8. dollar   franc   shilling   meter   peso
9. rose   zinnia   rhododendron   azalea   lilac
10. attack   stroke   assault   sally   raid
11. Ray   Carol   Jean   Mary   Robin
12. earl   senator   duke   count   marquis
13. learning   erudition   degree   scholarship   knowledge
14. crowd   mob   galaxy   horde   throng
15. *Norma   La Bohème   Tosca   Madame Butterfly   Manon Lescaut*
16. land   earth   ground   soil   property
17. highway   avenue   street   boulevard   parkway
18. intuition   insight   perception   apprehension   judgment
19. apple   peach   tomato   plum   apricot
20. mohair   rayon   nylon   dacron   acrilan
21. cube   triangle   square   circle   pentagon
22. pious   religious   faithful   devout   reverent
23. *Die Walküre   Siegfried   Parsifal   Lohengrin   Der Freischutz*
24. president   governor   king   emperor   rajah
25. iris   tulip   jonquil   pansy   hyacinth

Answers are on page 266.

	21 to 25 — S
	16 to 20 — T
	10 to 15 — A
Answers	5 to 9 — N
Correct	1 to 4 — D

TRY IT ON A FRIEND!

1. Place some sticks (matches or toothpicks) like this: VII − V = VI. This equation is obviously not correct. But you can make it correct by moving *one* stick to another position, using all 12 matches with which you started.

2. A train left New York for Philadelphia and made the trip in 80 minutes, traveling at a uniform rate and making no stops. At the same moment another train left Philadelphia for New York traveling on a parallel track at the same rate, also making no stops. But the second train took one hour and twenty minutes. Can you explain this phenomenon?

3. Take an empty match box. Ask a friend of yours for a dollar bill and give him a dollar bill of your own. Instruct him to fold the two dollar bills together and place them in the empty match box. Take the box from him, pass it from one hand to the other behind your back, say a little mumbo jumbo over it, rub it hard with one of your hands, then offer to sell your friend the box and its contents for a dollar and a half. In case he is skeptical, let him examine the contents of the box, and then repeat the mumbo jumbo performance. You will be surprised to find how many persons will fall for it!

4. Place fourteen matches or toothpicks like this: IV − III = VIII. But 4 minus 3 does not equal 8! Again by moving just one match to another position you can make this equation work.

5. What animal is it such that if all animals of that kind, and all seed of that animal, were destroyed, it would reappear in a matter of a few months?

6. What do you sit on, go to sleep in and brush your teeth with?

Answers are on page 266.

DE UNO MULTUM

From each word below make as many words of at least four letters as you can. Only one form of a word is allowed — either *mean* or *meant*, but not both. Don't make words by adding the letter *s* to another word. You may not use proper nouns, foreign words, abbreviations, contractions or slang. Answers are on page 266.

DEFENSELESS

22 or more — S
19 to 21 — T
14 to 18 — A
Answers 10 to 13 — N
Correct   1 to 9 — D

DISCERNMENT

95 or more — S
75 to 94 — T
44 to 74 — A
Answers 24 to 43 — N
Correct   1 to 23 — D

FRATERNIZATION

55 or more — S
40 to 54 — T
22 to 39 — A
Answers 16 to 21 — N
Correct   1 to 15 — D

ALL MIXED UP

Hidden in the column below are the names of flowers. How many of them can you unscramble? Answers are on page 266.

1. i t u p l _____
2. n e r v e a b _____
3. a y s d i _____
4. n a t c h h i y _____
5. r e l o a n e d _____
6. p s t w e e e a _____
7. u n m i t r a u t s _____
8. o o h h l l k y c _____
9. n y o p e _____
10. s l l o i g a u d _____
11. u n m m m h h y s t e a r c _____
12. n n a a t r i c o _____
13. s s i i b c u h _____
14. m e a n j s i _____
15. a a a l n n t _____
16. i n p u t a e _____
17. a b e g i n o _____
18. a r e a d i n g _____
19. a a c e i l l m _____
20. a a i l l m r s y _____
21. c d h i o r _____
22. a a d e g h n r y _____
23. e i l o v t _____
24. a d f d f i l o _____
25. a a g i l m n o _____

21 to 25 — S
17 to 20 — T
10 to 16 — A
Answers   4 to 9 — N
Correct   1 to 3 — D

WORDS! WORDS! WORDS!

From the four possibilities, select the correct meaning for each word at the left.

1. condolence — pity solace sympathy lament
2. maxim — law motto epigram rule
3. surmise — consider suspect imagine suppose
4. equanimity — serenity toleration poise patience
5. jeopardy — insecurity peril exposure risk
6. posthaste — rashly swiftly nimbly actively
7. abase — degrade stoop submit belittle
8. oblivion — forgetfulness pardon amnesty amnesia
9. fragrance — balm incense perfume scent
10. bane — mischief injury curse ruin
11. diffidence — shyness caution fear wariness
12. labyrinth — passage mesh maze intricacy
13. refuge — asylum safety escape shelter
14. ductile — plastic docile malleable durable
15. scourge — torture whip affliction thong
16. vindicate — assert defend justify acquit
17. gourmet — epicure trencherman gorger glutton
18. knack — trick aptitude competence cleverness
19. linger — dawdle defer delay remain
20. frustrate — outwit hinder spoil thwart
21. intuition — reasoning perception impulse apprehension
22. parsimony — frugality avarice care economy
23. necrology — mortality demise obituary fatality
24. traction — affinity draught hauling towage
25. wallow — grovel welter immerse flounder

Answers are on page 267.

Answers are on page 267.

22 to 25 — S
18 to 21 — T
10 to 17 — A
Answers 5 to 9 — N
Correct 1 to 4 — D

CAN YOU COUNT TO TEN?

How many sums ending in 0 (that is, 10, 20, 30, 40, etc.) can you make by adding at least three consecutive numbers in this chart? The numbers you add must be all together in the same line, that is horizontal or vertical, but not diagonal. Answers are on page 267.

15	23	8	5	19	26	10	6	12	20
11	3	15	16	10	18	4	26	11	27
12	9	4	25	1	15	21	12	24	10
6	22	10	17	20	2	16	3	4	21
22	13	2	24	14	11	9	7	22	2
25	13	16	5	8	21	18	24	15	20
13	19	4	7	14	23	3	17	13	24
8	25	12	18	7	19	20	9	7	16
9	17	28	1	27	14	8	23	5	8
24	11	5	25	14	20	19	6	23	18
27	21	6	18	10	28	7	3	10	16
15	17	9	5	22	6	26	25	12	22

85 or more — S
73 to 84 — T
46 to 72 — A
Answers   30 to 45 — N
Correct   1 to 29 — D

SPLIT LINKS

Joe Doaks checked into an inn in a town where he planned to spend eight days. He discovered that he had lost his wallet, or it had been stolen. The innkeeper demanded advance payment for the first night and assurance that Joe would be able to pay him for the following six nights. Joe had a watch with an 18-carat gold chain consisting of seven links, which he offered to use as security until he got home and could send money to replace the chain. The innkeeper agreed, but insisted on payment each night — not advance payment for the week. Since the chain was a valuable heirloom, Joe wanted to make as few cuts in it as possible. What is the smallest number of cuts he could make in the chain to separate the links and still pay each night for his lodging for that night?

Answer is on page 267.

CAN YOU COUNT WHAT YOU CAN'T SEE?

Near each pile write the number of blocks in it. If there is a block missing from the outside of the pile and you can't tell what is behind or below it, assume that all the blocks in that row or column are missing. Answers are on page 267.

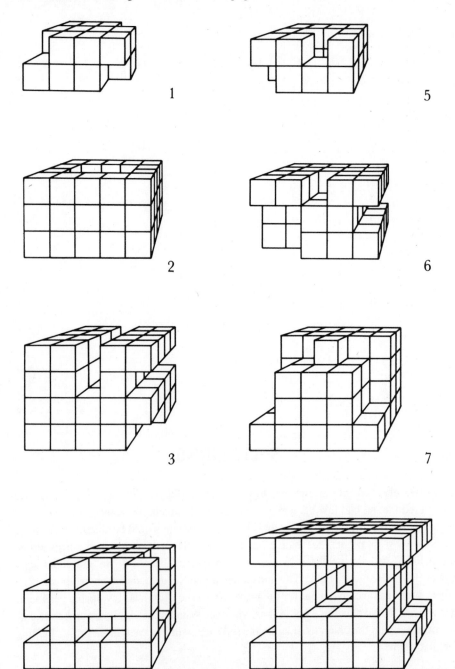

1

5

2

6

3

7

4

8

BOY MEETS GIRL

After each name below write F if it is a female name, M if for a male, FM if it is spelled the same for both. If both are not the same, write the corresponding name for the opposite sex, if any. Answers are on page 267.

1. Adrian   F _____
2. Andrew   M _____
3. Antoinette _____
4. Bernard   M _____
5. Carol   F _____
6. Cecil _____
7. Colette _____
8. Cornelius _____
9. Dale _____
10. Denise _____
11. Evelyn _____
12. Francis _____
13. Gail _____
14. Henry _____
15. Hilary _____
16. Jean _____
17. Jesse _____
18. Lee _____
19. Leslie _____
20. Louis _____
21. Marion _____
22. Meredith _____
23. Ray _____
24. Robin _____
25. Shirley   F _____
26. Sidney _____
27. Terry _____
28. Vivian _____

	50 or more — S
	43 to 49 — T
	31 to 42 — A
Answers	21 to 30 — N
Correct	1 to 20 — D

WORDS PLUS

From each word and the letter after it make a new word, with at least one change in the order of the letters of the original word. Answers are on page 267.

1.	rose	c	_____
2.	lapsed	d	_____
3.	plasters	s	_____
4.	earful	i	_____
5.	winter	t	_____
6.	carets	s	_____
7.	gander	e	_____
8.	diners	c	_____
9.	novelties	a	_____
10.	galley	r	_____
11.	dinner	g	_____
12.	jounce	r	_____
13.	oriented	s	_____
14.	canister	o	_____
15.	larger	u	_____
16.	sacred	u	_____
17.	garnet	a	_____
18.	chlorine	c	_____
19.	painters	m	_____
20.	manger	t	_____
21.	reduction	d	_____
22.	hearse	w	_____
23.	latrine	c	_____
24.	figure	n	_____
25.	kneads	p	_____
26.	maintain	o	_____
27.	imbues	l	_____
28.	trounce	s	_____
29.	nailed	h	_____
30.	assemble	l	_____

26 to 30 — S
17 to 25 — T
9 to 16 — A
Answers   4 to 8 — N
Correct   1 to 3 — D

TOOTHPICKS WILL DO!

You can work with the diagrams below, or you may prefer to use matchsticks or tooth-picks, which you can move around freely. Answers are on page 267.

1. Move two sticks so that you will have eight squares of the original size.
2. In how many more ways can you move two sticks so that you will have eight squares?
3. Move one stick so that you will still have seven squares.
4. Move four sticks so that you will have seven squares.
5. Move three sticks so that you will have eight squares.
6. In how many ways can you remove two sticks and have six squares?

7. Move one stick and have nine squares.
8. Move two sticks and have ten squares.
9. Move two sticks and have eight squares.
10. Move two sticks and have nine squares.
11. Remove two sticks and have eight squares.

12. Move one stick and have nine squares.
13. Move three sticks and have ten squares.
14. Move two sticks and have nine squares.
15. Remove one stick and have eight squares.
16. Remove two sticks and have eight squares.

FOR FUN EXPRESS THESE "SIVES"

For each clue below write one word ending in *sive*. The answer to the first one is *expensive*. Answers are on page 268.

1. costly   _____
2. causing separation   _____
3. very large   _____
4. tending to become larger   _____
5. stately   _____
6. vast, extreme   _____
7. slanderous   _____
8. apathetic, resigned   _____
9. deceptive   _____
10. pugnacious   _____
11. shifty, equivocal   _____
12. backward   _____
13. foul, unsavory   _____
14. all-embracing   _____
15. wanting to own   _____
16. serene   _____
17. clannish   _____
18. slippery, tricky   _____
19. clear cut   _____
20. one after the other   _____
21. mocking   _____
22. final   _____
23. thoughtful   _____
24. answering   _____
25. tyrannical   _____

	21 to 25 — S
	16 to 20 — T
	10 to 15 — A
Answers	5 to 9 — N
Correct	1 to 4 — D

LET'S PLAY HANKY PANKY!

After each expression write the *two rhyming words* to which it refers.

 1. correct cork   _____
 2. extended carol   _____
 3. irritable supervisor   _____
 4. thin locks   _____
 5. villainous tramp   _____
 6. choosy ill-behaved girl _____
 7. sober pillar   _____
 8. mature musical instrument _____
 9. shrewd substitute   _____
10. unattached fowl   _____
11. shaggy sprite   _____
12. more unusual trough   _____
13. sufficient specimen   _____
14. more timid lecturer   _____
15. amiable bird   _____
16. sham hose   _____
17. clever song   _____
18. happy parrot   _____
19. flower-shaped ocean deposit _____
20. weaker artist   _____
21. larger archeologist   _____
22. taller aviator   _____
23. gory pal   _____
24. biased craftsman   _____
25. benevolent plan   _____

Answers are on page 268.

Answers Correct
22 to 25 — S
18 to 21 — T
10 to 17 — A
5 to 9 — N
1 to 4 — D

GEM

What country has the smallest army in the world? How large is that army?
Answer is on page 268.

WHAT NEXT?

The numbers in each line below form a series. Write the next two numbers in each series.

1. **1   3   6   10   15** ____   ____
2. **3   2   5   6   7   10** ____   ____
3. **4   5   9   14   23** ____   ____
4. **1   3   7   13   21** ____   ____
5. **66   8   51   7   38   6** ____   ____
6. **2   5   4   8   6   11   8** ____   ____
7. **80   65   48   37   24** ____   ____
8. **1/2   1/3   5/6   1-1/6   2   3-1/6** ____   ____
9. **5   10   15   25   40** ____   ____
10. **1   5   7   11   13   17   19** ____   ____
11. **360   180   60   15** ____   ____
12. **2   4   3   10   4   18** ____   ____
13. **7   4   8   3   6   5   9   2** ____   ____
14. **10   25   17   62   26   123** ____   ____
15. **2   5   9   3   7   12   4** ____   ____

Answers are on page 268.

	13 to 15 — S
	10 to 12 — T
	7 to 9 — A
Answers	4 to 6 — N
Correct	1 to 3 — D

FAIR IS FAIR

After one of the more acrimonious of the Lincoln-Douglas debates prior to the Civil War, Douglas is supposed to have become so infuriated that he challenged Lincoln to a duel. Their seconds met to discuss the details of the duel — where and when it was to be held, the weapons to be used, and so on. Douglas's seconds insisted on the use of pistols. To that Lincoln's seconds would not agree. They argued that the use of pistols would be eminently unfair.

"Why?" asked Douglas's seconds. "What difference does it make what weapons are used?"

Lincoln's men answered: "Lincoln is a much taller man than Douglas. Lincoln would have only a small target to aim at, while Douglas would have a large target to aim at. That, you must agree, is hardly fair."

For the moment Douglas's men were stumped. They went into a huddle. Then they came up with what to them was a happy solution. "We'll draw a line on Lincoln's chest representing Douglas's height. Any shot above that won't count."

RIGHT ON!

Examine each sequence both horizontally and vertically and figure out the pattern. Then fill in the vacant spaces correctly.

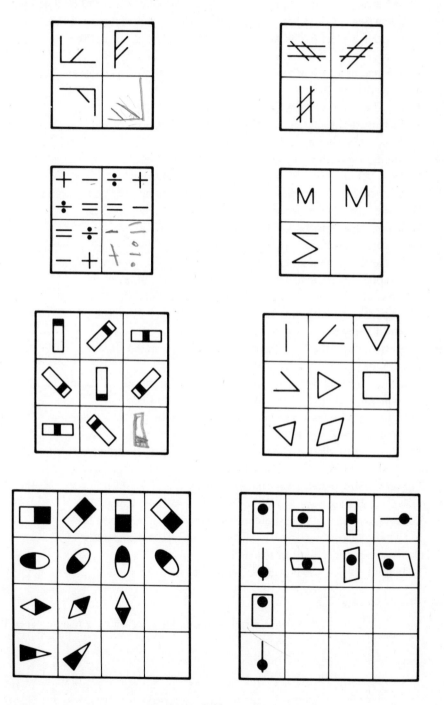

WHAT DO YOU KNOW?

Select the correct one of the four possible answers to each item.

1. The high rate of evaporation of water causes the saltiest water to be found in:
   1) Salton Sea   2) Red Sea   3) Gulf of Mexico   4) Mediterranean Sea
2. Nomination for admission to the U. S. Military Academy at West Point must be made by:
   1) principal of a high school   2) state Senator   3) school counselor
   4) U. S. Senator
3. The head of the Canadian Government is:
   1) the Governor General   2) Prime Minister   3) Queen of England
   4) President of Queen's Privy Council for Canada
4. The form of government in Israel is best described as:
   1) labor   2) republic   3) communistic   4) dictatorship
5. A major conflict between U. S. troops and Indians in 1890 took place at:
   1) Rapid City   2) Cheyenne   3) Fort Pierce   4) Wounded Knee
6. Which of these Presidents did not serve in the Civil War?
   1) Pierce   2) Harrison   3) Garfield   4) Hayes
7. Plato, the Greek philosopher, was a disciple of:
   1) Aristotle   2) Archimedes   3) Socrates   4) Pythagoras
8. Which of the following is most likely to cause pollution?
   1) the plastic in which bread is wrapped   2) bread   3) orange peels
   4) brown paper bag
9. Congress ordered the U. S. Navy to seize French armed ships in:
   1) 1773   2) 1785   3) 1798   4) 1812
10. What piece of land was purchased by the U. S. at the rate of 2¢ an acre?
    1) Louisiana   2) Northwest   3) Alaska   4) Southwest
11. The Women's Rights Amendment was approved by the U. S. Senate in:
    1) 1965   2) 1968   3) 1970   4) 1972
12. The first English dictionary was produced by Samuel Johnson in:
    1) 1755   2) 1776   3) 1785   4) 1800
13. The area with the greatest population density is:
    1) Japan   2) Singapore   3) West Germany   4) Hong Kong
14. The religion with the largest number of adherents in the world is:
    1) Hindu   2) Roman Catholic   3) Protestant   4) Mohammedan
15. One of the summer signs of the zodiac is:
    1) Taurus   2) Leo   3) Aquarius   4) Sagittarius

Answers are on page 268.

142

OPPOSITES ATTRACT

After each word below write its opposite, beginning with the letter *p*.

1. pleasure _____
2. affluent _____
3. defective _____
4. safety _____
5. careless _____
6. urban _____
7. discontinue _____
8. mental _____
9. inexcusable _____
10. awkwardness _____
11. active _____
12. annual _____
13. theoretical _____
14. turbulent _____
15. improbable _____
16. liberal _____
17. genuine _____
18. whole _____
19. tasteless _____
20. mature _____
21. unappetizing _____
22. discourteous _____
23. irrelevant _____
24. discontent _____
25. compassionate _____
26. significant _____
27. slow _____
28. unattractive _____
29. condemnation _____
30. uncertain _____

Answers are on page 268.

	25 to 30 — S
	19 to 24 — T
	12 to 18 — A
Answers	6 to 11 — N
Correct	1 to 5 — D

WORDS! WORDS! WORDS!

Select the one correct meaning in each group for each word at the left.

1. egress — outbreak   leakage   exit   shipment
2. remiss — negligent   indolent   slow   shiftless
3. legend — motto   folklore   inscription   myth
4. fortitude — firmness   bravery   valor   courage
5. brusque — coarse   unrefined   abrupt   uncivil
6. obstreperous — violent   vehement   intense   unruly
7. avocation — profession   calling   hobby   summons
8. taciturn — concise   unsociable   reticent   curt
9. denunciation — curse   condemnation   menace   defiance
10. vilify — belittle   defame   traduce   detract
11. motif — theme   reason   purpose   inducement
12. sanction — license   approval   probity   authorization
13. guilt — wrongdoing   outrage   fault   sin
14. copious — full   abundant   sufficient   adequate
15. garnish — decorate   trim   enrich   polish
16. .requisite — indispensable   urgent   insistent   basic
17. blemish — deformity   injury   defect   fault
18. hackneyed — trite   habitual   usual   frequent
19. nefarious — base   shameful   immoral   wicked
20. append — increase   attach   supplement   follow
21. credence — acceptance   recognition   faith   belief
22. habit — aptitude   skill   usage   way
23. innocent — immaculate   pure   blameless   simple
24. yearn — need   long   care for   prefer
25. zealous — ready   willing   partisan   ardent

Answers are on page 268.

Answers
Correct

22 to 25 — S
18 to 21 — T
10 to 17 — A
5 to 9 — N
1 to 4 — D

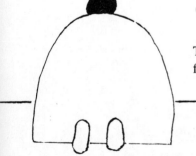

GEM

The figure at the left is supposed to be one of Victor Hugo's famous doodles. Can you tell what it is?

Answer is on page 268.

DE UNO MULTUM

From each word below make as many words of at least four letters as you can. Only one form of a word is allowed — either *mean* or *meant*, but not both. Don't make words by adding *s* to another word. Don't use proper nouns, foreign words, abbreviations, contractions or slang. Answers are on page 269.

ASSESSMENT

32 or more — S
27 to 31 — T
16 to 26 — A
Answers   10 to 15 — N
Correct   1 to 9 — D

REVOLUTION

50 or more — S
40 to 49 — T
20 to 39 — A
Answers   14 to 19 — N
Correct   1 to 13 — D

FACETIOUS

29 or more — S
26 to 28 — T
15 to 25 — A
Answers   10 to 14 — N
Correct   1 to 9 — D

SPOT THE STRANGER

Which picture in each group does not belong with the other four?

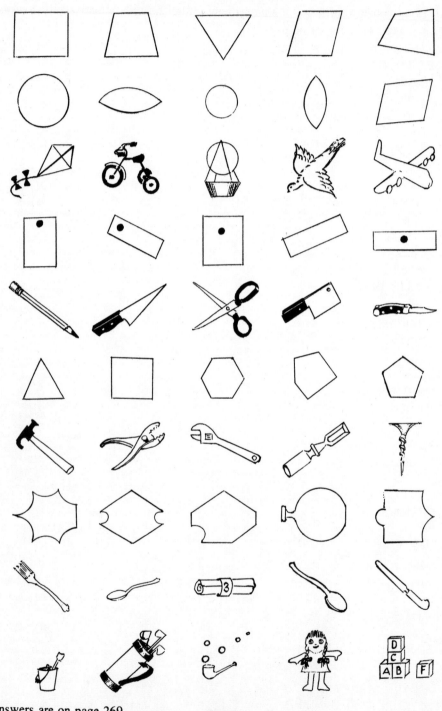

SYNONYMS

For each word give a synonym beginning with the letter *h*.

1. dexterous   _____
2. agreement   _____
3. precipitous   _____
4. lift   _____
5. customary   _____
6. mirth   _____
7. dupe   _____
8. rumor   _____
9. pledge   _____
10. meek   _____
11. throaty   _____
12. innocuous   _____
13. mongrel   _____
14. danger   _____
15. atrocious   _____
16. yoke   _____
17. cruel   _____
18. forerunner   _____
19. accumulate   _____
20. bargain   _____
21. likeness   _____
22. pagan   _____
23. frightful   _____
24. cordial   _____
25. submission   _____

Answers are on page 269.

Answers Correct

22 to 25 — S
18 to 21 — T
11 to 17 — A
5 to 10 — N
1 to 4 — D

GEM

A bookworm burrowed its way through the six volumes of a set of books, starting at page one of the first volume and stopping at the last page of the sixth volume. The pages of each volume were 2 inches thick, and each cover was ⅛ inch thick. How long a distance did the bookworm travel? Answer is on page 269.

THROUGH THE LOOKING GLASS

There are three mirror reflections given for each figure below. Only one reflection is correct. Pick the one image that is the way the original figure would appear in a looking glass. Answers are on page 269.

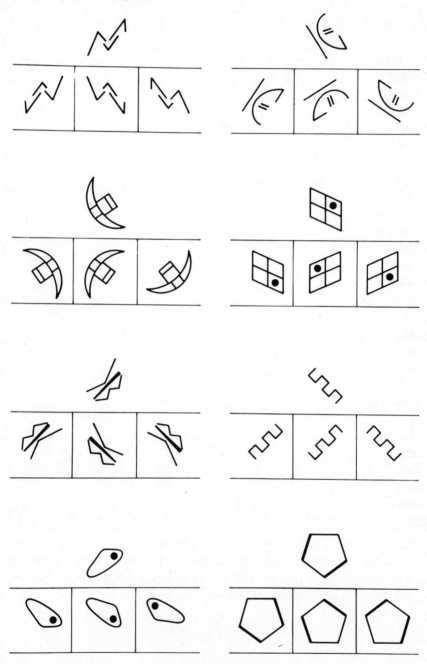

GROW-A-WORD

"Grow-a-Word" by adding a letter to the preceding word, as well as changing the sequence of its letters. The number of letters in each word is indicated by the number of dashes. Answers are on page 269.

1. dine   — — —
   damage   — — — —
   vital organ   — — — — —
   warm over   — — — — — —
   composed of clay   — — — — — — —
   a supporter   — — — — — — — —
   given courage   — — — — — — — — —
   warned   — — — — — — — — — —
2. pertaining to   — —
   period of time   — — —
   degree of speed   — — — —
   gaze fixedly   — — — — —
   female milk gland   — — — — — —
   exchanges   — — — — — — —
   mediators   — — — — — — — —
   attorney   — — — — — — — — —
3. conjunction   — —
   large body of water   — — —
   satisfy   — — — —
   fruits   — — — — —
   steps   — — — — — —
   began   — — — — — — —
   diverts, disparages   — — — — — — — —
   dispersed   — — — — — — — — —
4. parent   — —
   headgear   — — —
   a food   — — — —
   paired   — — — — —
   grouped together   — — — — — —
   settle disputes   — — — — — — —
   destroy many of   — — — — — — — —

SCRAMBLE

Make as many words as you can from the letters on each line, using all the letters each time. Answers are on page 269.

1. a d e l _____
2. a b d e r _____
3. a e g r s _____
4. a e g l r _____
5. c d e i r _____
6. a e d r _____
7. a c d e r s _____
8. b e o r s _____
9. a d e i n l _____
10. c d e e e r _____
11. d e o r s u _____
12. a b d e g r _____
13. s t i d e _____
14. e f i l r t _____
15. a b d e e l t _____
16. c e i l n s t _____
17. d e i r s _____
18. c e o r s s u _____
19. d e e i r s v _____
20. c d e e s u _____
21. a e e n r s t _____
22. e g i n o r s _____
23. c e i n o s t _____
24. a e l p r s t _____
25. e e l r s t w _____

65 or more — S
50 to 64 — T
28 to 49 — A
Answers   16 to 27 — N
Correct   1 to 15 — D

TONGUE TANGLE

Which witch wished which witch itched?

CAN YOU COUNT WHAT YOU CAN'T SEE?

Near each pile write the number of blocks in it. If there is a block missing from the outside of the pile and you can't tell what is behind or below it, assume that all the blocks in that row or column are missing. Answers are on page 269.

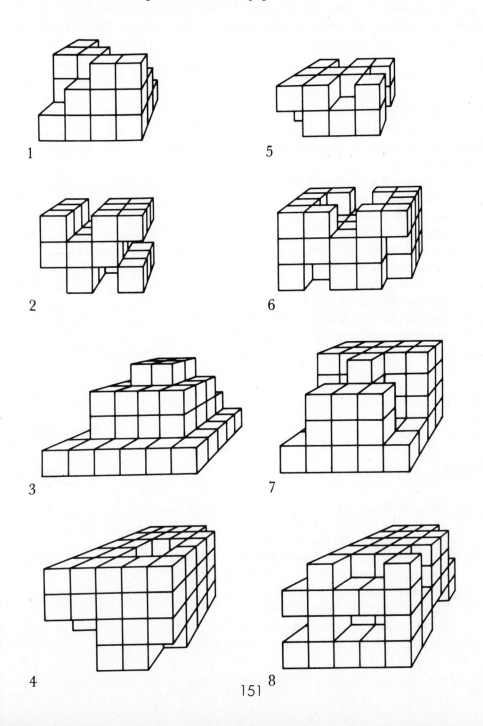

1

5

2

6

3

7

4

8

WHAT STATE ARE YOU IN?

The answer to each of the following clues is the abbreviation of the name of a state, possession or territory of the United States. For instance, the answer to No. 1 is CAL — the nickname of former president Calvin Coolidge — which is also the abbreviation of California. (In a few instances, the clue is followed by the notation sp. In such cases the spelling of the abbreviation and the item referred to are not the same, although the pronunciation is the same.) Answers are on page 269.

1. nickname of a former president _____
2. objective case of the ego _____
3. where the farmer may be found (sp) _____
4. character from the Arabian Nights (sp) _____
5. the one to whom the character from the Arabian Nights prayed (sp) _____
6. to read studiously and with great care _____
7. a French eminence _____
8. an infant's vocalization _____
9. mode of address _____
10. what small boys don't like to do _____
11. non-alternating electricity _____
12. Frenchman's equivalent for "scram" _____
13. without automotive form of conveyance _____
14. guarantee of the perpetuity of the animal species _____
15. democratic method of selecting legislators _____
16. greeting _____

	14 to 16 — S
	11 to 13 — T
	7 to 10 — A
Answers	*4 to 6 — N*
Correct	*1 to 3 — D*

GEM

Answers are on page 269.

1. Name an 8-letter word that contains five s's. _____
2. Name a 5-letter word containing one vowel and four consonants, three of the four consonants being the same letter. _____
3. Name a 5-letter word containing two vowels and three consonants, all three consonants being the same letter.

_____

TOOTHPICKS WILL DO!

You can work with the diagrams below, or you may prefer to use matchsticks or tooth-picks, which you can move around freely.

1. Move two sticks and have eleven squares.
2. Move two sticks and still have ten squares.
3. Move four sticks and have twelve squares.
4. Remove three sticks and have eight squares.

5. Remove six sticks and have nine squares.
6. Remove four sticks and have eight squares.
7. Move three sticks and have eleven squares.
8. Remove four sticks and have ten squares.

9. Move one stick and still have ten squares.
10. Move one stick and have eleven squares.
11. Move two sticks and have twelve squares.
12. Remove three sticks and have eight squares.
13. Remove two sticks and have nine squares.
14. Remove four sticks and have eight squares.

Answers are on page 269.

DO YOU HAVE THE TIME?

1. Mr. Doaks took a plane from New York City to Denver. The plane left at 2 P. M. eastern standard time. He knew that the trip was to take 6½ hours. Denver was on daylight saving time. At what time (Denver time) would he expect to reach Denver? How early or late could he expect to be for a 7:30 date, if he allowed a half hour to get from the airport to his date?

2. The plane stopped in Chicago on the way to Denver. A passenger who boarded the plane took the seat next to Mr. Doaks and asked him: "What time do we land in Denver?" What should he have told her?

3. If Doaks wanted to phone a client in a city in California that was on standard time, could he expect to be able to reach him after arriving at Denver if his client's office closed at 6 o'clock in the evening?

4. Jansen who lives in San Francisco eats his breakfast between 7:15 and 7:45 in the morning. Tompkins in New York plans to make a business call to Jansen. San Francisco is on standard time while New York is on daylight time. At what time in New York City must Tompkins call Jansen at his home in San Francisco while he is having his breakfast?

5. Barton makes a phone call from Denver, which is on daylight saving time, to his home office in a town in New Jersey, which is on standard time. At what time should he place his call in Denver to reach his party in New Jersey at 3:30 P.M.?

6. Mr. Looks took a plane that was to leave Los Angeles at 6 A.M. for New York City. The trip was scheduled to take 4 hours. Allowing 5 hours for him to get into New York, transact his business, and get back to the airport, what is the earliest he can expect to be back at the Los Angeles airport the same day — assuming he has a reservation on a plane that will leave New York City for Los Angeles just one hour after he gets back to the airport at New York City? (New York and Los Angeles are both on daylight saving time.)

Answers are on page 270.

WHO SAID THAT?

For each quotation below write the letter of its source.

_____ 1. They that can give up essential liberty to obtain a little temporary safety, deserve neither liberty nor safety.

_____ 2. I wish to preach, not the doctrine of ignoble ease, but the doctrine of the strenuous life.

_____ 3. The price of wisdom is above rubies.

_____ 4. History is bunk.

_____ 5. The miserable have no other medicine, but only hope.

_____ 6. God can't be always everywhere; and so, he invented Mothers.

_____ 7. Poverty is the parent of revolution and crime.

_____ 8. A good name is rather to be chosen than great riches.

_____ 9. A prophet is not without honor, save in his own country.

_____10. They do not love that do not show their love.

_____11. There never was a good war nor a bad peace.

_____12. The bullet that will kill me is not yet cast.

_____13. Physician, heal thyself.

_____14. Truth is truth to the end of reckoning.

_____15. Pay the income-tax and break your heart upon 't.

_____16. There is a homely adage which runs: "Speak softly and carry a big stick; you will go far."

_____17. The spirit indeed is willing, but the flesh is weak.

_____18. There's small choice in rotten apples.

_____19. An honest man's the noblest work of God.

_____20. The race is not to the swift nor the battle to the strong.

a. Old Testament
b. Shakespeare
c. Aristotle
d. Francis Bacon
e. Benjamin Franklin
f. New Testament
g. Woodrow Wilson
h. Napoleon
i. Eleanor Roosevelt
j. Robert Burns
k. John Ruskin
l. Theodore Roosevelt
m. Plato
n. Henry Ford
o. Edwin Arnold
p. Elizabeth B. Browning

Answers are on page 270.

Answers are on page 270.

Answers Correct	
16 to 20	— S
11 to 15	— T
7 to 10	— A
4 to 6	— N
1 to 3	— D

SYNONYMS

For each word below give a synonym beginning with the letter *o*.

1. paddle   _____
2. comment   _____
3. happen   _____
4. frequently   _____
5. skip   _____
6. protest   _____
7. withstand   _____
8. delighted   _____
9. trial   _____
10. responsibility   _____
11. repulsive   _____
12. salve   _____
13. consequence   _____
14. pledge   _____
15. discretionary   _____
16. extra   _____
17. belief   _____
18. start   _____
19. antiquated   _____
20. source   _____
21. unyielding   _____
22. prospect   _____
23. impromptu   _____
24. upset   _____
25. inhabit   _____
26. law   _____
27. surpass   _____
28. odious   _____
29. exclude   _____
30. persecute   _____

Answers are on page 270.

Answers are on page 270.

	26 to 30 — S
	20 to 25 — T
	13 to 19 — A
Answers	6 to 12 — N
Correct	1 to 5 — D

LEFT, RIGHT! LEFT, RIGHT!

Do you know left from right? Write R for right and L for left.

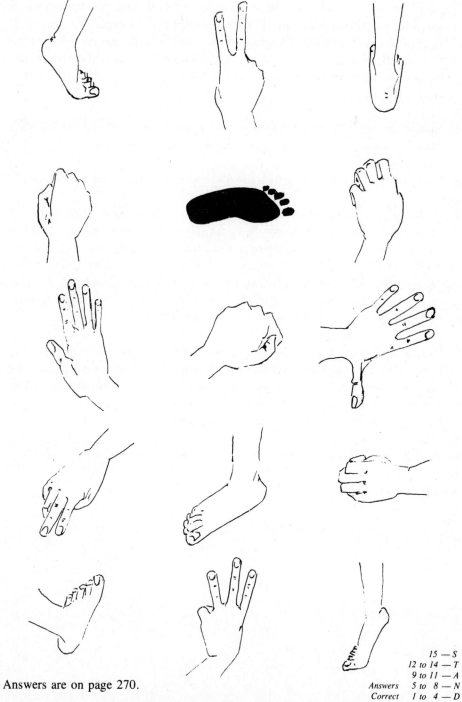

Answers are on page 270.

Answers are on page 270.

	15 — S
	12 to 14 — T
	9 to 11 — A
Answers	5 to 8 — N
Correct	1 to 4 — D

HOW ODD?

1. A service man who was bored with the customary pastime of "rolling the bones" offered, as a variation, to bet the others on the chances of his rolling just one 6 in a roll of five dice. In other words, he would win if on the roll of the five dice only one 6 appeared, and he would lose if no 6, or two or more 6's, appeared. The others took up the offer, but after a while decided that they were being too generous in the odds they had offered because the challenger was winning a sizable sum of money. If you had been in the group, what odds would you have offered in order to have an even chance of winning?

2. Suppose the bet had been on throwing exactly two 6's in a roll of five dice, what would have been fair odds to give you an equal chance of winning?

3. What are the odds in favor of getting five 6's or no 6's on a single throw of five dice?

4. A group of men were at a bar about to order drinks. One suggested that they "roll horses" to see who should pay for the drinks. That means that each man would roll five dice and the one who had the largest number of dice of the same size showing would win. If two had the same number of dice of the same size (for example, one has three 5's and the other three 3's), the one with the higher number (5's in this case) would win. Suppose one man threw three 4's, what are the chances that the next man would beat him? In this game the ace (the 1) is high.

5. Usually in this game a player has three throws, and he can keep dice from a previous throw. Thus if on the first throw he gets two 6's, he can keep them out and throw the other three dice in an effort to get more 6's. Suppose you were "rolling horses" and had thrown the five dice once, turning up two 4's. What are the chances of getting at least one 4 on the next throw of the remaining three dice?

6. What are the chances of getting two 4's on the second throw of the three dice?

Answers are on page 270.

DE UNO MULTUM

From each word below make as many words of at least four letters as you can. Only one form of a word is allowed — either *mean* or *meant*, but not both. Don't make words by adding the letter *s* to another word. You may not use proper nouns, foreign words, abbreviations, contractions or slang. Answers are on page 270.

EXTRANEOUS

45 or more — S
38 to 44 — T
23 to 37 — A
Answers 13 to 22 — N
Correct 1 to 12 — D

COMPREHENSIVE

75 or more — S
60 to 74 — T
39 to 59 — A
Answers 21 to 38 — N
Correct 1 to 20 — D

INTERRUPTION

60 or more — S
46 to 59 — T
34 to 45 — A
Answers 19 to 33 — N
Correct 1 to 18 — D

WORDS PLUS

From each word and the letter after it make a new word, with at least one change in the order of the letters of the original word. Answers are on page 270.

1. rumble   h   _____
2. palate   u   _____
3. goatherd   f   _____
4. sachet   e   _____
5. entrails   o   _____
6. rustle   c   _____
7. indirect   g   _____
8. canticle   h   _____
9. parish   t   _____
10. softer   g   _____
11. priest   a   _____
12. entering   a   _____
13. sacred   a   _____
14. passer   t   _____
15. altering   s   _____
16. leases   m   _____
17. parcel   i   _____
18. levers   a   _____
19. denature   v   _____
20. madder   i   _____
21. ocelot   s   _____
22. arbiters   r   _____
23. quails   d   _____
24. lisped   o   _____
25. nature   c   _____
26. conspire   i   _____
27. trudgers   o   _____
28. flounder   w   _____
29. trainers   t   _____
30. reunited   l   _____

26 to 30 — S
17 to 25 — T
9 to 16 — A
Answers   4 to 8 — N
Correct   1 to 3 — D

SPOT THE STRANGER

Which word in each group does not belong with the other four?

1. football   soccer   hockey   baseball   basketball
2. balsam   spruce   eucalyptus   elm   hemlock
3. galley   stern   bedroom   porthole   deck
4. polyester   acrilan   nylon   wool   rayon
5. tomatoes   peas   carrots   cauliflower   eggplant
6. Rio Grande   Salton   Wabash   Colorado   Ohio
7. Indian   Hudson   Biscay   Fundy   Bengal
8. jade   coral   amethyst   quartz   turquoise
9. turnip   rutabaga   beet   potato   bean
10. butler   salesclerk   domestic   maid   charwoman
11. attract   bewitch   enamor   cherish   enchant
12. petunia   marigold   rose   pansy   daisy
13. Paris   London   Rome   Athens   Monte Carlo
14. azalea   poinsettia   rhododendron   lilac   forsythia
15. Oklahoma   Florida   Oregon   California   South Carolina
16. Bermuda   Cuba   Puerto Rico   Haiti   New Orleans
17. *American Home*   *House and Garden*   *Better Homes and Gardens*
    New Yorker   *Good Housekeeping*
18. Eisenhower   Grant   Pershing   Lee   Farragut
19. oxfords   slippers   boots   sandals   mules
20. psychiatrist   oculist   obstetrician   urologist   internist
21. adding machine   calculator   abacus   slide rule   typewriter
22. Alaska   Florida   Iceland   Jutland   Iberia
23. pipe   cigar   cigarette   cigarillo   tobacco
24. egg   gene   larva   roe   seed
25. TV   cinema   slides   radio   stereoptican views

Answers are on page 271.

Answers
Correct

21 to 25 — S
16 to 20 — T
10 to 15 — A
5 to 9 — N
1 to 4 — D

RHYME TIME

"Evolution," quoth the monkey,
"Makes all mankind our kin.
There's no chance at all about it.
Tails we lose and heads they win."

SCRAMBLE

Make as many words as you can from the letters on each line, using all the letters each time. Answers are on page 271.

1. d i k s _____
2. a c e r t _____
3. e e h r t _____
4. b e i r s u _____
5. a c e p r s _____
6. e g o r _____
7. a c e i m n _____
8. a d e p r t _____
9. c d l o s _____
10. c e h i t s _____
11. b e l r s t u _____
12. a c e i l p r _____
13. c d e o r _____
14. a c d e i l t _____
15. a e n r s _____
16. a d e i n s t _____
17. a d e i l r _____
18. a b d e g i r _____
19. a e g i n r t _____
20. a d e l o p r _____
21. a e i l r s t _____
22. a c d e e i m t _____
23. a e e g n r s t _____
24. a e i n p r s t _____
25. r g a a m l n i _____

65 or more — S
50 to 64 — T
28 to 49 — A
Answers   16 to 27 — N
Correct   1 to 15 — D

TRY IT ON A FRIEND!

1. You have eight stacks of coins, each consisting of 8 silver dollars. One entire stack is counterfeit, but you have forgotten which stack it is. You know how much a silver dollar weighs, and you do remember that each counterfeit dollar weighs one ounce less than it should. You have available a balance scale. What is the smallest number of weighings by means of which you can tell which is the counterfeit stack?

2. Doaks took an early train home one day and arrived at his suburban station at 4:30 instead of 5:30 when his wife always met him with the family car. Since it was a nice day, he decided to walk instead of calling his wife. He followed the route his wife always took and met her on the way. He got into the car. She turned around and they arrived home just 20 minutes earlier than they usually did. Assuming a constant rate of driving speed, at what time did his wife pick him up?

3. Can you tell what coins a man has (in American money) if he has $4.99 in change but can not change a dollar, a half dollar, a quarter, a dime, or a nickel?

4. Can you arrange the digits from one to nine in a 3 x 3 square so that the three numbers in each row (horizontal, vertical or diagonal) add up to 15?

5. When numbers are arranged in a square so that the sum of the numbers in any direction is the same it is called a magic square. Can you arrange the numbers from 1 to 25 in a 5 x 5 square so that the sum of any column, row or diagonal is 65?

6. You are driving a taxicab in New York City and you pick up a fare at Madison Avenue and 37 Street. You have to stop for a red light at 52 Street, at 68 Street, and again at 82 Street. The passenger leaves the taxicab at 85 Street, after paying her fare and a generous tip of 50¢. How old is the taxicab driver?

Answers are on page 271.

DO YOU KNOW "OUS"?

For each clue write a word ending in *ous*.

1. fault finding _____
2. talkative _____
3. promoting health _____
4. desiring to inflict harm _____
5. savage _____
6. corresponding in some respect _____
7. stingy _____
8. of one mind _____
9. generous _____
10. noisy _____
11. foreign _____
12. thin or slender in form _____
13. odious _____
14. greatly troubled _____
15. harmless _____
16. peevish _____
17. servile _____
18. gallant _____
19. accidental _____
20. extremely steep _____
21. discreet _____
22. indistinct, hazy _____
23. predatory _____
24. skillful _____
25. tuneful _____

Answers are on page 271.

Answers Correct

20 to 25 — S
16 to 19 — T
10 to 15 — A
5 to 9 — N
1 to 4 — D

GEM

What seven weights (when used singly or in combinations of two or more at a time) will weigh any object from 1 ounce to 7 pounds 15 ounces?

Answers are on page 271.

FORWARD AND BACKWARD!

How many of the more than 40 words of three or more letters can you find that are also words backward, e.g. *spat–taps*. All the letters of each word must be together in one line, horizontal, vertical or diagonal, and may overlap. Answers are on page 271.

R	E	R	A	I	M	L	I	V	E	D	S
E	L	A	I	D	R	S	T	S	O	T	E
P	O	S	V	E	A	E	E	O	N	R	A
E	S	T	L	I	V	E	M	A	D	A	M
L	T	U	B	E	D	R	A	I	N	M	E
S	E	N	O	L	E	V	E	R	T	H	E
L	E	V	E	L	H	E	R	I	S	A	T
O	R	L	D	U	E	N	D	T	I	D	E
O	M	A	N	O	S	E	R	U	K	U	N
P	O	G	O	T	A	M	O	B	A	I	T
S	A	E	A	P	R	I	T	E	Y	L	A
O	T	R	E	F	E	R	A	R	A	E	B
G	U	R	T	N	Q	U	O	L	K	E	S
H	A	D	A	O	N	O	O	N	E	K	E
E	M	B	O	W	M	I	S	E	R	I	F

35 to 39 — S
30 to 34 — T
23 to 29 — A
Answers   16 to 22 — N
Correct   1 to 15 — D

OPPOSITES ATTRACT

After each word below write a word that means the opposite. Each answer must begin with the letter *t*. Answers are on page 271.

1. falsehood _____
2. savage _____
3. prompt _____
4. mend _____
5. freeze _____
6. short _____
7. renter _____
8. slimness _____
9. ungrateful _____
10. opaque _____
11. now _____
12. practical _____
13. learner _____
14. comic _____
15. timidity _____
16. tough _____
17. diplomatic _____
18. upset _____
19. permanent _____
20. insensitive _____
21. density _____
22. heir _____
23. relaxed _____
24. loquacious _____
25. incomplete _____
26. cold _____
27. loyalty _____
28. final _____
29. unmanageable _____
30. celestial _____

Answers
Correct

25 to 30 — S
19 to 24 — T
12 to 18 — A
6 to 11 — N
1 to 5 — D

CRACK THE CULPRIT

Jack D. was killed on a lonely road 2 miles from Podunk at 3:30 A.M., March 17, 1972. Shorty M., Tony V., Ben R., Joey F. and Red J. were arrested a week later and questioned. Each of these men made four statements, three of which were absolutely true, and only one was false. One of these men killed Jack D. Which one was guilty?

Shorty: I was in Chicago when D was murdered. I never killed anyone. Red is the guilty man. Joey and I were pals.

Ben: I did not kill D. I never owned a revolver in my life. Red knows me. I was in Philadelphia the night of March 17.

Tony: Ben lied when he said he never owned a revolver. One of us is guilty. Shorty was in Chicago at that time. The murder was committed on St. Patrick's Day.

Joey: I did not kill D. Red has never been in Podunk. I never saw Shorty before. Ben was in Philadelphia with me the night of March 17.

Red: I did not kill D. I have never been in Podunk. I never saw Ben before now. Shorty lied when he said I'm guilty. Answer is on page 271.

X MARKS THE SPOT

A psychologist was working in a civilian capacity for one of the armed services during World War II. Bored with the work he was doing, he decided to have himself a bit of fun. He cut a stencil of a typical mess hall, and had copies run off. Taking one copy, he marked a number of X's on it. Next to each X he made a circle. In each circle he wrote a number. Then he prepared a memorandum explaining that each X represented a spot where flypaper had been hung from the ceiling of the mess hall. The number in the circle near the X was the number of flies which had been counted on the flypaper at the end of the week when the paper was replaced by fresh flypaper. The psychologist then "bucked" the memorandum to some higher echelon.

Nothing happened. The next Friday he marked up another copy of the imaginary mess hall diagram with his X's, circles and numbers, prepared a new memorandum and sent it on its way. Again nothing happened. When after four weeks nothing happened, he got tired of the whole business and gave it up. Two weeks later, he received a memorandum asking where the "fly reports" were for the preceding two weeks!

PSYCHOANALYSIS FINALLY EXPLAINED

Psychoanalysis, which is easier to understand than to spell, tells us what we really think when we think we think a thing. Without psychoanalysis we should never know that when we think a thing, the thing we think we think is not the thing we think we think, but only the thing that makes us think we think the thing we think we think.

It is all a question of the Unconscious. The Unconscious enables us to think we are thinking about the thing we think we want to think about, while all the time the thing we really want to think about is being thought about unconsciously by the Unconscious.

The Unconscious is a survival from our barbaric ancestry and has no manners.

As the sort of thing the Unconscious thinks about is not the sort of thing we care to think about, the Unconscious takes care not to let us think it is thinking about what it is thinking about. If we are in danger of thinking that we are thinking about what we are really thinking about, the thing we are thinking about is sublimated into something we don't mind thinking we are thinking about.

Actually the Unconscious is divided into parts: the part that thinks the thing, and the part that prevents our thinking we are thinking the thing. This preventing of our thinking we are thinking the thing we do not care to think we are thinking is called Repression.

Repression is due to the Super-Ego, which is very genteel.

There is friction between the Super-Ego and the Coarse part of the Unconscious, or the Id. The Id thinks a thing that the Super-Ego thinks it ought not to think, and the Super-Ego represses the thing that the Id thinks, so that we never think we think it. But unless the Id thinks we are thinking it, the Id becomes dissatisfied and causes trouble.

As whatever the Id thinks we can only think we are thinking the sort of thing the Super-Ego thinks we ought to think, we have to make the Id think we are thinking that we are thinking the thing Id thinks, by thinking we are thinking something that is something like the thing the Id is thinking. If we can fool the Id we are all right. If not, there is no thinking what we may be thinking.

It comes, then, to this: The things to think we think are the things that the Super-Ego thinks are the things to think, and that the Id thinks are the things *it* thinks.

I think that's perfectly clear.

Author Unknown

TRY IT ON A FRIEND

1. You will need: three participants (No. 1, No. 2, and No. 3); twenty-four matches; and three objects — e.g., a button (Small), a coin (Medium), a key (Large).

    Lay out the twenty-four matches and the three objects on a table. Then say:

    "In order to remember who is who, I am giving No. 1 one match, No. 2 two matches, and No. 3 four matches. Please put these matches in a pocket so I won't be able to see them."

    Then turn your back to the table and continue the instructions:

    "No. 1, take any one of the three objects on the table. No. 2, take any one of the other two objects. No. 3, take the remaining object. Now, whoever took the button, take *just* as many matches from the table as I gave you; whoever took the coin, take *twice* as many matches as you were given; whoever took the key, take *four* times as many matches as you were given. Hold the matches in a closed fist so that I can't see them."

    When they have done this, turn and look into the eyes of each participant, as though reading his mind. At the same time, sneak a look at the table and note the number of matches left; that number will tell you which of the three volunteers has the button, which one has the coin, and which has the key! Can you figure out the key to the trick?

    A French mathematician, Claude G. Bachet, first published this trick in 1612 in a book entitled *Problèmes plaisants et délectable.*

2. Ask a volunteer to place a penny and a nickel on a table in front of him while your back is turned. Then, with your back still to the volunteer and the table, give him these instructions:

    "Place either hand — but don't tell me which one — on your head and keep it there. Stand up straight and tall with your chest out and your shoulders back. Keep the other hand down at your side." Allow a few seconds to elapse. Then say: "Now place the hand that is at your side on the penny, and the hand that is on your head on the nickel."

    As soon as the volunteer tells you that he has followed your instructions and the coins are covered, quickly turn and point to the hand that is on the nickel. No matter how many times this is done, you will always pick the correct hand. Do you know how to do it?

Answers are on page 272.

WORDS PLUS

From each word and the letter after it make a new word. You must make at least one change in the order of the letters of the original word. Answers are on page 273.

1.	ache	b	_____
2.	pace	h	_____
3.	glue	b	_____
4.	acre	m	_____
5.	fines	u	_____
6.	perch	y	_____
7.	flier	l	_____
8.	scone	a	_____
9.	round	t	_____
10.	berth	a	_____
11.	domes	t	_____
12.	grime	a	_____
13.	tines	c	_____
14.	chest	e	_____
15.	reaps	h	_____
16.	guests	g	_____
17.	lavers	e	_____
18.	waters	d	_____
19.	signet	w	_____
20.	angler	u	_____
21.	repast	t	_____
22.	thorns	e	_____
23.	cyanid	m	_____
24.	listen	c	_____
25.	cigaret	n	_____
26.	pirates	a	_____
27.	iterating	a	_____
28.	algebra	u	_____
29.	cremation	p	_____
30.	dueling	d	_____

25 to 30 — S
20 to 24 — T
10 to 19 — A
Answers   5 to 9 — N
Correct   1 to 4 — D

171

WHERE IN THE WORLD?

After each point of interest write the letter of the place on the facing map where it is located. Answers are on page 273.

1. Stonehenge   _____
2. The Alhambra   _____
3. The Parthenon   _____
4. Eiffel Tower   _____
5. The Colosseum   _____
6. Picadilly Circus   _____
7. Fjords   _____
8. Big Ben   _____
9. The Peace Palace   _____
10. Leaning Tower   _____
11. Blarney Stone   _____
12. Bridge of Sighs   _____
13. King Arthur's Round Table   _____
14. Vesuvius   _____
15. North Cape   _____
16. Black Forest   _____
17. The Kremlin   _____
18. Waterloo   _____
19. Andorra   _____
20. The Louvre   _____
21. Loch Ness Monster   _____
22. Blue Grotto   _____
23. The Tyrol   _____
24. Birthplace of Napoleon   _____
25. El Prado   _____
26. Monte Carlo   _____
27. The Matterhorn   _____
28. Crete   _____
29. Hans Christian Andersen's Home   _____
30. Van Gogh's Home   _____

	25 to 30 — S
	20 to 24 — T
	10 to 19 — A
Answers	5 to 9 — N
Correct	1 to 4 — D

TONGUE TANGLE

The shrewish scold screamed and scowled as she scorched the scallions.

DE UNO MULTUM

From each word below make as many words of at least four letters as you can. Only one form of a word is allowed — either *make* or *makes*, but not both. You may not use proper nouns, foreign words, abbreviations, contractions, or slang. Answers are on page 273.

TELEGRAMS

Answers
Correct

110 or more — S
85 to 109 — T
50 to 84 — A
25 to 49 — N
1 to 24 — D

ABSOLVENT

Answers
Correct

110 or more — S
85 to 109 — T
50 to 84 — A
25 to 49 — N
1 to 24 — D

HYPOCHONDRIAC

Answers
Correct

110 or more — S
85 to 109 — T
50 to 84 — A
25 to 49 — N
1 to 24 — D

DO IT WITH NUMBERS

1. Multiply any number by 9. Then add the digits of the product. What do you discover? For example, multiply 57×9. The product is 513. Add the digits. The sum is 9. Multiply 3826 by 9. The product is 34434. The sum of the digits of the product is 18. The sum of those digits is 9. Is that always true?

2. Multiply 9×9 and you get 81. Now put a 9 before the 8 and a 0 between the 8 and the 1, and you get 9801, which is the product of 99×99. Put another 9 in front of the number 9801, and another 0 before the 1, and you get 998001, which is the product of 999×999. What do you think is the product of 9999×9999?

3. The number of days in the year (365) can be obtained by adding the squares of *three* consecutive numbers. What are they? It can also be obtained by adding the squares of which *two* consecutive numbers?

4. To multiply 142857×3 all you have to do is move one digit. Which one?

5. How can you tell (without dividing) whether a number is evenly divisible by —

2?	5?
3?	6?
4?	8?
	9?

6. In the expression $x^2 - y^2$ the letters x and y represent numbers, and the expression means the difference between the squares of two numbers. You may remember from your study of algebra that $x^2 - y^2$ can also be written $(x + y)(x - y)$, which means the sum of two numbers (x and y) multiplied by their difference. Under what conditions does $(x + y)(x - y) = (x + y)$?

7. The following is a series in which one item is lacking: O T T F F S S E N. Can you provide the missing item?

8. What digits do the letters represent in these addition tasks?

A B E	L M N	R S T U
B D E	O N L	U S T R
F G E B	P Q Q Q	V W W V

9. A cow is tied to a 30-foot rope in a large 4-acre field. Over how large an area can the cow graze?

10. There were ten crows on a fence. A farmer shot one of them. How many remained?

Answers are on page 275.

LET'S PLAY HANKY PANKY!

After each expression below write the *two rhyming words* to which the expression refers. For example, *ample material* is *enough stuff*. Answers are on page 275.

1. ample material   _____
2. healthy dog   _____
3. evil plan   _____
4. infective cynic   _____
5. strange sweetening   _____
6. dirty loot   _____
7. lively alcohol drink   _____
8. metal beast   _____
9. complete groove   _____
10. competent animal   _____
11. finer woolen garment   _____
12. wet label   _____
13. larger excavator   _____
14. satisfactory lumber   _____
15. more reluctant pilot   _____
16. sugary dessert   _____
17. humane pawnbroker   _____
18. reddish flower   _____
19. Belgian scar   _____
20. agile finger protector   _____
21. gymnastic art lover   _____
22. royal dog   _____
23. counterfeit bills   _____
24. shiny cow   _____
25. thin pawnbroker   _____
26. ultimate explosion   _____
27. wise vital organ   _____
28. unattached horned animal   _____
29. chubby darling   _____
30. verdant partition   _____

	25 to 30 — S
	20 to 24 — T
	10 to 19 — A
Answers	5 to 9 — N
Correct	1 to 4 — D

SCRAMBLE

See how many words you can make out of each group of letters, using all the letters each time. From the letters *a e g l n*, for example, you can make the words *angel, angle,* and *glean.* Answers are on page 276.

1.	a e g l n	_____
2.	t n s e	_____
3.	a t p s	_____
4.	a t b e	_____
5.	s e t w	_____
6.	r p d o	_____
7.	a r n d	_____
8.	e d m a i	_____
9.	t d e h a	_____
10.	a b e r s	_____
11.	l e s t p	_____
12.	l r b e a	_____
13.	g e d r i	_____
14.	i f d l e a	_____
15.	a i n n o t	_____
16.	r c c e l i	_____
17.	a c e l r t	_____
18.	b d e i r n	_____
19.	d s e l i m	_____
20.	s p l e e a	_____
21.	e f f l r t u	_____
22.	d i o p r s t	_____
23.	a d e g i n r	_____
24.	e a e l m n s s	_____
25.	a c g i n o s t	_____
26.	a d e i l t t u	_____
27.	a c d e i o n t u	_____
28.	b d e n o r s u	_____
29.	a c e i l r s v	_____
30.	a e i n r r s t	_____

25 to 30 — S
20 to 24 — T
10 to 19 — A
Answers   5 to 9 — N
Correct   1 to 4 — D

177

SYNONYMS

After each word write a word with the same meaning that starts with *l*. Answers are on page 276.

1. praise   _____
2. rent   _____
3. accountability   _____
4. flabby   _____
5. indolent   _____
6. precise   _____
7. toilsome   _____
8. outline   _____
9. slacker   _____
10. myth   _____
11. high   _____
12. generosity   _____
13. sole   _____
14. enduring   _____
15. fate   _____
16. loiter   _____
17. easy   _____
18. position   _____
19. reasonable   _____
20. permit   _____
21. cave   _____
22. faithful   _____
23. prevaricate   _____
24. raze   _____
25. fluid   _____
26. shining   _____
27. listless   _____
28. clear   _____
29. suitor   _____
30. oiling   _____

	25 to 30 — S
	20 to 24 — T
	10 to 19 — A
Answers	5 to 9 — N
Correct	1 to 4 — D

178

PUT IT ALL TOGETHER

Draw lines in each figure to show how it is made by putting together the pieces at the right of it. Answers are shown on page 277.

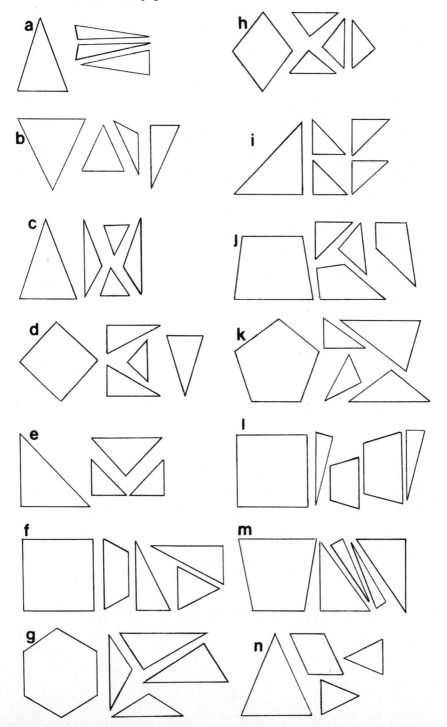

WHAT NEXT?

For each row write the two numbers that come next. Answers are on page 277.

1. **7   8   10   13   17**   ____   ____
2. **96   80   66   54   44**   ____   ____
3. **40   39   41   38   42**   ____   ____
4. **30   32   31   35   32   38**   ____   ____
5. **360   180   60   15**   ____   ____
6. **12   21   14   20   16   19**   ____   ____
7. **4   8   3   6   2   4**   ____   ____
8. **8   9   10   11   10**   ____   ____
9. **1   2   4   8   16**   ____   ____
10. **43   35   28   22   17**   ____   ____
11. **240   120   60   30**   ____   ____
12. **8   6   3   8   6   3**   ____   ____
13. **125   25   64   16   27**   ____   ____
14. **3600   600   120   30   10**   ____   ____
15. **1   1   4   8   9   27**   ____   ____
16. **25   7   24   8   22   10   19**   ____   ____
17. **1440   144   1296   162   1134   189**   ____   ____
18. **26   18   11   5   0   5**   ____   ____
19. **1   2   2   6   4   16   8**   ____   ____
20. **−2   −1   6   25   62   123**   ____   ____

	17 to 20 — S
	13 to 16 — T
	9 to 12 — A
Answers	5 to 8 — N
Correct	1 to 4 — D

TONGUE TANGLE

Paddy Pipper packed the popper after popping popcorn for the picnic.

OPPOSITES ATTRACT

For each word below write the opposite word that begins with the letter *e*. Answers are on page 277.

1. cause _____
2. virile _____
3. consistent _____
4. inflexible _____
5. compulsive _____
6. depression _____
7. ignorant _____
8. unqualified _____
9. tardy _____
10. enlarge; add _____
11. disappear _____
12. incompetent _____
13. absorb _____
14. spiritual _____
15. dismiss _____
16. junior _____
17. prodigality _____
18. limited _____
19. entrance _____
20. enslave _____
21. disparity _____
22. none _____
23. contraction _____
24. lessen _____
25. vulgarity _____
26. unimportant _____
27. admit _____
28. confuse _____
29. inadequate _____
30. disclose _____

25 to 30 — S
20 to 24 — T
10 to 19 — A
Answers   5 to 9 — N
Correct   1 to 4 — D

CREATE EQUALITY

Each line below has several numbers and arithmetic signs: $+$, $-$, $\times$, $\div$, $(\,)$, $\sqrt{\ }$. Every line has an equal sign $(=)$. Make an equation of the numbers and signs in each line, using all of them only once each, as in this example:

$$1 \quad 2 \quad 5 \quad 8 \quad = \quad - \quad \div \qquad\qquad \underline{8 \div 2 = 5 - 1}$$

1. 2 3 3 4 5 = + − × _____
2. 2 3 4 5 25 = + − × ( ) _____
3. 5 8 8 24 = − ÷ _____
4. 2 4 4 5 6 6 = + − × × ( ) ( ) _____

5. 2 3 4 4 5 8 = + + + × _____
6. 2 2 2 2 3 10 = − × ÷ ( ) _____
7. 2 3 5 8 17 = − ÷ ÷ ( ) _____
8. 2 2 3 3 3 7 = + − × ( ) _____
9. 2 2 2 3 3 4 = + × × ( ) _____
10. 2 2 3 3 4 6 = + + − × ( ) ( ) _____

11. 2 2 3 3 3 5 = + + × ( ) _____
12. 3 3 3 4 5 8 = + − × ( ) _____
13. 2 2 3 3 3 4 5 = + + × ( ) _____
14. 2 2 2 5 9 9 = + + × $\sqrt{\ }$ ( ) _____
15. 2 2 3 4 5 5 10 = + − × ÷ ( ) ( ) _____

Answers are on page 277.

	13 to 15 — S
	10 to 12 — T
	7 to 9 — A
Answers	4 to 6 — N
Correct	1 to 3 — D

GEM

Which state of the United States has a point that is farther north, one that is farther west, and one that is farther east than any of the other states? Answer is on page 283.

IT TAKES TWO

Take the two words in each line, rearrange the order of the letters, and make one word using all the letters. For instance, from the words *tap* and *lash* you can make *asphalt*. Answers are on page 278.

1. tap + lash   _____
2. gnat + peon   _____
3. invite + lose   _____
4. treat + wage   _____
5. cafe + urn   _____
6. mica + led   _____
7. most + dice   _____
8. cease + pad   _____
9. soda + bride   _____
10. lone + since   _____
11. tram + late   _____
12. malt + suite   _____
13. claim + ripe   _____
14. peon + oats   _____
15. antic + near   _____
16. aimed + timely   _____
17. score + pipe   _____
18. front + dreams   _____
19. vain + stage   _____
20. grain + muse   _____
21. ibid + coal   _____
22. tinge + staid   _____
23. mogul + noose   _____
24. lowly + refund   _____
25. frenetic + sneer   _____
26. loam + barn   _____
27. peel + honest   _____
28. action + dime   _____
29. biped + laces   _____
30. scene + regime   _____

	25 to 30	— S
	20 to 24	— T
	10 to 19	— A
Answers	5 to 9	— N
Correct	1 to 4	— D

WHAT GIVES?

In which of these pictures is something missing or wrong, and what is it? Answers are on page 278.

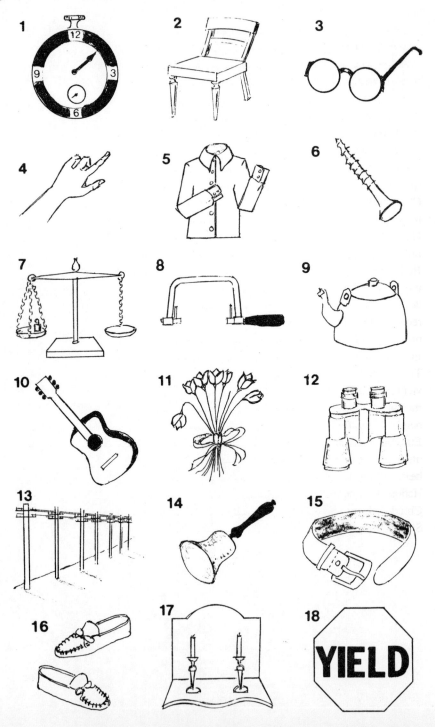

SPOT THE STRANGER

Cross out the one word in each group that does not belong with the other four. Answers are on page 278.

1. Jupiter   Athena   Juno   Venus   Vulcan
2. Rembrandt   Vermeer   Hals   Breugel   Gauguin
3. Washington   Fillmore   Arthur   Coolidge   John Adams
4. Angola   Nigeria   Kenya   Afghanistan   Rhodesia
5. infantry   navy   artillery   armor   signal corps
6. peevish   furious   irritable   impatient   moody
7. corn   pea   bean   lentil   peanut
8. Satan   Lucifer   Mephistopheles   Devil   Mammon
9. Ottawa   Paris   Melbourne   Vienna   Moscow
10. sphere   prism   cylinder   cube   triangle
11. Chippendale   Hepplewhite   Duncan Phyfe   Colonial   Sheraton
12. biography   novel   story   romance   fiction
13. Garfield   Lincoln   Taft   Kennedy   McKinley
14. orange   tomato   grapefruit   lemon   citron
15. Buddhism   Confucianism   Bahai   Christianity   Shintoism
16. payment   salary   wages   stipend   remuneration
17. doctor   surgeon   dentist   nurse   druggist
18. recite   narrate   recapitulate   recount   relate
19. prophecy   prediction   augury   premonition   prognostication
20. Earl Warren   John Marshall   Charles Hughes   William Taft   O. W. Holmes
21. Tokyo   Melbourne   Rio de Janeiro   Montreal   New York
22. violin   harp   cello   viola   bass viol
23. mutiny   revolt   insurrection   gyration   rebellion
24. peach   nectarine   quince   almond   apricot
25. Ethiopia   Brazil   Switzerland   Ireland   Israel
26. otter   beaver   mink   ermine   lemming
27. bean   spinach   pea   carrot   lettuce
28. Hawthorne   Du Maurier   Melville   Lewis   Hemingway
29. Chevalier   Barrymore   Marie Dressler   Mary Martin   Fairbanks
30. Shaw   Galsworthy   Stevenson   Shakespeare   Coward

	25 to 30	— S
	20 to 24	— T
	10 to 19	— A
Answers	5 to 9	— N
Correct	1 to 4	— D

BETTER LATE __!

For each clue write a word ending in *late*. The answer to No. 1 is *speculate*. The rest of the answers are on page 278.

1. engage in conjectural thought   _____
2. gather; collect   _____
3. surrender unconditionally   _____
4. insert   _____
5. barren; deserted   _____
6. handle with skill   _____
7. increase by steps   _____
8. curdle; congeal   _____
9. spotlessly clean   _____
10. filter   _____
11. disfigure   _____
12. reduce to nothing   _____
13. remonstrate   _____
14. rise and fall in waves   _____
15. absorb   _____
16. segregate   _____
17. require as an essential condition   _____
18. cheerless; gloomy   _____
19. utter distinctly   _____
20. puff or blow up   _____
21. review by an orderly summary   _____
22. observe thoughtfully   _____
23. transform; convert   _____
24. express in precise terms   _____
25. pretend   _____
26. pass from place to place   _____
27. provide with fresh air   _____
28. try to equal or excel   _____
29. rouse to action   _____
30. swing; vibrate   _____

	25 to 30 — S
	20 to 24 — T
	10 to 19 — A
Answers	5 to 9 — N
Correct	1 to 4 — D

AND FOUR TO GO

From the illustrations on the right, choose the figure in each row that bears the same relationship to the third figure as the second does to the first. Answers are on page 279.

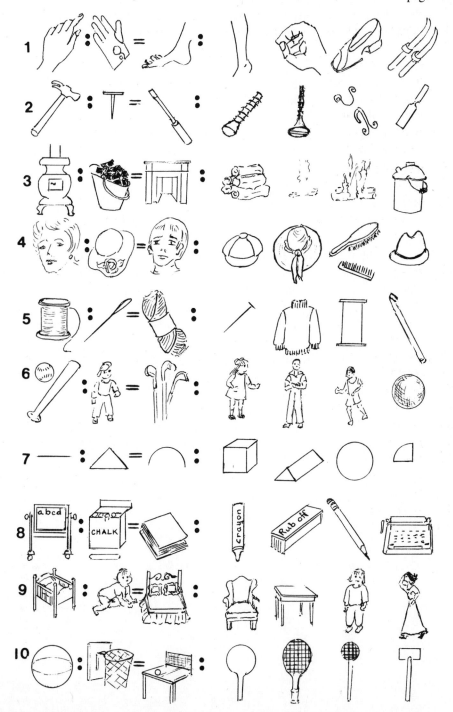

WHAT DO YOU KNOW?

Select the correct one of the four possible answers for each item. Answers are on page 279.

1. Which kind of retail store is most numerous in the United States?
   1) liquor   2) women's apparel   3) eating and drinking places
   4) food stores
2. The state with the largest Indian population is
   1) Oklahoma   2) New Mexico   3) California   4) Arizona
3. Which of these is the longest-lived animal?
   1) elephant   2) chimpanzee   3) lion   4) rhinoceros
4. The U.S. Military Academy at West Point was founded in
   1) 1776   2) 1802   3) 1861   4) 1875
5. If you were born in July, your birthstone is the
   1) garnet   2) topaz   3) ruby   4) opal
6. The oldest national park in the United States is
   1) Yosemite   2) Sequoia   3) Crater Lake   4) Yellowstone
7. Which football stadium has a capacity of over 100,000?
   1) Gator Bowl   2) Rose Bowl   3) Sugar Bowl   4) Orange Bowl
8. An applicant for U.S. citizenship must have been a lawful resident of the country
   continuously for how many years?
   1) two   2) three   3) five   4) eight
9. The Argentine revolution in which the dictator Perón was overthrown took place
   in
   1) 1941   2) 1946   3) 1955   4) 1960
10. The country that leads in the production of crude petroleum is
    1) Saudi Arabia   2) United States   3) U.S.S.R.   4) Iran
11. The Grand Canyon of the Colorado River is located in
    1) Arizona   2) New Mexico   3) Colorado   4) Utah
12. The largest increase in arrests between 1971 and 1972 in the U.S. was for
    1) drunkenness   2) vagrancy   3) forcible rape
    4) driving under the influence
13. The first U.S. President to be assassinated was
    1) Harrison   2) Garfield   3) Lincoln   4) McKinley
14. The Polar Star is
    1) Venus   2) Jupiter   3) Mars   4) the North Star
15. Of the following Gulf ports, the one handling the most shipping is
    1) Baton Rouge   2) New Orleans   3) Houston   4) Tampa

WORDS! WORDS! WORDS!

Select the correct meaning for each word at the left. Answers are on page 279.

1. giddy   vacillating   fickle   flighty   volatile
2. lavish   excessive   profuse   overabundant   prodigal
3. choleric   irascible   touchy   angry   diseased
4. sibilant   whistling   rustling   hissing   wheezy
5. illusory   imaginary   visionary   fancied   deceptive
6. plaintive   woeful   sad   mournful   wistful
7. zany   clown   half-wit   boor   wiseacre
8. animus   animism   antagonism   attitude   courage
9. kaput   violated   overthrown   ruined   head
10. nubilous   marriageable   nebulous   smoky   cloudy
11. deceit   stratagem   hypocrisy   fraud   stealing
12. urbane   mannerly   civil   complaisant   suave
13. ostensible   professed   showy   manifest   obvious
14. hearten   foster   encourage   promote   applaud
15. vindictive   apologetic   resentful   revengeful   palliative
16. bleak   depressing   windy   dark   desolate
17. weird   spectral   unworldly   queer   spooky
18. facade   cover   face   aspect   front
19. tenuous   thin   makeshift   gaseous   temporary
20. morbid   diseased   gloomy   unwholesome   sickly
21. yammer   yelp   declaim   lament   complain
22. emollient   soothing   medicinal   tranquilizing   mild
23. sanguine   bloody   calm   cheerful   bloodthirsty
24. jagged   craggy   notched   irregular   sharp
25. reciprocal   mutual   correlative   interchanging   complementary
26. define   specify   interpret   explain   deduce
27. pivot   turn   hinge   revolve   focus
28. vouch   protect   attest   defend   warrant
29. sedate   composed   serious   demure   calm
30. indite   accuse   prescribe   compose   arraign

25 to 30 — S
20 to 24 — T
10 to 19 — A
Answers   5 to 9 — N
Correct   1 to 4 — D

WORDS PLUS TWO

If you have done the anagram games Words Plus in other *Pencil Puzzles,* you are probably ready for something a bit more difficult. Here are more Words Plus, but this time the "plus" is *two* additional letters instead of one. Answers are on page 280.

1.	moon	i	k	_____
2.	weep	h	n	_____
3.	grout	a	e	_____
4.	lager	i	f	_____
5.	adult	e	f	_____
6.	neigh	a	r	_____
7.	reason	l	p	_____
8.	prime	h	w	_____
9.	berth	c	u	_____
10.	moose	h	w	_____
11.	chained	n	r	_____
12.	ridges	a	c	_____
13.	aspic	e	z	_____
14.	sheet	e	t	_____
15.	matters	a	g	_____
16.	crave	a	i	_____
17.	slain	d	e	_____
18.	rounds	a	q	_____
19.	malign	a	o	_____
20.	stamen	f	i	_____
21.	pretext	a	i	_____
22.	elevator	i	n	_____
23.	tangle	t	u	_____
24.	agnostic	o	u	_____
25.	details	s	u	_____
26.	laments	d	i	_____
27.	scaled	i	t	_____
28.	plastic	e	k	_____
29.	saltier	e	v	_____
30.	printers	e	e	_____

25 to 30 — S
20 to 24 — T
10 to 19 — A
Answers   5 to 9 — N
Correct   1 to 4 — D

TEST YOUR MEMOR-EYE

Look at the picture on this page for *two minutes*. Time yourself carefully. Then turn to the next page and answer as many of the questions there as you can, without looking back to the picture.

Answer these questions without looking back at the picture on the preceding page. Answers are on page 280.

1. Where is this scene?
2. Is the day gray or sunny?
3. How many people are there in the picture?
4. How many tables are there?
5. How many benches?
6. Is there any other structure besides the tables and benches?
7. How many trees are there at the back on the left side?
8. What is on the table at the back?
9. How many articles are there on the benches?
10. What are they?
11. Is there a sign pointing toward the background?
12. Are there any instructions anywhere in the picture? What are they?
13. Would it be easy to move the benches? Why or why not?
14. What is on one of the tables?
15. Is there a place to buy drinks? Where?
16. How many fireplaces are there in the picture?
17. What are the adults doing?
18. What are the children doing?
19. How many trees are there in the lower left corner of the picture?
20. Where must picnickers dispose of their garbage?
21. What kind of hat is the man in the rowboat wearing?
22. Who is doing the rowing?
23. Who is watching the little boy playing with the ball?
24. How many bottles are on the counter of the refreshment stand?
25. How many persons are sitting at the tables?

	20 to 25 — S
	15 to 19 — T
	10 to 14 — A
Answers	5 to 9 — N
Correct	1 to 4 — D

TONGUE TANGLE

She said Sheila shouldn't shake and shiver in her shabby shift.

CATEGORIES

Under each letter try to write at least one name or word starting with that letter for each category listed. Answers are on page 280.

Category	A	B	C	D	E
Vegetables					
Colors					
Countries					
Painters					
School Subjects					
Musical Instruments					
Trees					
Presidents (U.S.)					
Flowers					
Occupations					

38 to 50 — S
28 to 37 — T
18 to 27 — A
Answers 10 to 17 — N
Correct   1 to 9 — D

NAMES OR WORDS?

For each description below write the word to which it refers. The word must *also* be a proper name or nickname. The letter after the description tells whether the name is masculine or feminine. Answers are on page 281.

1. to diminish gradually (m) _____
2. an amatory card (m) _____
3. first appearance of daylight (f) _____
4. calmness in waiting; quiet perseverance (f) _____
5. a sortie of troops (f) _____
6. a newly married man (m) _____
7. a narrow beam of light (f,m) _____
8. large units of distance (m) _____
9. a covered vehicle for moving furniture (m) _____
10. a flower; (slang) an effeminate man (f) _____
11. (slang) an instrument for amplifying sound (m) _____
12. (slang) the human rear end (f) _____
13. an Egyptian dancing girl (f) _____
14. an account of money owed (m) _____
15. a flower; (slang) something fine or first-rate (f) _____
16. (slang) an old Ford car (f) _____
17. a moving picture award (m) _____
18. to spread out for drying (m) _____
19. a notch or groove (m) _____
20. a high-ranking army officer (m) _____
21. an umbelliferous aromatic plant (f) _____
22. a bird that talks and likes crackers (f) _____
23. to treat with insolence; to torment (m) _____
24. tap lightly under the chin; a cut of beef (m) _____
25. a granular substance used for grinding (m) _____
26. a picturesque English dance (m) _____
27. on the right side (m) _____
28. a case containing a collection of tools (f) _____
29. a characteristic of a good beach (f,m) _____
30. a division or a district of a city or town (m) _____

	25 to 30 — S	
	20 to 24 — T	
	10 to 19 — A	
Answers	5 to 9 — N	
Correct	1 to 4 — D	

194

WITH THAT KIND OF FRIEND . . .

In front of each name in the column at the left write the letter of the person in the column at the right about whom it could be said: "With that kind of friend, he needed no enemies." Answers are on page 281.

_____ 1.	Brutus	a.	John T. Scopes
_____ 2.	Stalin	b.	William H. Taft
_____ 3.	Theodore Roosevelt	c.	Abraham Lincoln
_____ 4.	Carmen	d.	Julius Caesar
_____ 5.	Rasputin	e.	Othello
_____ 6.	Henry Cabot Lodge	f.	King David
_____ 7.	Stephen Douglas	g.	Mao Tse-tung
_____ 8.	Aaron Burr	h.	Leon Trotsky
_____ 9.	Elizabeth I	i.	Samson
_____ 10.	King Saul	j.	José
_____ 11.	Lin Paio	k.	Anne Boleyn
_____ 12.	William J. Bryan	l.	Nicholas II
_____ 13.	Judas	m.	St. John
_____ 14.	John Dean	n.	Woodrow Wilson
_____ 15.	Albert B. Fall	o.	Jesus
_____ 16.	Cain	p.	Sir Walter Raleigh
_____ 17.	Iago	q.	Alexander Hamilton
_____ 18.	Salome	r.	Abel
_____ 19.	Hernando Cortes	s.	Richard Nixon
_____ 20.	Delilah	t.	Robin Hood
_____ 21.	Napoleon	u.	Moses
_____ 22.	Henry VIII	v.	Calvin Coolidge
_____ 23.	Faust	w.	Josephine
_____ 24.	Pharaoh	x.	Catherine the Great
_____ 25.	Carl Jung	y.	Richard the Lion-Hearted
_____ 26.	Judith	z.	Montezuma
_____ 27.	Sheriff of Nottingham	A.	Sigmund Freud
_____ 28.	Major Esterhazy	B.	Alfred Dreyfus
_____ 29.	Potemkin	C.	Marguerite
_____ 30.	King John	D.	Holofernes

	25 to 30 — S
	20 to 24 — T
	10 to 19 — A
Answers	5 to 9 — N
Correct	1 to 4 — D

FRAME THEM!

Each frame can be cut into the parts to the right of it. Draw lines in each frame to show that this is so. Answers shown on page 283.

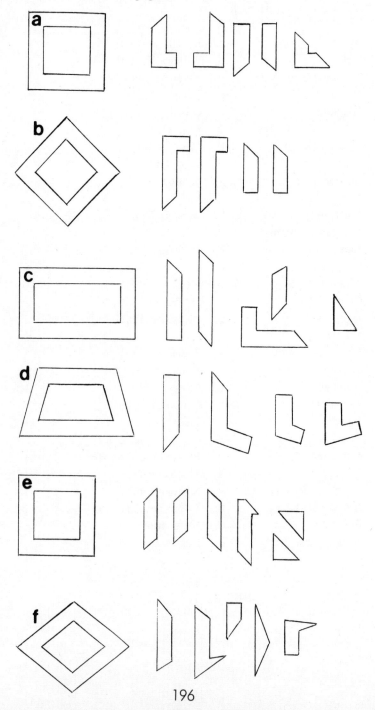

WHO'S WHO?

In one wing of a motel there were four suites of rooms in a row, each named after a state. Each suite was occupied by a family from a different state (not the same state as the name of the suite). Each family arrived on a different day of the week; each had a different destination; and each had a different kind of dog. Now read these nine statements and see if you can answer the questions that follow. Answers are on page 272.

1. The family that came from Kansas occupied the suite to the left of the Idaho suite.
2. The family from New Jersey arrived on Tuesday; they were heading for Mesa Verde.
3. The family with the poodle occupied the Arizona suite.
4. The family occupying the Idaho suite came from Maine and had a fox terrier.
5. The family that was headed for Yosemite was in the second suite just to the right of the family from New Jersey.
6. The family with the poodle was to the left of the family from Maine.
7. The family that was headed for Canada was in the next to the last suite, which was named Arizona.
8. The family that arrived on Friday had a beagle and stayed in the Florida suite, to the left of the family with the poodle.
9. The family in the Idaho suite arrived on Saturday.

      Which family came from Indiana? _____

      Which family arrived on Wednesday? _____

      Which family was heading for Yellowstone? _____

      Which family had the cocker spaniel? _____

GEM

How many errors in grammar are there in each of these sentences?
1. Them houses there ain't built like these houses here is.
2. "Ain't got any eggs, is you?" "Ain't said I ain't, is I?" "Ain't asked you is you is. Asked you is you ain't. Is you?"

Answers are on page 283.

GROW-A-WORD

"Grow-a-Word" by adding a letter to the preceding answer word, as well as changing the sequence of its letters. For example, *it, tie, rite*, etc. The number of letters in each word is indicated by the number of dashes after it. Answers are on page 281.

1. concerning   — —
   auditory organ   — — —
   degree of speed   — — — —
   very small amount   — — — — —
   wagon driver   — — — — — —
   change direction of light   — — — — — — —
   more cunning   — — — — — — — —
2. regret   — — —
   employer   — — — —
   waken   — — — — —
   more acid   — — — — — —
   ploverlike bird   — — — — — — —
   source of supply   — — — — — — — —
3. part of a circle   — — —
   mark left by a healed wound   — — — —
   is concerned   — — — — —
   wading birds   — — — — — —
   type of farms   — — — — — — —
   persons who alter   — — — — — — — —
   seeking   — — — — — — — — —
4. parent   — —
   simian   — — —
   fruit   — — — —
   hanging cloth   — — — — —
   coupled   — — — — — —
   hoped   — — — — — — —
   eden   — — — — — — — —
   belittle   — — — — — — — — —

TONGUE TANGLE

The two tiny torpid turtles trudged through the trackless thicket.

DE UNO MULTUM

From each word below make as many words of at least four letters each as you can. Only one form of a word is allowed. You may not use proper nouns, foreign words, abbreviations, contractions, or slang. Answers are on page 274.

EVALUATIONS

	75 or more — S
	60 to 74 — T
	39 to 59 — A
Answers	21 to 38 — N
Correct	1 to 20 — D

DETERIORATE

	60 or more — S
	51 to 59 — T
	31 to 50 — A
Answers	19 to 30 — N
Correct	1 to 18 — D

SCINTILLATE

	75 or more — S
	60 to 74 — T
	39 to 59 — A
Answers	21 to 38 — N
Correct	1 to 20 — D

SCRAMBLE

See how many words you can make out of each group of letters, using all the letters each time. Answers are on page 276.

1. e   r   t   i   _____
2. a   g   h   s   _____
3. a   t   b   u   _____
4. i   p   n   s   _____
5. a   k   c   l   _____
6. a   f   s   o   _____
7. e   v   d   r   i   _____
8. c   e   d   t   i   _____
9. e   o   r   t   u   _____
10. e   d   e   r   f   _____
11. d   d   r   a   e   _____
12. a   e   f   l   s   _____
13. h   e   r   c   o   _____
14. a   i   l   o   r   t   _____
15. a   e   e   h   r   t   _____
16. e   h   i   r   t   w   _____
17. e   o   r   r   s   t   _____
18. e   i   l   n   s   v   _____
19. e   o   r   s   t   v   _____
20. d   e   g   g   t   a   _____
21. d   e   e   e   t   p   s   _____
22. a   c   g   i   n   r   t   _____
23. a   c   e   i   m   r   s   t   _____
24. e   f   i   l   r   s   t   _____
25. a   c   e   i   n   n   s   t   _____
26. d   e   n   r   s   s   u   _____
27. c   e   e   l   r   o   s   t   _____
28. a   i   l   o   r   s   t   y   _____
29. a   e   n   o   p   r   s   s   t   _____
30. c   g   i   i   n   n   o   o   t   _____

25 to 30 — S
20 to 24 — T
10 to 19 — A
Answers   5 to 9 — N
Correct   1 to 4 — D

200

WHICH IS WHICH?

Each figure at the right is the same as the box at the left, but opened up. The letters A and B in the figure at the right are the same edges as the letters A and B on the box at the left. Study the figures, and then match the numbers of the edges of the open box with the letters of the edges of the unopened box. Write X for edges that don't show. Answers are on page 281.

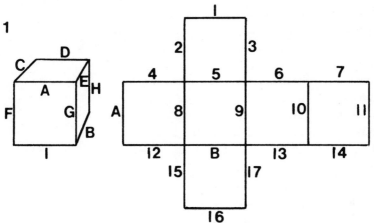

1   2   3   4   5   6   7   8   9   10   11   12   13   14   15   16   17

— — — — — — — — — — — — — — — — —

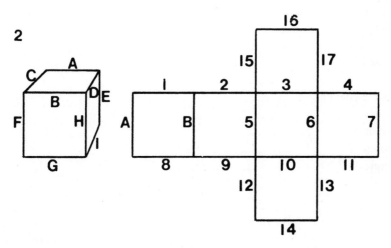

1   2   3   4   5   6   7   8   9   10   11   12   13   14   15   16   17

— — — — — — — — — — — — — — — — —

30 to 34 — S
22 to 29 — T
16 to 21 — A
Answers   9 to 15 — N
Correct   1 to 8 — D

SYNONYMS

After each word write a word with the same meaning that starts with *d*. Answers are on page 276.

1. argument _____
2. merit _____
3. devilish _____
4. postpone _____
5. delicate _____
6. excavate _____
7. lacking _____
8. adornment _____
9. monotonous _____
10. doctrine _____
11. goal _____
12. fearless _____
13. fraud _____
14. sediment _____
15. doubtful _____
16. poniard _____
17. vanquish _____
18. diverge _____
19. rot _____
20. energetic _____
21. pleasant _____
22. elude _____
23. dawdle; idle _____
24. control _____
25. erase _____
26. double-dealing _____
27. recite _____
28. extent _____
29. loosen _____
30. perplexity _____

	25 to 30	— S
	20 to 24	— T
	10 to 19	— A
Answers	5 to 9	— N
Correct	1 to 4	— D

FIND THE DEFINITE "SION"

For each clue below write a word ending in *sion*. Answers are on page 279.

1. false belief or opinion _____
2. sight _____
3. secret agreement; conspiracy _____
4. very strong emotion _____
5. stretching; straining _____
6. shutting; keeping out _____
7. something added _____
8. a hollow _____
9. injury; wound _____
10. orderly sequence _____
11. sympathy _____
12. ownership _____
13. slow wearing or eating away _____
14. offensive action or procedure _____
15. surrender _____
16. imposing residence _____
17. a particular account of some matter _____
18. a strong effect _____
19. important time or event _____
20. repugnance; dislike _____
21. being driven forward _____
22. advising against an action _____
23. retirement _____
24. prolongation _____
25. act of yielding _____
26. a harmful invasion _____
27. pardon _____
28. backward movement _____
29. turning aside _____
30. temporary economic decline _____

25 to 30 — S
20 to 24 — T
10 to 19 — A
Answers   5 to 9 — N
Correct   1 to 4 — D

203

WHAT DO YOU KNOW?

Select the correct one of the four possible answers for each item. Answers are on page 279.

1. Which candidate for the presidency received more *electoral* votes than any other candidate?
   1) Lyndon Johnson   2) Richard Nixon   3) John Kennedy
   4) Franklin Roosevelt

2. The forcible transportation of four thousand Acadians from Nova Scotia to Louisiana by the British in 1755 is commemorated in the poem
   1) *Evangeline*   2) *Pippa Passes*   3) *Home Thoughts from Abroad*
   4) *Incident of the French Camp*

3. The newspaper with the largest daily circulation is the
   1) *Los Angeles Times*   2) *Chicago Tribune*   3) *New York News*
   4) *New York Times*

4. The continent with the largest area is
   1) Asia   2) Africa   3) North America   4) South America

5. What fraction of the population of the entire world lives in Asia (approximately)?
   1) one-fourth   2) more than one-half   3) one-fifth   4) two-thirds

6. Which of the following is the highest waterfall?
   1) Sutherland (New Zealand)   2) Gietroz (Switzerland)   3) Glass (Brazil)
   4) Yosemite (U.S.)

7. The first U.S. Vice-President to resign while in office was
   1) Burr   2) Johnson   3) Dawes   4) Agnew

8. The number of persons employed in agriculture in the United States in 1970 was about what fraction of the number employed in agriculture in 1920?
   1) nine-tenths   2) two-thirds   3) one-third   4) one-fifth

9. Which state has neither a state income tax nor a state inheritance tax?
   1) Nevada   2) Alabama   3) Hawaii   4) West Virginia

10. The first use of aircraft in war was made by
    1) Italy in 1911   2) England in 1914   3) Germany in 1914   4) U.S. in 1917

11. The airline distance between New York and Melbourne is about how many miles?
    1) 3000   2) 5000   3) 10,000   4) 14,000

12. The area of Alaska is about what fraction of the area of the entire U.S.?
    1) one-twentieth   2) one-twelfth   3) one-tenth   4) one-sixth

13. The most populous Indian tribe is the
    1) Sioux   2) Cherokee   3) Navajo   4) Chippewa

14. The state with the smallest population is
    1) Hawaii   2) Alaska   3) Nevada   4) Wyoming

15. Which of these states has no city with a population of at least 100,000?
    1) Arkansas   2) Delaware   3) Kansas   4) Louisiana

WORDS PLUS

From each word and the letter after it make a new word, with at least one change in the order of the letters of the original word. Answers are on page 273.

1. gift   h   _____
2. mass   p   _____
3. alms   l   _____
4. lass   h   _____
5. trash   e   _____
6. river   a   _____
7. grail   c   _____
8. paced   r   _____
9. spine   t   _____
10. lavas   i   _____
11. douse   x   _____
12. score   f   _____
13. remit   b   _____
14. chest   i   _____
15. tread   h   _____
16. carter   i   _____
17. person   d   _____
18. umpire   m   _____
19. finale   t   _____
20. gambol   u   _____
21. paints   i   _____
22. signer   o   _____
23. direst   v   _____
24. taxied   o   _____
25. streams   t   _____
26. railing   o   _____
27. president   l   _____
28. uncaged   i   _____
29. debacle   h   _____
30. sprouted   a   _____

25 to 30 — S
20 to 24 — T
10 to 19 — A
Answers   5 to 9 — N
Correct   1 to 4 — D

TONGUE TANGLE

The scornful sculptor scuffed the scholar's scruff.

205

PUT IT ALL TOGETHER

A part of each square below has been cut out and then cut into two pieces. These sixteen pieces are shown below the squares, together with several extra pieces. Write the number of each square on the two parts cut from it. Answers are shown on page 277.

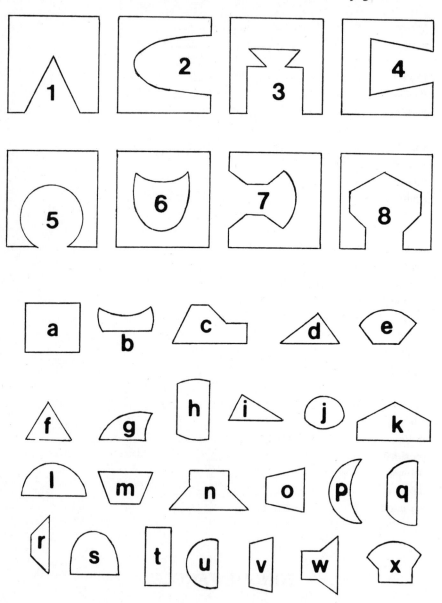

WORDS! WORDS! WORDS!

Select the correct meaning for each word at the left. Answers are on page 279.

1. garble   falsify exaggerate distort pervert
2. mitigate   soften lessen temper moderate
3. sparse   meager sporadic infrequent few
4. herald   leader pioneer predict messenger
5. overhaul   explore replace renew repair
6. creed   formula belief authority trust
7. ultimate   crowning extreme farthest conclusive
8. noxious   harmful virulent malignant evil
9. eccentric   peculiar irregular insane neurotic
10. precursor   omen introduction forerunner antecedent
11. impunity   acquittal nerve courage exemption
12. amatory   erotic ardent fond loving
13. inclement   stormy merciless violent pitiless
14. pacific   untroubled tranquil conciliatory mild
15. toady   parasite sycophant adulator cringer
16. disengage   cut extricate release liberate
17. snarl   dilemma tangle jumble threat
18. liability   casualty chance obligation possibility
19. ruminate   abscond meditate consult chew
20. whet   excite rouse stimulate sharpen
21. brazen   impudent bold shameless defiant
22. luxuriant   profuse fruitful rank rich
23. flaccid   unyielding flabby elastic soft
24. rebate   abatement excision refund allowance
25. vitiate   cancel destroy corrupt impair
26. juvenile   undeveloped puerile immature young
27. wane   fail decline ebb contract
28. acumen   discernment wisdom knowledge perception
29. ethical   legal philosophic right moral
30. rectitude   equity straightness correctness justice

	25 to 30 — S
	20 to 24 — T
	10 to 19 — A
Answers	5 to 9 — N
Correct	1 to 4 — D

207

DO IT WITH NUMBERS

1. Do you know that sometimes when you have to multiply two numbers, you can write the answer without doing the actual multiplying? Suppose you have to multiply two numbers such as:

75	87	38	94	65	59	42	86
×75	×83	×32	×96	×65	×51	×48	×84

Note that the first digit is the same in both numbers, and the second digits add up to 10. You can write the answer by multiplying the first digit by one more than itself; then multiply that product by 100; and then add the product of the two second digits. For example, in the first task (75 × 75) you would multiply 7 by 8, multiply that product, 56, by 100, and then add 25. The answer is 5625. In the second task you would multiply 8 × 9, write 21 after it, and get an answer of 7221. The answer to the third one is 1216. Can you write the answers to the last five tasks without doing the actual multiplying?

2. What pupil (or adult, for that matter) isn't made unhappy by having to multiply by 9's, 8's, or 7's? Think of the irritation caused by multiplication tasks such as:

99	97	998	989	996	988
×98	×94	×993	×992	×994	×995

But you can write the answers without doing the multiplying! How?
Using the first task as an example: *Think* of the complement of 99 (to 100), subtract that complement from 98, write the difference (97), multiply by 100, and add the product of the two complements (2 × 1). The answer is 9702.
In the second task subtract either 3 from 94 or 6 from 97; in either case you get 91. Multiply by 100 and add the product of the two complements (3 × 6). The answer is 9118. In the third task the complements are taken to 1000. So you write 991 (that is, either 993 − 2 or 998 − 7), multiply by 1000, and add 14. The answer is 991014. In like manner you find the answer to the fourth task to be 981008; that is, 989 − 8 (or 992 − 11) multiplied by 1000 plus 88. Can you write the answers to the other tasks without doing all the multiplication?

Answers are on page 275.

CREATE EQUALITY

Make an equation from all the numbers and arithmetic signs in each line, using each number and sign only once. Answers are on page 278.

1. 2 3 5 5 8 = + + ( ) _____
2. 3 3 3 5 12 = − × ÷ ( ) _____
3. 1 2 2 2 3 4 = + − _____
4. 1 2 2 2 2 2 8 = + + + × ( ) ( ) _____

   _____

5. 1 2 3 3 15 = + × ÷ ( ) _____
6. 2 3 3 3 6 9 = + − × × ( ) ( ) _____

   _____

7. 2 5 6 9 12 = − × × ( ) _____
8. 2 2 3 3 4 20 = + − × ( ) _____
9. 2 3 3 4 5 6 = + − _____
10. 3 5 6 7 19 = − ÷ ÷ ( ) _____
11. 1 2 3 4 16 = + − $\sqrt{}$ _____
12. 2 2 3 5 10 30 = + − ÷ ( ) _____
13. 2 3 3 4 9 10 = + − × $\sqrt{}$ ( ) _____
14. 1 2 2 3 3 4 4 = + + × × ( ) ( ) _____

   _____

15. 4 5 8 10 20 = − ÷ ÷ ( ) _____

13 to 15 — S
10 to 12 — T
7 to 9 — A
Answers   4 to 6 — N
Correct   1 to 3 — D

GEM

Read the following:

STARS TWINKLE IN THE THE SKY

PRIDE GOES BEFORE A A FALL

TOO MANY COOKS SPOIL THE THE BROTH

Now read it again, but this time read it one word at a time and point to each word as you say it. Try this experiment on a number of different people. What happens? Answer is on page 283.

SPOT THE STRANGER

Cross out the one word in each group that does not belong with the other four. Answers are on page 278.

1. George Eliot   Daphne DuMaurier   Victor Hugo   George Sand   Willa Cather
2. H. H. Humphrey   Alben Barkley   Andrew Johnson   George Clinton   Levi P. Morton
3. Arizona   Wyoming   Tennessee   Georgia   Iowa
4. Tunney   Ketchel   Dempsey   Louis   Patterson
5. furrow   groove   channel   flute   notch
6. reflect   imitate   copy   ape   mimic
7. physics   psychology   history   bookkeeping   mathematics
8. unequal   matchless   uneven   disparate   different
9. Axminster   Brussels   Wilton   Linoleum   Chenille
10. Austria   Poland   Bulgaria   Romania   Hungary
11. esprit   priest   respite   sprite   stripe
12. knoll   hummock   mound   hillock   height
13. Maxwell   Overland   Pontiac   Hudson   Essex
14. Egypt   Syria   Libya   Turkey   Jordan
15. indubitable   evident   clear   obvious   manifest
16. Kipling   Millay   Longfellow   Tagore   Christie
17. Pekingese   hound   Skye terrier   shepherd   setter
18. June 21   December 22   March 21   September 23   October 21
19. tower   promontory   headland   bluff   mount
20. Khartoum   Nairobi   Pretoria   Salisbury   Tanzania
21. tennis   badminton   Ping-Pong   volleyball   shuttlecock
22. Georgia   Estonia   Uzbek   Moldavia   Kirghiz
23. immortal   perpetual   deathless   imperishable   undying
24. oboe   piccolo   saxophone   flute   recorder
25. nihilism   oligarchy   autocracy   monarchy   republic
26. Proust   Steinbeck   Maugham   Walter Scott   Kipling
27. lacrosse   soccer   water polo   softball   badminton
28. Saudi Arabia   Angola   Kenya   Gabon   Nigeria
29. Madrid   Prague   The Hague   Dublin   Oslo
30. basset   mastiff   collie   dugong   boxer

	25 to 30	— S
	20 to 24	— T
	10 to 19	— A
Answers	5 to 9	— N
Correct	1 to 4	— D

OPPOSITES ATTRACT

For each word below write the opposite word that begins with the letter q. Answers are on page 277.

1. barely; hardly   _____
2. ordinary; modern   _____
3. agreement   _____
4. certainty   _____
5. professional   _____
6. steady (in voice)   _____
7. product   _____
8. stillness   _____
9. easygoing   _____
10. accord   _____
11. sip daintily   _____
12. answer; reply   _____
13. patriot   _____
14. normal   _____
15. noisy   _____
16. slow   _____
17. continue   _____
18. freedom   _____
19. at rest; still   _____
20. malapropism   _____
21. original   _____
22. sureness   _____
23. hunter   _____
24. cultivate   _____
25. down-to-earth   _____
26. dry, hard ground   _____
27. riot; rebel   _____
28. narrate; respond   _____
29. unsuited   _____
30. real   _____

	25 to 30 — S
	20 to 24 — T
	10 to 19 — A
Answers	5 to 9 — N
Correct	1 to 4 — D

TURNABOUTS

For each clue write a word that is exactly the same spelled forward or backward. Answers are on page 282.

1. a kind of haircut; a float for a fishing line   _____
2. look slyly; a bird's sound   _____
3. choke; joke   _____
4. small child; small quantity   _____
5. observes   _____
6. silent   _____
7. member of the family   _____
8. midday   _____
9. accomplished   _____
10. a polite term of address   _____
11. female sheep   _____
12. make lace   _____
13. an act; legal document   _____
14. a racing boat; a carriage   _____
15. to sound a wind instrument   _____
16. father   _____
17. direct the attention   _____
18. soft food for infants   _____
19. sister   _____
20. a fool (slang)   _____
21. period just preceding an important event   _____
22. young dog   _____
23. adored as a god   _____
24. part of a ship; a deck   _____
25. having an even surface   _____
26. spot on a playing card   _____
27. electronic detecting device   _____
28. wet with condensed moisture   _____
29. there are only two of them   _____
30. taken out   _____

	25 to 30 — S
	20 to 24 — T
	10 to 19 — A
Answers	5 to 9 — N
Correct	1 to 4 — D

AND FOUR TO GO

From the illustrations on the right, choose the figure in each row that bears the same relationship to the third figure as the second does to the first. Answers are on page 279.

WHAT NEXT?

Write the two numbers that come next in each row. Answers are on page 277.

1. 1   2   4   8   16   ____   ____
2. 32   41   52   65   80   ____   ____
3. 6   7   5   8   9   7   ____   ____
4. 1   8   27   64   ____   ____
5. 1   3   9   27   81   ____   ____
6. 1/3   2/4   3/5   4/6   ____   ____
7. 810   270   90   30   ____   ____
8. 2   4   8   3   9   27   ____   ____
9. 1   2   6   24   120   ____   ____
10. 1   2   5   10   17   ____   ____
11. 5   10   30   120   ____   ____
12. 720   120   24   6   ____   ____
13. 27   28   30   33   37   ____   ____
14. 12   9   10   15   12   13   18   ____   ____
15. 2   9   28   65   ____   ____
16. 12   11   9   15   14   12   18   ____   ____
17. 1   8   9   64   25   ____   ____
18. 42   7   6   30   6   ____   ____
19. 1   3   2   4   1   9   4   16   ____   ____
20. 2   3   10   15   26   ____   ____

17 to 20 — S
13 to 16 — T
9 to 12 — A
Answers   5 to 8 — N
Correct   1 to 4 — D

SEEMS APPROPRIATE

At five o'clock one morning a young Latin teacher was leaving the hospital after his baby was born. As the doctor who had delivered the baby walked out with him, he asked the new father: "What are you thinking of now?" Without hesitation the young Latin teacher answered: "It occurred to me that a good motto for a maternity hospital would be the old Latin saying *'Sine Labore Nihil'* " (Without labor, nothing).

LET'S PLAY HANKY PANKY!

After each expression below write the *two rhyming words* to which the expression refers. Answers are on page 275.

1.   Latin actor   _____
2.   narrow auto-wheel protector   _____
3.   more saccharine welcomer   _____
4.   pleasant segment of bread   _____
5.   tardy spouse   _____
6.   odd holy person   _____
7.   repeated hard luck   _____
8.   flexible colossus   _____
9.   more stupid pipe fixer   _____
10. sedate female   _____
11. uninterested nobleman   _____
12. weak coloring matter   _____
13. actual impression   _____
14. wonderful rendezvous   _____
15. broad shute   _____
16. less fast fan   _____
17. muffled noise   _____
18. salty nut confection   _____
19. less heavy pugilist   _____
20. mislaid inventory   _____
21. lively insect   _____
22. irritated pig   _____
23. unfastened rope   _____
24. giddy girl   _____
25. good film   _____
26. comfortable insect   _____
27. broad, slippery surface   _____
28. stylish girl   _____
29. central musical instrument   _____
30. greasy ornamental napkin   _____

                                              25 to 30 — S
                                              20 to 24 — T
                                              10 to 19 — A
                                   Answers   5 to 9 — N
                                   Correct   1 to 4 — D

215

WORDS PLUS

From each word and the letter after it make a new word, with at least one change in the order of the letters of the original word. Answers are on page 273.

1. lead   b   _____
2. dean   c   _____
3. mars   w   _____
4. also   s   _____
5. groan   e   _____
6. clout   c   _____
7. tones   f   _____
8. filth   g   _____
9. sager   e   _____
10. start   i   _____
11. ether   a   _____
12. bards   u   _____
13. least   e   _____
14. nasty   x   _____
15. wraps   i   _____
16. racing   h   _____
17. astern   i   _____
18. stiles   h   _____
19. marine   t   _____
20. parson   t   _____
21. lances   e   _____
22. hunter   a   _____
23. verbal   y   _____
24. carves   i   _____
25. blemish   t   _____
26. tarriers g   _____
27. moorings n   _____
28. denting   i   _____
29. violets   n   _____
30. lordosis l   _____

25 to 30 — S
20 to 24 — T
10 to 19 — A
Answers   5 to 9 — N
Correct   1 to 4 — D

GEM

Can you write a sentence ending with what looks like three prepositions? Answer is on page 283.

TEST YOUR MEMOR-EYE

Look at the picture on this page for *two minutes*. Time yourself carefully. Then turn to the next page and answer as many of the questions as you can, without looking back to the picture on this page.

Answer these questions without looking back at the picture on the preceding page. Answers are on page 280.

1. How many different kinds of occupations appear in the picture?
2. What are they?
3. What ad is on the side of the building?
4. What is the tailor doing?
5. How many persons are shown in the picture?
6. How many are adults?
7. How many are children?
8. In front of which store is there a fire hydrant?
9. Is the dog walking on the sidewalk or in the street?
10. Is it on a leash?
11. The door of which store is open?
12. How many adults are carrying packages?
13. How many wigs are on display?
14. Which store has a recessed entrance?
15. Which store is offering a bargain?
16. How many mannequins are there in the store windows?
17. Who is entering the tailor shop?
18. Are the women wearing pants or dresses?
19. Are the men wearing jackets?
20. What is the larger child carrying?
21. At which office window can you see a typist?
22. What is the mannequin displaying?
23. What is the man near the fire hydrant doing?
24. In which hand is the woman with the dog holding her purse?
25. What kind of hat is the man inside the office building entrance wearing?
26. How many offices and shops are on the second floor?
27. What are they?

	22 to 27 — S
	16 to 21 — T
	10 to 15 — A
Answers	5 to 9 — N
Correct	1 to 4 — D

YOU SAID IT!

When a teacher asked her class for examples of the word *redundancy*, a bright boy raised his hand and came up with this:

A customer said to the waiter: "Bring me a black demitasse of coffee." And as the waiter started toward the kitchen, the customer called out: "No sugar or cream."

WORDS! WORDS! WORDS!

Select the correct meaning for each word at the left. Answers are on page 279.

1.	gibe	deride taunt slight jeer
2.	drudge	work exert slave strive
3.	morose	crabby sour gloomy sullen
4.	appease	pacify allay moderate please
5.	naive	simple unsophisticated genius natural
6.	founder	fall sink stumble flounder
7.	relapse	yield revert regress fall back
8.	quaff	drink swig guzzle drain
9.	grotesque	bizarre deformed odd misshapen
10.	cajole	flatter delude wheedle deceive
11.	waive	abandon forgo forsake surrender
12.	homage	obedience submission veneration devotion
13.	ordinance	enactment command obedience law
14.	vagary	monstrosity whim caprice freak
15.	buttress	bracket strut support defense
16.	purport	intent profess import object
17.	itinerant	journeying peripatetic nomadic wayfaring
18.	scrimp	stint husband save retrench
19.	rapport	connection alliance relation analogy
20.	educe	evoke extract elicit develop
21.	usurp	pretend encroach dispossess eject
22.	moiety	portion share fragment half
23.	lacerate	hurt tear cut mangle
24.	temerity	fear audacity timidity rashness
25.	devious	circuitous indirect rambling wandering
26.	bias	warp oblique line partiality unfairness
27.	unctuous	waxy suave oily fatty
28.	meander	deviate stray digress wander
29.	docile	teachable weak willing gentle
30.	yeanling	cub lamb young juvenile

25 to 30 — S
20 to 24 — T
10 to 19 — A'
Answers 5 to 9 — N
Correct 1 to 4 — D

TRY IT ON A FRIEND

1. What is the smallest number of persons among whom all these family relationships can exist?

    mother sister daughter niece father cousin
    uncle brother son aunt nephew

2. What four numbers add up to 64 if the result is the same when you add 3 to the first number, subtract 3 from the second number, multiply the third one by 3, and divide the last one by 3?

3. The removal of tonsils is called tonsilectomy; the removal of an appendix is called appendectomy. What do you call the removal of a growth from the top of the head?

4. The sticks lettered *a* to *x* are so arranged that they make nine squares, all the same size, inside one large square. You are to find *two* ways to solve this puzzle: Take away six sticks, leaving three squares; then take away two more sticks leaving only two squares.

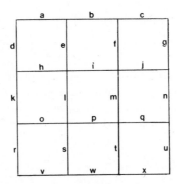

5. In the diagram below there are two empty spaces in the top row, followed by four spaces in which there are nickels, followed by four spaces in which there are pennies. Move the nickels and pennies, two adjacent ones at a time, until you alternate the pennies and nickels, filling the first eight spaces in place of the last eight. What is the smallest number of moves in which you can do it?

		N	N	N	N	P	P	P	P	
P	N	P	N	P	N	P	N			

6. There is a "taxpayer" on Main Street consisting of ten stores. One day during the Great Depression of the 1930s, a man entered the first store, a haberdashery, and picked out a tie that sold for seventy-five cents. It had cost the storekeeper fifty

cents. The customer found that he had left his wallet and all his change home. The storekeeper agreed to take a check for one dollar (the customer was superstitious about making out a check for less than a dollar), and to give the customer twenty-five cents in change.

A few minutes later the first storekeeper entered his neighboring store to buy a birthday gift for his son. He purchased a seventy-five cent penknife (for which that storekeeper had paid fifty cents), paid for it with the same one-dollar check, and received twenty-five cents in change. Each successive storekeeper purchased a seventy-five-cent item from the next neighboring store (for which that storekeeper had paid fifty cents), paid for the item with the same one-dollar check, and received twenty-five cents in change.

On Friday the ten storekeepers met for lunch as they did every week. The last storekeeper arrived a bit late and announced that he had just come from the bank where he learned that the much-used one-dollar check had bounced. The other nine agreed that they should all chip in and pay the last storekeeper whatever amount was necessary so that he would lose no more than any of the others.

Question: How much should each of the other nine storekeepers pay the tenth one so that they would all come out even; and how much did each one gain or lose on the transaction?

7. Here's an oldie. Draw a line without a break that crosses every line of this figure, but only once.

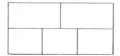

8. Mr. A told his son Don that if he started saving one penny this week and doubled the amount he saved each week after that, he, Mr. A, would double the amount Don had saved by the end of six months. How much would Mr. A have to give Don to keep his promise?

9. Mr. B entered a store to buy a tie. The one he picked out sold for eight dollars. He found that he didn't have that much with him. He told the storekeeper that he would buy the tie if the latter would lend him as much as he then had in his pocket. The storekeeper agreed to do so and Mr. B bought the tie. Mr. A thought that was a lot of fun. So he made the same offer in three successive stores, where he bought a cap, a penknife, and a book, each for eight dollars. After paying for the book, he didn't have any money in his pocket. How much did he have when he entered the first store?

10. How many boys and how many girls are there in a family if each boy has one fewer sisters than he has brothers, and each girl has two brothers fewer than twice the number of sisters she has?

Answers are on page 272.

FRAME THEM!

Draw lines in each frame to show how it is made by putting together the pieces at the right of it. Answers shown on page 283.

DE UNO MULTUM

From each word below make as many words of at least four letters as you can. Only one form of a word is allowed. Do not use proper nouns, foreign words, abbreviations, contractions, or slang. Answers are on page 274.

ALTERNATIVE

85 or more — S
68 to 84 — T
42 to 67 — A
Answers 25 to 41 — N
Correct 1 to 24 — D

EXTRAVAGANCE

70 or more — S
65 to 69 — T
36 to 64 — A
Answers 19 to 35 — N
Correct 1 to 18 — D

EMPIRICAL

85 or more — S
68 to 84 — T
42 to 67 — A
Answers 25 to 41 — N
Correct 1 to 24 — D

SCRAMBLE

See how many words you can make out of each group of letters, using all the letters each time. Answers are on page 276.

1. i l n o _____
2. h n c i _____
3. a p t r _____
4. a c e m _____
5. o h e s _____
6. a s n p _____
7. r m t a s _____
8. e e t g r _____
9. t d p e a _____
10. a l y s p _____
11. t v e c i _____
12. o l s p o _____
13. o o t s r _____
14. e o p r s t _____
15. b d e i r s _____
16. a e f s s t _____
17. c e f o r s _____
18. a d e i m n _____
19. a d e r r t _____
20. a e e l r s _____
21. a c e i n r s t _____
22. a b d e e s t _____
23. a e e g n r t _____
24. a c e e r r t _____
25. a c e e h r s t _____
26. a e l r s t t _____
27. a e i p r s t _____
28. a d e e r r s t _____
29. a c d e e o r t _____
30. a b e g i l n t _____

	25 to 30 — S
	20 to 24 — T
	10 to 19 — A
Answers	5 to 9 — N
Correct	1 to 4 — D

224

SYNONYMS

After each word write a word with the same meaning that starts with *u*. Answers are on page 277.

1. single-handed _____
2. impartial _____
3. scold _____
4. shameless _____
5. futile _____
6. incompatible _____
7. savage _____
8. result _____
9. farthest _____
10. courteous _____
11. genuine _____
12. superior _____
13. weird _____
14. uprising _____
15. completely _____
16. homogeneous _____
17. weaponless _____
18. turmoil _____
19. clumsy _____
20. citified _____
21. honorable _____
22. excessive _____
23. offense _____
24. below _____
25. support _____
26. crucial _____
27. experience _____
28. overturn _____
29. doubtful _____
30. imposter _____

	25 to 30 — S	
	20 to 24 — T	
	10 to 19 — A	
Answers	5 to 9 — N	
Correct	1 to 4 — D	

225

TIME FOR "ANCE"RS!

For each clue write a word ending in "ance." Answers are on page 279.

1. overbearing pride _____
2. sweet scent _____
3. scanty income; mite _____
4. bigotry; dogmatism _____
5. obstruction _____
6. oversupply; wealth _____
7. illustration; example _____
8. disinclination _____
9. weighing instrument _____
10. opposition _____
11. brilliance; luster _____
12. something that disturbs; nuisance _____
13. divergency; discrepancy _____
14. provide capital for _____
15. moderation _____
16. look quickly _____
17. nutrition _____
18. move the feet rhythmically _____
19. decree; law _____
20. knowledge _____
21. love story _____
22. position (in golf) _____
23. significance _____
24. annoyance; pest _____
25. aspect; appearance _____
26. caper; dance _____
27. casualness _____
28. persistence _____
29. space interval _____
30. separation _____

	25 to 30 — S
	20 to 24 — T
	10 to 19 — A
Answers	5 to 9 — N
Correct	1 to 4 — D

WHAT GIVES?

In which of these pictures is something missing or wrong. What is it? Answers are on page 278.

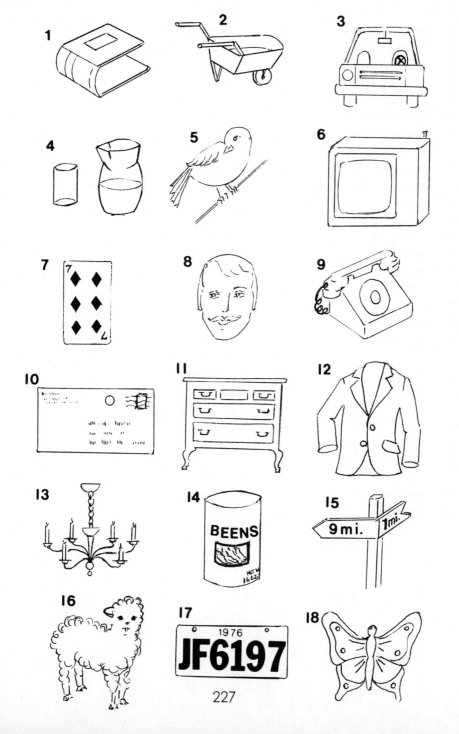

1

2

3

4

5

6

7
7

8

9

10

11

12

13

14 BEENS

15 9 mi. 1 mi.

16

17 1976 JF6197

18

OPPOSITES ATTRACT

For each word below write the opposite word that begins with the letter *j*. Answers are on page 277.

1. fresh   _____
2. applaud   _____
3. dignified   _____
4. classical music   _____
5. stimulating   _____
6. talk distinctly   _____
7. liquefy   _____
8. safety   _____
9. rejoicing   _____
10. smooth   _____
11. serious   _____
12. white   _____
13. flotsam   _____
14. specialist   _____
15. pacifist   _____
16. amulet   _____
17. prisoner   _____
18. inequity   _____
19. unenvious   _____
20. calm   _____
21. senior   _____
22. dry   _____
23. unfair   _____
24. loose   _____
25. orderly arrangement   _____
26. separation   _____
27. cheerless   _____
28. harmonize   _____
29. apprentice   _____
30. mature   _____

25 to 30 — S
20 to 24 — T
10 to 19 — A
Answers 5 to 9 — N
Correct 1 to 4 — D

WORDS PLUS

From each word and the letter after it make a new word, with at least one change in the order of the letters of the original word. Answers are on page 273.

1.	dais	e	_____
2.	rags	u	_____
3.	apes	k	_____
4.	idly	e	_____
5.	unite	m	_____
6.	stain	m	_____
7.	cores	t	_____
8.	tired	o	_____
9.	adore	l	_____
10.	glean	f	_____
11.	vocal	e	_____
12.	caned	s	_____
13.	bleat	t	_____
14.	liver	s	_____
15.	since	c	_____
16.	corals	h	_____
17.	greats	o	_____
18.	averse	o	_____
19.	result	h	_____
20.	tables	i	_____
21.	flares	u	_____
22.	batons	i	_____
23.	loosen	c	_____
24.	seeing	n	_____
25.	hurtles	s	_____
26.	mordants	s	_____
27.	secretes	n	_____
28.	officer	u	_____
29.	recaning	o	_____
30.	sainted	v	_____

229

DO IT WITH NUMBERS

1. A coin is tossed nine times and always turns up tails. What are chances of a head on the tenth toss?

2. Ask a friend to note the two numbers of dots on a domino, without your seeing the domino. Tell him to multiply one of the two numbers by 5. Then tell him to add 7 to the product, multiply the sum by 2, and add to this product the other number on the domino. Then ask him to tell you the number he finally has. Subtract 14 from that number. The result will be a two-digit number — the two digits being the two numbers on the domino!

   For example, suppose the numbers are 5 and 2. Your friend multiplies 5×5, getting 25, to which he adds 7, getting 32. He then multiplies by 2, which gives him 64, to which he adds the other number on the domino (2) to get 66. From this you mentally subtract 14. Your answer is 52 — the two digits you started with. Can you explain why this "trick" will work with all digits of 9 or less?

3. Assume that the earth is a perfect sphere, with a metal band snug around the equator. If the circumference of the band were increased by 1 foot, would a mouse be able to crawl between the earth and the metal band?

4. The difference between the squares of two numbers must be larger than the difference between the two numbers. But with fractions that is not always so. In fact, in this illustration: $3/5 - 2/5 = 1/5$; $(3/5)^2 - (2/5)^2 = 9/25 - 4/25 = 5/25 = 1/5$ the difference between the two fractions 3/5 and 2/5 is the *same* as the difference between the squares of the same two fractions. In this illustration the two fractions have the same denominator (5), and the denominator is equal to the sum of the two numerators. Let's try another pair of fractions with the same denominator, which is also the sum of the two numerators:
   $$5/8 - 3/8 = 2/8; (5/8)^2 - (3/8)^2 = 25/64 - 9/64 = 16/64 = 2/8$$
   Can you show that this must always be true?

5. Which weighs more, a pound of feathers or a pound of gold?

6. Mrs. Housewife bought a 2-pound poundcake at the bakers, for which she paid $1.20 a pound. When she got home she measured the cake and found it was 12 inches long, 4 inches wide, and 4 inches high. She cut it in half and found a large hole in the middle of the cake that was 6 inches long, 2 inches wide, and 2 inches deep. By how much had the baker overcharged her?

Answers are on page 275.

230

ON THE SQUARE

Each figure at the right can be cut up into pieces that can be rearranged to form the square at the left. Draw lines to show how you would cut up each figure at the right; then draw the lines in the square to show how the pieces fit into it. Answers are shown on page 282.

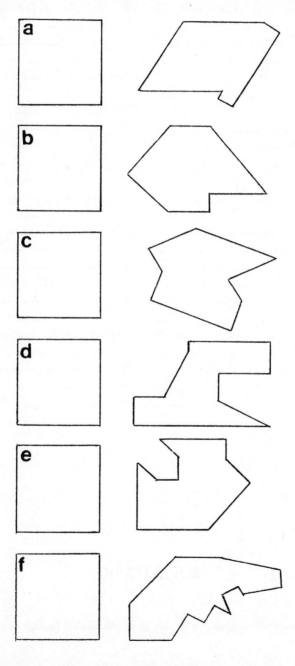

DON'T LOOK!

Can you write the names of all fifty states of the United States, followed by the capital of each state — *without looking them up?* Answers are on page 282.

1. _____
2. _____
3. _____
4. _____
5. _____
6. _____
7. _____
8. _____
9. _____
10. _____
11. _____
12. _____
13. _____
14. _____
15. _____
16. _____
17. _____
18. _____
19. _____
20. _____
21. _____
22. _____
23. _____
24. _____
25. _____

26. _____
27. _____
28. _____
29. _____
30. _____
31. _____
32. _____
33. _____
34. _____
35. _____
36. _____
37. _____
38. _____
39. _____
40. _____
41. _____
42. _____
43. _____
44. _____
45. _____
46. _____
47. _____
48. _____
49. _____
50. _____

	45 to 50 — S
	38 to 44 — T
	32 to 37 — A
Answers	*25 to 31 — N*
Correct	*1 to 24 — D*

A STATISTIC

If all the people who eat in boarding houses were placed side by side at a long table, they would r-e-a-c-h!

SPOT THE STRANGER

Cross out the one word in each group that does not belong with the other four. Answers are on page 278.

1. Aldebaran   Pluto   Neptune   Jupiter   Saturn
2. soldier   sailor   policeman   messenger   fireman
3. McCord   Hunt   Barker   Liddy   Ellsberg
4. Miss Muffet   Old Woman   Peter Pan   Jack Horner   My Son John
5. Marquesas   Gilbert   Galápagos   Society   Ellice
6. tardy   posthumous   delayed   belated   overdue
7. Lewis Carroll   O. Henry   Mark Twain   Disraeli   Mr. Dooley
8. Everglades   Grand Canyon   Yosemite   Mesa Verde   Joshua Tree
9. meter   foot   liter   hectare   gram
10. beauty   symmetry   balance   proportion   harmony
11. sausage   veal   beef   lamb   pork
12. Czar Nicholas II   Leon Trotsky   Czar Alexander II
    Mayor William J. Gaynor   Archduke Francis Ferdinand
13. Datsun   Mazda   Honda   Toyota   Opel
14. gambol   frisk   chance   frolic   romp
15. Mediterranean   Caspian   Persian   Baltic   Yellow
16. Honduras   Guinea   Nicaragua   Costa Rica   Panama
17. Quebec   Manitoba   Saskatchewan   Alberta   Yukon
18. dog   cow   goose   kitten   pig
19. wickedness   iniquity   sin   transgression   guilt
20. dividers   thermometer   weighing scale   ruler   barometer
21. Hawaii   Arizona   Washington   New Mexico   Alaska
22. henna   cardinal   red   vermilion   crimson
23. attenuate   decay   weaken   lessen   dilute
24. lyric   sonnet   limerick   rhyme   ballad
25. greeting card   telephone   telegram   letter   cablegram
26. Somalia   Afghanistan   Mongolia   Japan   Laos
27. protest   object   contradict   repudiate   disapprove
28. Orion   Cassiopeia   Taurus   Gemini   Jupiter
29. instigate   provoke   simulate   incite   urge
30. Caspian   Black   Superior   Victoria   Chad

25 to 30 — S
20 to 24 — T
10 to 19 — A
Answers   5 to 9 — N
Correct   1 to 4 — D

IT TAKES TWO

Make a new word from the two words in each line, using all the letters each time. Answers are on page 278.

1. den + nab   _____
2. poets + rim   _____
3. should + hoe   _____
4. iron + stein   _____
5. moor + heil   _____
6. juice + and   _____
7. aged + brain   _____
8. milk + rice   _____
9. clean + nip   _____
10. laid + flues   _____
11. rent + crape   _____
12. thug + real   _____
13. lure + grail   _____
14. gas + tonic   _____
15. reap + meet   _____
16. army + chap   _____
17. latch + sock   _____
18. round + recess   _____
19. tinge + trash   _____
20. said + lime   _____
21. rain + jot   _____
22. sore + pants   _____
23. odor + rate   _____
24. hens + farm   _____
25. rein + secant   _____
26. audit + once   _____
27. sent + relay   _____
28. sit + eating   _____
29. niche + army   _____
30. lean + tinge   _____

	25 to 30 — S
	20 to 24 — T
	10 to 19 — A
Answers	5 to 9 — N
Correct	1 to 4 — D

234

WHICH IS WHICH?

Each figure at the right is the same as the box at the left, but opened up. The letters A and B are the same edges in both figures. Match the numbers of the edges of the open box with the letters of the edges of the unopened box. Write X for edges that don't show. Answers are on page 281.

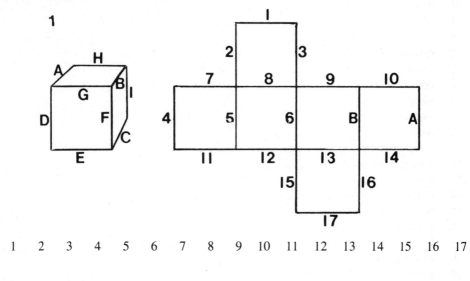

1   2   3   4   5   6   7   8   9   10   11   12   13   14   15   16   17

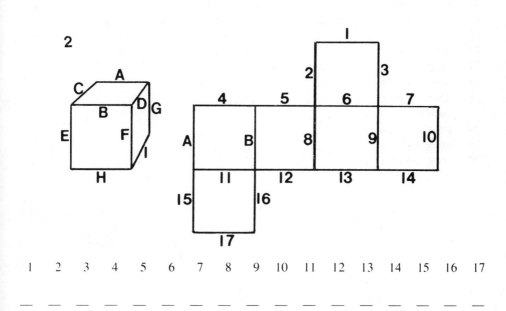

1   2   3   4   5   6   7   8   9   10   11   12   13   14   15   16   17

30 to 34 — S
22 to 29 — T
16 to 21 — A
Answers   9 to 15 — N
Correct   1 to 8 — D

WORDS PLUS TWO

From each word and the two letters after it make a new word with at least one change in the order of the letters in the original word. Answers are on page 280.

1.	glue	a	e	_____
2.	leaks	c	h	_____
3.	roach	l	s	_____
4.	admire	i	n	_____
5.	flower	p	u	_____
6.	agent	a	m	_____
7.	endear	l	v	_____
8.	sleep	i	l	_____
9.	cartel	a	e	_____
10.	glare	c	i	_____
11.	denotes	c	g	_____
12.	broad	e	f	_____
13.	taboo	r	w	_____
14.	hampers	e	o	_____
15.	moons	i	u	_____
16.	demise	t	n	_____
17.	lovers	a	l	_____
18.	treating	i	a	_____
19.	farce	l	u	_____
20.	pride	f	y	_____
21.	meeting	a	r	_____
22.	mossy	b	l	_____
23.	hotter	i	s	_____
24.	cones	b	e	_____
25.	article	n	o	_____
26.	paint	e	u	_____
27.	candor	l	u	_____
28.	polish	a	t	_____
29.	cheater	a	h	_____
30.	promotes	i	l	_____

25 to 30 — S
20 to 24 — T
10 to 19 — A
Answers   5 to 9 — N
Correct   1 to 4 — D

GROW-A-WORD

"Grow-a-Word" by adding a letter to the preceding synonym, as well as changing the sequence of its letters. The number of letters in each word is indicated by the number of dashes after it. Answers are on page 281.

1. musical note   — —
    piece of earth (with grass)   — — —
    wands   — — — —
    people who perform   — — — — —
    herds   — — — — — —
    evacuators   — — — — — — —
    dissolutions of marriages   — — — — — — — —
    act of finding out   — — — — — — — — —

2. moved swiftly   — — —
    close by   — — — —
    amount of variation   — — — — —
    semiprecious red stone   — — — — — —
    kind of rock   — — — — — — —
    warning   — — — — — — — —
    three-sided figures   — — — — — — — — —

3. a pronoun   — —
    join   — — —
    location   — — — —
    prongs   — — — — —
    introduce   — — — — — —
    a discolorer   — — — — — — —
    stones   — — — — — — — —
    affirming   — — — — — — — — —
    persons' names as written   — — — — — — — — — —

4. disencumber   — — — —
    awful   — — — — —
    lamented   — — — — — —
    assessed; appraised   — — — — — — —
    penetrated   — — — — — — —
    feeble; broken down   — — — — — — — —
    acknowledged payment   — — — — — — — — —

DE UNO MULTUM

From each word below make as many words of at least four letters as you can. Only one form of a word is allowed. Do not use proper nouns, foreign words, abbreviations, contractions, or slang. Answers are on pages 274–275.

BACKGROUND

60 or more — S
46 to 59 — T
34 to 45 — A
Answers   19 to 33 — N
Correct   1 to 18 — D

DISCONSOLATE

160 or more — S
125 to 159 — T
85 to 124 — A
Answers   35 to 84 — N
Correct   1 to 34 — D

EARNESTLY

70 or more — S
65 to 69 — T
36 to 64 — A
Answers   19 to 35 — N
Correct   1 to 18 — D

CATEGORIES

Under each letter try to write at least one name or word starting with that letter for each category listed at the left. Answers are on page 281.

Category	F	G	H	L	M
Rivers					
Colleges					
States					
Composers					
Authors (U.S.)					
Fruits					
Automobiles					
Household Furnishings					
Sports					
State Capitals					

38 to 50 — S
28 to 37 — T
18 to 27 — A
Answers 10 to 17 — N
Correct   1 to 9 — D

AND FOUR TO GO

For each line, *a* through *t*, draw in the fourth figure. It must bear the same relationship to the third figure as the second bears to the first. Answers are on page 283.

a ◯ : ◖ = △ :

b ▢ : ▭ = ◯ :

c ▽ : ◇ = ⬠ :

d ◯ : ◗ = ▢ :

e ⟩ : ∨ = ⟨ :

f ⬡ : ◗ = ▱ :

g ╲ : ‖ = ⫽ :

h ▯ : ▢ =) :

i ◊ : ◯ = ▽ :

j) :) =) :

k ⌢ : ⌒ = ▽ :

l ◇ : ◇ = ⟩ :

m — : ╱ = — :

n ⟩ : ⌃ =) :

o ▢ : ▢ = ▯ :

p ◯ : ◖ = ⋈ :

q ◊ : ◇ = ◇ :

r ◁ : ⬡ = ▢ :

s ⬠ : ◯ = ⬡ :

t ⋈ : ⧖ = ⋈ :

240

WORDS! WORDS! WORDS!

Select the correct meaning for each word at the left. Answers are on page 279.

1. hoyden   lass tomboy brat wench
2. languid   dull faint heavy weak
3. nurture   foster feed provide furnish
4. dross   rubbish garbage refuse leavings
5. orient   east place locate origin
6. murky   dirty airless unclear dark
7. astute   bright quick intelligent shrewd
8. septic   infected contaminated unhealthy epidemic
9. franchise   freedom favor privilege prerogative
10. calumny   sarcasm censure slander scandal
11. broach   suggest begin embark launch
12. welsh   elude avoid escape evade
13. ravenous   omnivorous voracious greedy hungry
14. gauge   estimate evaluate measure compute
15. nonage   adolescence minority childhood youth
16. tenure   possession ownership monopoly tenancy
17. pungent   sharp tart caustic acrid
18. caprice   quirk vagary whim notion
19. querulous   squeamish touchy complaining fretful
20. volatile   gaseous buoyant airy light
21. irascible   waspish fiery bad-tempered hasty
22. feral   fierce violent outlandish wild
23. empyrean   unworldly spiritual celestial heavenly
24. halyard   rope cable hawser filament
25. ubiquity   residence omnipresence saturation whereness
26. squirm   contort distort wriggle twine
27. cordial   cardiac sincere vigorous hearty
28. lassitude   weariness tedium fatigue monotony
29. tableau   view representation display picture
30. fallacious inaccurate deceptive unreasonable illogical

25 to 30 — S
20 to 24 — T
10 to 19 — A
Answers   5 to 9 — N
Correct   1 to 4 — D

THING OR PLACE?

Before each clue write the letter of the word (which is also a geographical name) that the clue refers to. Answers are on page 282.

_____ 1. a warlike woman; a large river

_____ 2. an Indian home; a Colorado city

_____ 3. a close-fitting shirt; a channel island

_____ 4. large stores; a Kansas city

_____ 5. a grape used for wine; seaport in southeast Arabia

_____ 6. a Spanish sword; a Spanish city

_____ 7. a kind of hemp; a large city

_____ 8. a fowl; an Asian country

_____ 9. a fishing net; a river

_____10. a grassy plain; a seaport

_____11. hard black varnish; an oriental country

_____12. a kind of tableware; an oriental country

_____13. evade payment; pertaining to part of Britain

_____14. close-knitted woolen garment; eastern state

_____15. large animal; lake port

_____16. kind of weight; classical city

_____17. portable wheelless vehicle; French city

_____18. rich tapestry; French city

_____19. cage birds; group of islands in the Atlantic

_____20. glazed earthenware; Dutch city

_____21. golden (reddish) brown; a state prison

_____22. former coin, twenty-one shillings; west African country

_____23. a large fish (grouper); Polish city

_____24. kind of carriage; English county

_____25. higher in rank or degree; a lake

_____26. social dance; New England city

_____27. tropical Asian palm; ancient Syrian city

_____28. kind of loose gown; Italian city

_____29. concave molding; poetic Scotland

_____30. cotton fabric used for linings; region of central Europe

a. emporia

b. manila

c. amazon

d. turkey

e. japan

f. welsh

g. buffalo

h. pueblo

i. muscat

j. sedan

k. arras

l. guernsey

m. warsaw

n. china

o. savannah

p. toledo

q. auburn

r. seine

s. superior

t. jersey

u. guinea

v. silesia

w. palmyra

x. canaries

y. troy

z. scotia

A. delft

B. boston

C. mantua

D. surrey

25 to 30 — S
20 to 24 — T
10 to 19 — A
Answers   5 to 9 — N
Correct   1 to 4 — D

IT'S "NESS"ESSARY!

For each clue write a word ending in "ness." Answers are on page 279.

1. lack of hair   _____
2. inconstancy   _____
3. humility   _____
4. testifier   _____
5. egoism   _____
6. vertigo   _____
7. brightness; clarity   _____
8. freedom from craftiness   _____
9. superficiality   _____
10. sanctity   _____
11. pardon   _____
12. repulsiveness; unsightliness   _____
13. brevity   _____
14. anaesthesia   _____
15. despair   _____
16. anarchy   _____
17. condition of being dull   _____
18. ardor; enthusiasm   _____
19. irregularity   _____
20. inanity   _____
21. obscurity   _____
22. daring   _____
23. alacrity   _____
24. occupation   _____
25. homeliness   _____
26. void   _____
27. yoke; hitch up   _____
28. moderation   _____
29. acuity   _____
30. resemblance   _____

	25 to 30 — S
	20 to 24 — T
	10 to 19 — A
Answers	5 to 9 — N
Correct	1 to 4 — D

DON'T LOOK!

Can you write the names of all the countries of Asia and the Far East, followed by the capital of each country — *without looking them up?* Answers are on page 282.

1. _____		20. _____	
2. _____		21. _____	
3. _____		22. _____	
4. _____		23. _____	
5. _____		24. _____	
6. _____		25. _____	
7. _____		26. _____	
8. _____		27. _____	
9. _____		28. _____	
10. _____		29. _____	
11. _____		30. _____	
12. _____		31. _____	
13. _____		32. _____	
14. _____		33. _____	
15. _____		34. _____	
16. _____		35. _____	
17. _____		36. _____	
18. _____		37. _____	
19. _____		38. _____	

30 to 38 — S
22 to 29 — T
16 to 21 — A
Answers   10 to 15 — N
Correct   1 to 9 — D

YES, SIR!

Samuel Johnson on "The education of children and what was best to teach them first" (from James Boswell's *Journal,* 26 July 1763):

"Sir, there is no matter what you teach them first, any more than what leg you shall put into your breeches first. Sir, you may stand disputing which is best to put in first, but in the meantime your backside is bare. Sir, while you are considering which of two things you should teach your child first, another boy has learnt them both."

ON THE SQUARE

Each design below is made up of the little squares lettered *a* to *l*. In the grid to the right of each design write the letters of the squares that form the design. Answers are shown on page 282.

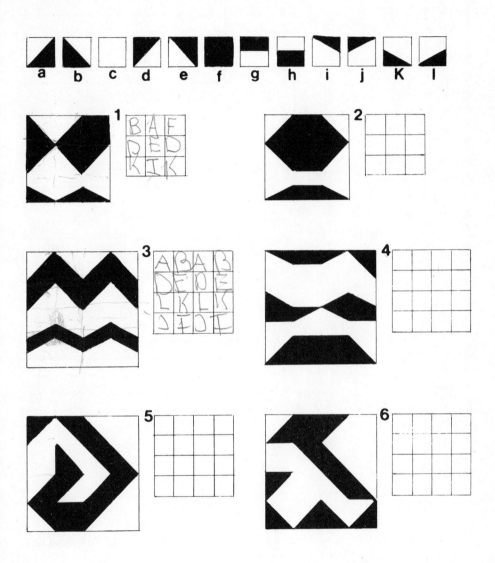

245

SCRAMBLE

See how many words you can make out of each group of letters, using all the letters each time. Answers are on page 276.

1. e l o s   _____
2. a e l m   _____
3. a s t c   _____
4. g a s n   _____
5. d e s i   _____
6. p t s o   _____
7. e d r a c   _____
8. a t l r e   _____
9. e o p r s   _____
10. s e d e n   _____
11. e o p s s   _____
12. e m s r a   _____
13. s s e a p   _____
14. a d e n r w   _____
15. a i l n p s   _____
16. e l o s t w   _____
17. i n n o s u   _____
18. e i n r s u   _____
19. a e l p s t   _____
20. d e o r s t   _____
21. e i i l m s s   _____
22. c e e f n o r r   _____
23. d e l m o r s   _____
24. b d e m o o r   _____
25. b e g h i n o r t   _____
26. a c e r s s t   _____
27. a e g l l r y   _____
28. a d e e l r t   _____
29. a a e i p r s t   _____
30. c e e i o r s t   _____

	25 to 30 — S
	20 to 24 — T
	10 to 19 — A
Answers	5 to 9 — N
Correct	1 to 4 — D

246

TRY IT ON A FRIEND

1. You have three boxes; each contains two marbles. One has two white marbles, one has one white marble and one blue marble, and the third has two blue marbles. The boxes were originally labeled WW, WB, and BB to show which marbles were in them. Somehow the labels got switched so that no box is now correctly labeled. What is the smallest number of marbles you can withdraw (one at a time, without looking into any box) in order to tell what is in each box?

2. Joe Doaks, who lives in Manhattan, has two girlfriends whom he likes equally. One lives in the Bronx, the other in Brooklyn. To call on either one he has to take the subway from a station near his home. He lets chance determine which girl he will visit each time. If the southbound train arrives first, he takes that and goes to Brooklyn. If the northbound train arrives first, he takes that and goes to the Bronx. Bronx trains arrive at that subway station every fifteen minutes. Brooklyn trains also arrive at the station every fifteen minutes. Joe reaches the platform at a random time every Sunday afternoon. Why does he find himself visiting the Bronx girl four times out of five?

3. Mr. C plans to plant a tree every three yards along both sides of a road for a distance of sixty yards. How many trees must he plan to plant?

4. Which is correct — "The yolk of an egg *is* white?" or "The yolk of an egg *are* white?"

Answers are on page 272.

SOUNDS GOOD

A psychologist completed the psychological testing of a girl of about ten whose family lived in a backwoods area of Tennessee. The psychologist was curious about the girl's first name, which he was told was Larseeney. He asked the mother whether the unusual name ran in the family. The mother explained: "No. The day she was born her father was sent to jail for larseeney. We liked the word so much that we made it her name."

LONG-DISTANCE COUCH

A young lady was undergoing psychiatric therapy. After several months of weekly visits to the psychiatrist she received an invitation to spend a month with some friends who lived a thousand miles away. Her psychiatrist urged her to accept the invitation because a vacation would be good for her. He assured her that the interruption in her therapy would not be serious. So she accepted the invitation and left to visit her friends. A week later, the psychiatrist received a telegram that asked: "I'm having a very good time. Why?"

WIFELY DUTY

Mrs. Doaks answered her doorbell one day and was surprised to find two children at her front door — a little girl of about five and a little boy who looked to be about three years old. She recognized them as children from the neighborhood. To her smiling inquiry: "What can I do for you, children?" the little girl replied: "We are playing house. I'm the mother and he's my husband. We would like to visit you."

Mrs. Doaks thought the children were very cute. She invited them in, got them comfortably settled in her living room, and brought milk and cookies. After they had talked a while and the children had finished their refreshments, the little girl stood up and said to Mrs. Doaks: "We have enjoyed visiting you. Thank you for the milk and cookies. You must excuse us now. I must take my husband home because he has just wet his pants!"

TONGUE TANGLE

Sally sang the slogan as she slid slowly down the slippery slope on her sled.

SOLUTIONS

The answers on the following pages are given consecutively, following the order of the puzzles in the book, and are keyed (in boldface type) to the pages on which the puzzles appear.

Page 12
1. aspect
2. estate
3. corner
4. style
5. abuse
6. causer
   saucer
7. crease
8. people
9. naught
10. respect
    scepter
    specter
11. chambers
12. reigns
    resign
    signer
    singer
13. person
14. opera
15. cipher
16. remote
17. applied
18. reason
19. ambler
    marble
    ramble
20. ending
21. binder
    inbred
    rebind
22. moisten
23. enlist
    listen
    silent
    tinsel
24. response
25. altruist
26. article
27. tapering
28. ardent
    ranted
29. caress
30. deranges
    grandees
    grenades

Page 13
1. Remove the 4 sticks from the two corners at top or bottom and the middle stick from opposite side.
2. Remove 2 sticks from any corner and middle stick from opposite side.
3. 8 ways; any two non-adjacent corners; and any corner and the adjacent middle square.
4. Move the 3 middle sticks to form a new square; or move any corner and the middle stick from the opposite side to form a new square.

5. Remove the middle stick from each side.
6. Remove the 2 corners on any one side and middle stick from opposite side.
7. Remove the 4 sticks from the middle row; or column; or one corner and two sticks from the opposite middles.

8. Move 2 of the middle sticks and use to complete incomplete squares; or move 2 sticks from any corner and use to complete incomplete squares.
9. Ten
10. Move 3 sticks from any square and use to complete an adjacent square and 2 opposite squares.
11. Eight

Page 14
1. nearing
2. endearing
3. scaring
4. reappearing
5. swearing
6. soaring
7. sparring
8. sugaring
9. starring
10. muttering
11. whispering
12. simpering
13. tapering
14. interfering
15. whimpering
16. loitering
17. entering
18. sauntering
19. pestering
20. bartering
21. catering
22. reassuring
    cheering
23. concurring
24. cluttering
25. searing

Page 16
1. black
   bleak
2. base
   basis
   basement
   bottom
3. bar
4. bury
5. bother
6. babble

Page 15
1. angel
   angle
   glean
2. evil
   live
   veil
   vile
3. pars
   raps
   rasp
   spar
4. gnus
   guns
   snug
   sung
5. inset
   stein
   tines
6. least
   slate
   stale
   steal
   taels
   tales
   teals
7. sinew
   swine
   wines
8. hales
   heals
   leash
   selah
   shale
9. argon
   groan
   orang
   organ
10. forest
    foster
    softer
11. enlist
    inlets
    listen
    silent
    tinsel
12. ablest
    bleats
    stable
    tables
13. drapes
    parsed
    rasped
    spader
    spared
    spread
14. reigns
    resign
    signer
    singer
15. deltas
    lasted
    salted
    slated
    slated
    staled
16. hornet
    throne
17. capitol
    optical
    topical
18. chaste
    cheats
    scathe
19. organist
    roasting
20. claimed
    decimal
    declaim
    medical
21. damned
    demand
22. painter
    pertain
    repaint
23. beater
    berate
    rebate
24. diaper
    paired
    repaid
25. options
    potions
    spitoon

7. blanch
   bleach
8. badge
9. baffle
10. balance
11. ballot
12. banish
13. bankrupt
14. barbarian
    brutal
    brutish
15. barren
16. barricade
17. bashful
18. bland
19. burst
20. broadcast
21. border
22. bulge
23. brevity
24. bound
25. bluff
26. bequest
27. belligerent
28. beneficial
29. beginning
30. blend

Page 17
1. 11, 13
2. 1, ½
3. 48, 66
4. 25, 36
5. 0, −15
6. 4, 10
7. 46, 42
8. 16, 5
9. 23, 46
10. 2, 8
11. 1, 1
12. 14, 22
13. 3, 2
14. 9, 5
15. 21, 34

PETER'S POSER
Since Adam and Eve were the only two souls in heaven that had not been born of woman, neither had an umbilicus (belly button).

250

Page 18

1. azure
2. jonquil
3. meter
4. temper
5. triangle
6. potato bugs
7. ship
8. *Fidelio*
9. Election Day
10. lamb
11. game
12. table
13. astronomy
14. minimize
15. idea
16. spider
17. shorts
18. obstinacy
19. lyre
20. lavender
21. Cointreau
22. *Cavalleria Rusticana*
23. criticism
24. heron
25. goat

GEM

aurora
aerate
bureau
cookie
hoodoo
iguana
opiate
oriole
peewee
unique
etc.

Page 19

Reading the reflections for each figure as 1, 2, 3 from left to right, the correct ones are given below:

1. 3
2. 1
3. 3
4. 1
5. 2
6. 2
7. 3
8. 2

Page 20

1. command
2. cold cool
3. clumsy
4. continue
5. confidence credence credit
6. curse
7. consent
8. concord
9. chaos
10. clean
11. convene
12. calm
13. contradict
14. condemnation criticism
15. cooperate concur
16. civil courteous
17. clamor clatter
18. cease
19. coarse
20. candor
21. construction creation
22. certain credible
23. contract curtail
24. cynic
25. convene collect
congregate
26. close compact
27. consistent
28. continuous
29. charitable
30. common

Page 21

DOMESTICATION

amen	cone	dint	made	mind	moot	sane	some	tine	inset	scion	taste	motion	citation
came	cost	does	maid	mine	most	sate	soon	toad	manic	smote	action	notice	comatose
cane	cote	dome	main	mint	name	scan	soot	tome	meant	snide	incest	notion	domestic
cant	dame	done	mane	mist	neat	scat	stem	tone	medic	staid	insect	nation	dominate
cast	damn	doom	mast	mite	nest	seam	tact	amend	mince	stain	intact	static	motioned
cite	date	dose	mate	moan	nice	seat	tame	ament	moist	state	maiden	dictate	dictation
coat	dent	dote	mead	moat	node	send	team	atone	motto	stead	mastic	diction	medication
coda	diet	edit	meat	mode	nose	side	teat	comet	satin	steam	median	instead	
code	dime	into	mesa	mood	note	site	tide	ditto	scant	stein	mitten	section	
coma	dine	mace	mica	moon	same	soda	time	enact	scent	stone	modest	station	

MEASUREMENT

amen	mart	mesa	neat	same	sere	team	true	enure	stere	master	stream	nearest
aten	mast	mete	nest	sane	sent	tear	turn	meant	stern	mature	summer	stammer
earn	mate	muse	rant	sate	stem	teem	urea	semen	tease	nature	tenure	steamer
ease	mean	must	rate	seam	stun	term	ament	smart	teens	resent	tureen	easement
east	meat	mute	ream	sear	sure	tern	amuse	stare	ensure	resume	unseat	meanest
mane	meet	name	rent	seem	tame	tram	aster	steam	manure	serene	uremia	measure
mare	mere	near	rest	seen	tare	tree	enter	steer	marten	stamen	earnest	

TRANSPARENT

aper	neat	pate	rapt	sane	spar	tarn	trap	panne	spear	taper	patent	spatter
aten	nest	pear	rare	sate	spat	tart	anent	parse	spent	taste	patter	
earn	pane	peat	rasp	sear	star	tear	apart	paste	sprat	treat	rattan	
east	pant	pert	rate	seat	step	teat	aster	prate	stare	arrant	repast	
nape	pare	pest	reap	sent	stet	tent	attar	snare	start	arrest	tanner	
neap	part	rant	rent	snap	tape	tern	nares	spare	state	errant	tartar	
near	past	rape	rest	span	tare	test	paean	spate	stern	parent	tenant	

Page 22

1. bertha	13. ruth
2. harry	14. roger
3. faith	15. colleen
4. warren	16. dean
5. kit	17. earl
kitty	18. duke
6. joseph	19. jimmy
7. opal	20. grant
8. frank	21. lily
9. hazel	22. timothy
10. jack	23. victor
11. carol	24. jenny
12. robin	25. eve

Page 23

1. $3 + 3 = 8 - 2$
   $3 + 2 = 8 - 3$
2. $14 - 2 = 3 \times 4$
3. $7 - 5 = 8 \div 4$
4. $12 - (4 \times 2) = 2 \times 2$
   $(2 \times 2) \times 2 = 12 - 4$
   $12 - (2 \times 2) = 4 \times 2$
5. $30 \div 5 = 18 \div 3$
6. $(4 + 3) \times 2 = (5 \times 3) - 1$
   $(5 \times 3) - 3 = (1 + 2) \times 4$
7. $(3 \times 2) + 2 = (5 \times 2) - 2$
8. $21 \div 3 = (5 \times 2) - 3$
9. $(15 - 3) \div 4 = 6 - 3$
10. $5 \times 2 = 3 + 3 + 2 + 2$

Page 24

1. fat rat
2. chief thief
3. grave brave
4. main lane
5. stupid cupid
6. waste paste
7. chaste taste
8. sane Dane
9. ready steady
10. nimble thimble
11. French wench
12. bright light
13. better letter
14. broad sword
15. asinine porcupine
16. double bubble
17. cuter tutor
18. frisky whiskey
19. sentimental oriental
20. blue Sioux
21. greater debater
22. free bee
23. large barge
24. loud crowd
25. funny bunny

Page 25

1. bearing
2. feign
3. hearty
4. scholarly
5. slavery
6. anointing
7. opinionated
8. free
9. antiquated
10. undefinable
11. rogue
12. bully
13. emaciated
14. authorization
15. hardy
16. unlawful
17. profound
18. hypothesis
19. worldly
20. safekeeping
21. free
22. sticky
23. kind
24. tone color
25. discernment

GEM

1. committee
2. bookkeeper
   bookkeeping

Page 26

1. 18
2. 15
3. 13
4. 19
5. 16
6. 14
7. 21
8. 18

Page 27

1. The second and third statements made by Dick and Tom couldn't all be true or all false. Therefore the first statements made by both are true. Therefore Harry broke the window.
2. Since Susie Smith was afraid of horses, the vet's nurse had to be Millie White — since Alice Jones was the dentist's nurse. Alice Jones could not be Dr. Smith's nurse (see statements c and d). Therefore Dr. Smith was the vet, and Dr. White the dentist.
3. Carl Nolan

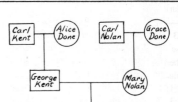

Page 28

1. image   resect
2. after   secret
3. false   5. repeat
      fleas   6. scratch
      leafs   7. conceal
4. erects   8. chapter
9. composed   direct
10. tower
11. sphere   15. forge
12. signal   16. unity
13. candied   17. resist
14. credit   18. verbal   sister
19. represent
20. sample
21. varied
22. alias
23. diverge
24. dignity
25. syringe
26. sailor
27. soprano
28. department
29. orchestra
30. disaster

Page 29

1. hazardous   euphoria
   horrendous   4. education
   stupendous   automobile
   tremendous   automotive
2. facetious   emulation
   abstemious   refutation
   adventitious   regulation
3. equation   revolutionary
speculation
ejaculation
mensuration
equitation
etc.
5. geese
   reeve
6. deeded
7. indivisibility
8. abracadabra
9. effervescence
   beekeeper
   interdependence
10. footstool
   foolproof
   bookroom
schoolroom
11. tumultuous
   unscrupulous
12. amalgamate
   jacaranda
   jambalaya
13. God be with you.
14. tough

Page 29 (cont.)

cough	mummy		
though	pappy		
through	poppy		
bough	puppy		
bought	17. aitch		
15. strengths	queue		
16. added	18. aerie		
asses	adieu		
esses	audio		
bobby	eerie		
daddy	maiou		
mammy	queue		

GEM

The line CE is a diagonal of the rectangle CDEO and is therefore the same length as the other diagonal, OD. The diagonal OD is a radius and is therefore 15 feet long. The line CE is also 15 feet long.

Page 32

1. horde	11. haughty	21. harsh
2. habit	12. heroic	22. hesitate
3. heedless	13. honest	23. hoodwink
4. hoard	14. haggard	24. humble
5. humane	15. hopeless	25. haphazard
6. halt	16. hymn	26. hallow
7. humid	17. harass	27. hamper
8. haggle	18. holiness	28. hoist
9. heathen	19. hostile	29. handy
10. hilarity	20. handsome	30. homage

Page 33

These times are necessarily only approximate, since often the two hands of a clock cannot be in exactly the same places when interchanged.

1. 12:15	5. 1:46	9. 1:01
2. 1:31	6. 7:13	10. 9:43
3. 4:22	7. 6:28	11. 10:04
4. 8:18	8. 4:42	12. 3:37

Page 30

1. 9
2. 4
3. 8
4. 12
5. 10
6. 3
7. 8
8. 15
9. 4
10. 4⁴/₉
11. 50
12. 6

Page 31

1. grandaunt; or grandmother
2. cousin
3. great grandmother
4. cousin
5. sister-in-law
6. self; or brother; or cousin
7. my son; or nephew
8. stepmother
9. self
10. grandfather
11. great grandfather
12. self; or brother; or sister
13. self; or no relation
14. self; brother; or no relation
15. cousin; or no relation

GEM

GEM

Hugo's doodle is a soldier with a musket over his shoulder and his dog at his side, just passing out of sight seen through an open doorway.

Page 34

1. fraternize	6. legalize	11. antagonize	16. generalize	21. familiarize	25. temporize
2. colonize	7. recognize	12. minimize	17. harmonize	22. pulverize	26. authorize
3. vaporize	8. scrutinize	13. ostracize	18. immunize	23. pauperize	27. penalize
4. cauterize	9. criticize	14. patronize	19. mesmerize	24. systematize	28. revolutionize
5. aggrandize	10. agonize	15. amortize	20. characterize	organize	29. symbolize
					30. economize

Page 35

1. gums	mire	spear	ulcer	garden	tones	signed
mugs	rime	8. merits	11. heaps	ranged	19. hares	singed
smug	5. flesh	mister	phase	15. lattice	hears	24. capes
2. mate	shelf	miters	shape	tactile	share	paces
meat	6. belied	mitres	12. retest	16. lemons	shear	space
tame	edible	remits	setter	melons	20. dentist	25. alignment
team	7. apers	smiter	street	solemn	stinted	lamenting
3. alts	pares	timers	tester	17. wider	21. contains	
last	parse	9. direr	13. seated	weird	sanction	
lats	pears	drier	sedate	wired	22. clouts	
salt	rapes	rider	teased	18. notes	locust	
slat	reaps	10. cruel	14. danger	onset	23. deigns	
4. emir	spare	lucre	gander	stone	design	

1. Remove the corner sticks from C and I; or remove the top and bottom sticks from B and H.
2. Remove the top and bottom sticks from either B or H, or the two side sticks from F, or the two corner sticks from C or I.
3. Move the outside stick from B or D or F to make a square to the left of D.
4. Move the corner sticks from A or C or G or I to form two squares to the left of F.

5. Remove the outside stick from each of B, E, H, and J; or C, E, H, J; or B, E, H, K; or C, E, H, K.
6. Four
7. Remove the outside stick from any of the following: B E H; C, E, H; B, E, J; C, E, J; B, E, K; C, E, K; E, H, J; E, H, K; B, H, K; C, H, K; B, H, J; C, H, J.
8. Remove the two corner sticks from any corner and one outside stick from a non-adjacent space.

9. Remove two corner sticks from any of these pairs: A, F; A, I; A, K; B, F; B, I; B, K; F, K; or the left one from F and 3 from I or J; or two each from B, D; or D, F; D, I; D, K; I, K.
10. Remove 5 sticks from F and I and 3 from J; or 5 from A and B and 3 from J; or 6 from J and K and 2 from A, B, D, F or I.
11. Remove the left hand stick from H.
12. Remove the left stick from H and 2 sticks from any one of A, B, D, or F.

Grids

```
A   B   C
        D
E   F   G

A   B   C   D
E   F   G   H
I   J   K   L

A   B   C
D   E   F
G   H   I
J   K   L
```

1. France
2. Scrabble
3. Huron
4. reckless
5. reader
6. nicotine
7. picture
8. kiosk
9. annoyed
10. termite
11. maple
12. facial tissue
13. lawn
14. contradiction
15. revolver
16. destination
17. Beethoven
18. *Tosca*
19. compromise
20. current
21. nylon
22. ink
23. ruby
24. solo
25. chartreuse

GEM
The two American coins, one of which is not a nickel, which add up to 15¢ are a dime and a nickel. (The dime is not a nickel.)

1. hay
2. tide
3. give
4. heads
5. gray
6. good
7. late
8. peny
9. light
10. waste
11. strike
12. mouth
13. nothing
14. bow
15. tales
16. weede
17. rolling
18. rob
19. Rome
20. bread
21. another
22. neede
23. wearing
24. eares
25. cake

1. arrest
2. accepting
3. artificial
4. aggressive
5. abridge
6. amass
7. accessible
8. assemble
9. absurd
10. accord agreement
11. ambiguity
12. adjoin
13. asymmetrical abnormal
14. abbreviate
15. assurance
16. antagonistic
17. alliance achieved
18. ardent
19. attest
20. attack
21. ask
22. artificial
23. aid
24. action
25. accomplished
26. admit accept
27. admire approve
28. applause approbation
29. alike
30. aversion

Read the states on pages 36 & 37 from top to bottom

1. Alaska
2. Illinois
3. South Carolina
4. Utah
5. Delaware
6. Montana
7. Michigan
8. North Dakota
9. Georgia
10. Florida
11. Colorado, or Wyoming
12. Idaho
13. Texas
14. New Hampshire
15. Kentucky
16. Oregon
17. Ohio
18. Alabama
19. Mississippi
20. Wisconsin
21. Colorado, or Wyoming
22. Vermont
23. Oklahoma
24. New Mexico

1. They were triplets. One had died.
2. One man threw his cigarette into the lake. That made the boat a cigarette lighter!
3. When the two trains met they were the same distance from New York—or from any other place.
4. The sum is 2120. Strangely, most men come up with the answer 3020; most women get the right answer.
5. Make a triangle from 3 of the matches. Then make a tent of the other 3, producing a three-dimensional figure of 4 equilateral triangles.
6. Percival, Montmorency, and Aloysius should give Algernon a $10 check. 3 checks of $10 each will settle the bills.

Page 42 (cont.)

GEM

The shorter Indian was the taller Indian's mother.

Page 44

1. disparage	10. unfeeling	19. malicious
2. glaring	11. amulet	20. renounce
3. related	12. waver	21. mitigate
4. sedative	13. construct	22. gibberish
5. misfortune	14. banter	23. breeze
6. shrewd	15. displeasure	24. serious
7. dilemma	16. imperfect	25. calm
8. accuse	17. base	
9. contestant	18. ripe	

Page 46

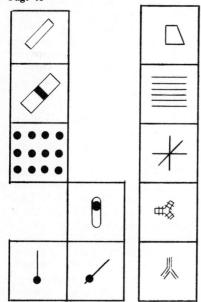

Page 43

1. ti	2. id	3. en	4. as
lit	die	net	sat
silt	lied	sent	past
lifts	tiled	stein	strap
stifle	dilate	inters	repast
filters	trailed	resting	parents
flitters	retailed	steering	patterns
		regiments	

Page 45

1. 12, 14	5. 10, 7	9. 3, 13	13. 4, 12
2. 15, 21	6. 40, 52	10. 19, 25	14. 9, 15
3. 16, 22	7. 10, 9	11. 28, 39	15. 5, 3
4. 17, 14	8. 12, 15	12. 8, 11	

Page 47

1. $2 + 3 = 10 - 5$
2. $2 \times 4 = 11 - 3$
3. $8 \div 2 = 6 - 2$
4. $3 + 7 - 6 = 2 \times 2$
5. $(5 \times 5) - 20 = (4 + 6) \div 2$
6. $(7 - 4) + 1 = 3 + (5 \div 5)$
7. $12 - (2 \times 3) = 2 + (2 \times 2)$
8. $2 \times 3 \times 4 = 6 \times (8 \div 2)$
9. $10 = 3 + 2 + (15 \div 3)$
10. $(3 \times 3) - (16 \div 2) = 1$
11. $3 + 4 = 14 \div 2$
12. $5 + 5 - 2 = 5 + (15 \div 5)$
13. $81 \div 3 = 3 \times 3 \times 3$
14. $(5 \times 2) + 2 = 3 \times 4$
15. $18 \div (3 + 3) = 3$
16. $12 - (3 \times 3) = (8 \div 4) + 1$
17. $(5 + 2) \times 3 = (8 \times 3) - 3$
18. $(18 - 6) \div 3 = 2 + 2$
19. $5 + 2 = (12 \div 4) + (2 \times 2)$
20. $4 \times 3 = (5 \times 2) + 2$

Page 48

1. 20
2. 28
3. 22
4. 25
5. 12
6. 20
7. 25 or 23
8. 50

Page 49

1. happy pappy
2. gabby tabby
3. merry ferry
4. legal beagle
5. prime time
6. crystal pistol
7. cross boss
8. real meal
9. nice vice
10. least feast
11. rotten cotton
12. pretty city .
13. ruddy buddy
14. smelly jelly
15. genial menial
16. craven raven
17. slower mower
18. taller caller
19. unique boutique
20. bare square
21. merrier terrier
22. major wager
23. narrow arrow
24. hidden midden
25. simple dimple

Page 50

SUBJECTIVE

beet	bite	cube	jibe	jute	stub	tube	vise	cubit	juice	bisect
best	bust	cute	jive	sect	suet	vest	beset	eject	sieve	justice
bice	cite	jest	just	site	suit	vice	civet	evict	suite	subject

ENDEARMENT

amen	date	dram	mart	mere	rant	rent	teem	anent	enter	dement	remand
dame	dean	drat	mate	name	rate	tame	tend	armed	trade	endear	tanner
damn	dear	earn	mean	nard	read	tare	tern	deter	tread	manned	tender
dare	deem	made	meat	near	ream	tarn	tree	dream	trend	manner	meander
darn	deer	mane	meet	neat	reed	team	amend	edema	ardent	marten	remnant
dart	dent	mare	mend	need	rend	tear	ament	emend	demean	redeem	

TIMELINESS

emit	lien	list	mile	mite	sent	slit	tine	limit	smelt	stile	tinsel
isle	lime	meet	mine	ness	silt	stem	inlet	seine	smile	enlist	missile
lent	limn	melt	mint	nest	sine	teem	inset	sense	smite	insist	tensile
less	line	mess	miss	seem	site	tile	islet	sleet	steel	listen	
lest	lint	mien	mist	seen	slim	time	istle	slime	stein	silent	

Page 51

1. 2	9. 3
2. 4	10. 4
3. 4	11. 1
4. 3	12. 1
5. 3	13. 4
6. 4	14. 2
7. 1	15. 3
8. 2	

Page 52

Think of the items in each row as numbered from 1 to 5. The answers given here tell the number of the right one in each row.

1. 2	6. 1
2. 2	7. 5
3. 4	8. 3
4. 3	9. 4
5. 1	10. 5

Page 53

1. safety	16. serene
security	smooth
2. sacred	
3. strong	17. silent
sturdy	speechless
4. spurn	18. sagacious
5. sad	19. sincere
sullen	20. steep
6. sorry	21. settler
7. strict	22. synonym
stern	23. stagnant
8. symmetry	stationary
9. smooth	24. skilled
10. suitable	skillful
11. separate	25. starboard
sever	26. solid
12. sallow	27. soak
13. stranger	28. savage
14. shiftless	29. serviceable
15. supple	30. shiny
	sharp

Page 54

1. attachment	27. placement
2. inducement	28. assortment
3. argument	29. compliment
4. condiment	30. adjustment
5. fragment	
6. apartment	
tenement	
7. assignment	
8. fulfillment	
accomplishment	
9. enactment	
10. liniment	
11. nourishment	
12. requirement	
13. entanglement	
14. establishment	
15. detachment	
16. ailment	
17. basement	
18. monument	
19. sediment	
20. arrangement	
21. sentiment	
22. banishment	
23. engagement	
24. punishment	
25. derangement	
26. management	

Page 55

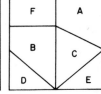
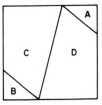

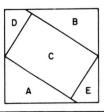

Page 56

1. emit	strap	16. rickets
item	traps	sticker
mite	9. laves	tickers
time	salve	17. introduce
2. ache	slave	reduction
each	vales	18. gyrated
3. thaw	veals	tragedy
what	10. acred	19. gradient
4. merit	arced	redating
miter	cared	treading
mitre	cedar	20. earned
remit	raced	endear
timer	11. skater	neared
5. aster	streak	21. piston
rates	takers	pitons
stare	12. rivets	points
tares	stiver	22. dearth
tears	strive	hatred
6. paste	13. sower	thread
pates	swore	23. brief
peats	worse	fiber
septa	14. craned	fibre
spate	dancer	24. caller
tapes	15. parses	cellar
7. bales	passer	recall
blase	repass	25. fidget
sable	spares	gifted
8. parts	sparse	
sprat	spears	

Page 57

1. Move left stick of F to B; or upper stick of F to E; or right stick of G to K; or lower stick of G to H; or top of C to B; or bottom of J to K.
2. Move 3 sticks from any corner to complete squares at three of B, E, H, or K.
3. Move 2 sticks from A, C, D, I, J, or L to complete squares at two of B, E, H, or K.
4. Remove 2 sticks from C, F, G, or J.
5. Move 4 sticks from R and S to make squares in G, H, L, A; or 3 sticks from E and 1 from B or C to make squares in G, H, L, M; etc.
6. Move 2 sticks from B and 1 from I to J and T; etc.
7. Remove top stick of D and left stick of N.
8. Remove 2 sticks from A or I or P or S.
9. Move 2 sticks from A to B and K; or 2 sticks from P to K and O; etc.
10. Move 3 sticks from A or C and 1 from F (or 2 from E and 2 from F) to form squares at H, K, and O.
11. Remove 3 sticks from A, or C, or N, or P.
12. Move left stick of J to K.
13. Move 3 sticks from A or C or L or N or P to H and K or H and B.
14. Four

Page 58

Read the states on pages 54 and 55 from top to bottom.

1. New York	8. Hawaii
2. West Virginia	9. Virginia
3. Washington	10. California
4. No. Carolina	11. Nebraska
5. Minnesota	12. Arizona
6. Maryland	13. Kansas
7. Connecticut	

Page 62

1. They are the same distance apart.
2. If you keep looking at the steps they will switch back and forth from being below you to being above you.
3. They are the same length.
4. You should see a part of a finger (like a small sausage) suspended in the air by itself.
5. Yes. The shading makes the right-hand one look wider.
6. The middle one.
7. They are all the same size.

Page 65

1. 44, 64	6. 20, 9	11. $14^2/_5$, 12
2. 12, 45	7. 16, 32	12. 85, 121
3. 16, 5	8. 125, 216	13. $^5/_6$, $^6/_7$
4. 23, 26	9. 6, 21	14. 12, 10
5. 5, 25	10. 16, 64	15. 5, 20

GEM

An Egyptian priest about 2000 B.C.

Page 57 (cont.)

A	B	C	D
E	F	G	H
I	J	K	L

A	B	C	D	E
F	G	H	I	J
K	L	M	N	O
P	Q	R	S	T

A	B	C	D
E	F	G	H
I	J	K	L
M	N	O	P

Page 59

1. New Jersey
2. Nevada
3. Indiana
4. Iowa
5. Maine
6. Rhode Island
7. Tennessee
8. Massachusetts
9. Louisiana
10. Missouri
11. Pennsylvania
12. South Dakota
13. Arkansas

Page 60

1. 2
2. 5
3. 8
4. 6
5. 3½
6. 1½
7. 6
8. $1^2/_5$
9. $^3/_4$
10. 7
11. 3½
12. 5

Page 63

1. 10 A.M.
2. 5:30 P.M.
3. 9 A.M.
4. 6 hours

Page 66

1. aristocrat
2. indifference
3. lazy
4. risk
5. adulterate
6. sensitive
7. loyalty
8. clear
9. exceed
10. briskness
11. forerunner
12. definite
13. sneering
14. boring
15. high-flown
16. inert
17. credulous
18. confirm
19. appropriate
20. criticism
21. entrap
22. destitution
23. issue
24. cowardly
25. experimental

Page 64

1. grandfather
2. grandnephew
3. self
4. no relation
5. cousin
6. cousin
7. uncle
8. no relation
9. cousin
10. grandfather; or no relation
11. grandnephew
12. brother; or no relation
13. no relation
14. sister; sister-in-law; or no relation
15. grandfather

Page 61

1. during
2. mattress
   smatters
3. resect
   secret
4. winter
5. sphere
6. recipe
7. wound
8. ghost
9. fruit
10. cleaned
11. cubism
12. refund
13. eyelid
14. neuter
    retune
    tenure
    tureen
15. contain
16. relying
17. denied
    indeed
18. integral
    relating
    triangle
19. creator
20. finger
    fringe
21. harvest
22. chasm
23. leaser
    resale
    reseal
    sealer
24. student
    stunted
25. gnawed
26. heading
27. justice
28. integrate
29. premise
30. ligaments

Page 67

Reading the reflections for each figure as 1, 2, 3 from left to right, the correct ones are given below:

1. 1
2. 3
3. 2
4. 2
5. 1
6. 3
7. 1
8. 3

Page 68

1. waver
2. warp
3. wink
4. wiry
5. woo
6. wrestle
7. worth
8. wry
9. wrap
10. waterfall
11. weariness
12. weave
13. whitewash
14. whim
15. wharf
16. whine
17. wince
18. wield
19. wickedness
20. wit
21. wonder
22. worn
23. wrath
24. whirl
25. wearisome

Page 70

WATERGATE	CELESTIAL	
area	alit	tell
agar	call	test
ewer	case	till
gate	cell	caste
gear	celt	cleat
grew	ease	elite
rage	else	islet
rate	isle	istle
tare	lace	lease
tart	last	least
tear	late	lilac
teat	less	scale
tree	lest	slate
wage	lice	sleet
ware	list	stall
wart	sail	steal
watt	sale	steel
wear	salt	still
were	sate	taste
agate	seal	telic
agree	seat	testa
attar	sell	celesta
eager	site	elastic
eater	tact	
grate	tael	
great	tail	
treat	talc	
wager	tale	
water	tall	
aerate	teal	

Page 69

1. Start at A and go in turn to B, C, D, B, E, D, A, C.

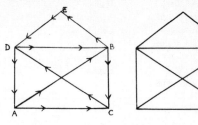

2. Mark Underhill
   Andover
   Massachusetts

3. Three socks. If the first two are the same color, he has a pair. If not, the third one must form a pair with one of the others.

4. H, H₁, and H₂ are the three Hungarians, H being the rower. S, S₁ and S₂ are the Swedes, S being the rower.

   S takes S_1 across
   S returns
   S takes S_2 across
   S returns
   H takes H_1 across
   H returns with S_1
   H takes S across
   H returns with S_2
   H takes H_2 across
   S returns
   S takes S_1 across
   S returns
   S takes S_2 across

5. Starting from the North Pole, he can walk south 200 miles then west 200 miles then north 200 miles and he will be back at the North Pole. He can start at a point 200 miles north of a parallel 200 miles in circumference just north of the South Pole. After walking around that parallel, he will walk north on the same parallel on which he had walked south.

   Starting north of a parallel that is 100 miles (or 50 miles, or 33¹/₃ miles) in circumference, he would walk 200 miles to that parallel and then walk around it to the west twice, (or three or four times, etc.) and then north back on the same meridian on which he had walked south.

SATURNINE

anti	rase	sane	stun	turn	saint	train	tennis
aunt	rate	sate	suit	anent	satin	trine	ursine
earn	rein	sear	tare	anise	siren	urine	
east	rent	seat	tarn	aster	stain	astern	
neat	rest	sent	tear	inert	stair	insert	
nest	rise	sine	tern	inset	stare	nature	
nine	rite	site	tine	inter	stein	retain	
rain	runt	star	tire	raise	stern	retina	
rant	rust	stir	tune	risen	suite	strain	

258

Page 71

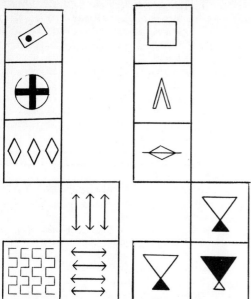

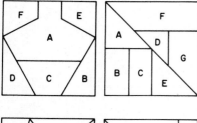

Page 72

1. are
   race
   clear
   lacier
   clavier
   cavalier
2. at
   tan
   rant
   train
   retain
   stainer
   strained
3. pa
   rap
   pear
   drape
   spared
   praised
   paradise
4. ore
   rope
   toper
   report
   prorate
   predator

Page 73

1. preface
2. deserted
3. rank
4. formless
5. blotched
6. insipid
7. frightful
8. coarse
9. worthless
10. stubborn
11. abusive
12. differing
13. delicious
14. odious
15. odd
16. grating
17. raillery
18. interpret
19. ardent
20. spirit
21. abstruse
22. drowsiness
23. transgress
24. imperative
25. precise

Page 74

1. gentle
2. greet
3. gain
4. gamble
5. garrulous
6. generous
7. gay
   genial
8. gradual
9. greed
10. guest
11. gloat
12. graceful
13. group
14. gigantic
15. grateful
16. genuine
17. gather
18. guile
19. gratify
20. gloom
21. grave
    glum
22. grandeur
23. grief
24. grand
25. general
26. gullible
27. genesis
28. glum
    gloomy
29. glamour
30. grimy

Page 75

1. 4	4. 4	7. 1	10. 2	13. 4
2. 3	5. 2	8. 1	11. 4	14. 3
3. 3	6. 3	9. 1	12. 2	15. 1

Page 76

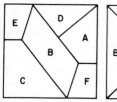

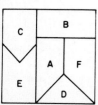

Page 77

1. narrate
2. perforate
3. liberate
4. separate
5. deteriorate
6. corroborate
7. obdurate
8. recuperate
9. regenerate
10. penetrate
11. elaborate
12. deliberate
13. lacerate
14. disintegrate
15. considerate
16. prorate
17. exaggerate
18. frustrate
19. inaugurate
20. accelerate
21. celebrate
22. operate
23. pirate
24. moderate
25. confederate

Page 78

1. spoil
2. burnt
3. melt
4. pride
5. more
6. ill
7. ear
8. will
9. well
10. cart
11. fear
12. shoemaker's
13. cloth
14. hound
15. beggars
16. strings
17. fool
18. fire
19. cat
20. buttered
21. dog
22. inch
23. swallow
24. leap
25. clean

Page 79

1. Indians
2. England
3. apple
4. nasturtium
5. movie
6. Brazil
7. tennis
8. Spain
9. carburetor
10. list
11. Maxwell
12. cup
13. lacrosse
14. chartreuse
15. temperature
16. chaise longue
17. carrots
18. Poland
19. cousin
20. India
21. courage
22. orange
23. gin rummy
24. raccoon
25. indictment

Page 80

1. diet, stanch, waddles
   edit, 8. claps, 17. demerit
   tide, clasp, merited
   tied, scalp, mitered
2. brute, 9. corona, 18. despoil
   buret, racoon, spoiled
   rebut, 10. esprit, 19. enlarge
   tuber, priest, gleaner
3. ester, ripest, general
   reset, spiter, 20. kitchen
   steer, sprite, thicken
   stere, stripe, 21. posture
   terse, tripes, pouters
   trees, 11. cruet, spouter
4. bluest, cuter, troupes
   bustle, truce, 22. weather
   sublet, 12. berated, whereat
   subtle, debater, wreathe
5. does, rebated, 23. construe
   dose, 13. copes, counters
   odes, copse, recounts
6. carets, scope, trounces
   caster, 14. chalets, 24. alerting
   caters, latches, altering
   crates, satchel, integral
   reacts, 15. early, relating
   recast, layer, triangle
   traces, relay, 25. nightcap
7. chants, 16. dawdles, patching
   snatch, swaddle

Page 81

1. 19
2. 34
3. 37
4. 93
5. 14
6. 43
7. 60
8. 93

Page 82

1. defined, 12. consider, 21. steadily
2. section, 13. stammer, 22. vintages
3. heading, 14. selecting, 23. enlarged
4. tricked, 15. unbar, 24. gondola
5. apostle, urban, 25. wreath
6. organic, 16. retail, 26. measuring
7. senator, 17. reduce, 27. massacre
8. clients, 18. detail, 28. inception
   stencil, dilate, 29. betrayal
9. stiffen, 19. stadium, 30. bachelors
10. entranced, 20. eductions
11. derelict, seduction

Page 83

1. abundant, 11. advance, 21. agree
   ample, 12. accidental, 22. aged
2. above, 13. ally, 23. answer
3. abstract, 14. active, 24. adequate
4. absolute, 15. adhere, ample
5. accept, 16. associate, 25. approximate
6. abhor, 17. actual, 26. accomplish
7. able, 18. arrive, achieve
   adept, 19. ancient, 27. antecedent
8. abolish, antique, 28. abolish
9. admonish, 20. afar, 29. acute
10. abrupt, away, 30. activity

Page 84

1. Yes
2. As you keep looking at the glass lines, a and c seem alternately to be in front of and behind b and d.
3. They are the same.
4. As you keep looking at it the surfaces change position.
5. They are the same.
6. They are equally light, as you will see if you cover the dark figure except for the circle and compare the two circles.

Page 85

INTRODUCE

cent, dine, ired, rite, tire, diner, trine
cite, dint, iron, rode, trod, edict, truce
code, dirt, nice, rout, true, inter, cornet
cone, done, node, rote, unto, niter, credit
core, dour, note, rude, count, nitre, direct
corn, duct, nude, tend, court, ounce, induce
cote, duet, once, tide, crude, outer, induct
cute, edit, rent, tied, cruel, route, trounce
dice, iced, rice, tier, cured, trice, reduction
diet, into, ride, tine, cuter, tried

EXCEPTION

cent, cope, into, note, otic, peon, tine, niece, pence, except
cite, cote, next, once, oxen, pine, tone, opine, piece, excite
cone, exit, nice, open, pent, pint, inept, optic, tonic, expect

FOREIGNERS

fine, goes, reef, seen, sing, feign, grief, singe, fringe, seeing, freeing
fire, gone, rein, seer, sire, forge, infer, sneer, refine, signer, reefing
fore, gore, rife, sign, song, gorse, refer, snore, resign, singer, foreign
free, grin, ring, sine, sore, green, reign, finger, rosier, foreign

Page 86

1. scamp, 16. sneer
2. sedate, scoff
   shy, 17. shatter
3. salary, 18. seethe
4. senior, 19. sinuous
5. seclusion, 20. safeguard
   solitude, 21. scanty
6. sham, 22. sovereign
7. sieve, 23. similarity
8. scarlet, semblance
9. shiver, 24. sleuth
10. sacred, 25. sallow
    sacrosanct, 26. signify
11. smother, 27. spoil
    suffocate, 28. salvation
12. scale, 29. sojourn
13. simulate, stay
14. seer, 30. scurrilous
15. sagacious

Page 90

1. R
2. L
3. L
4. L
5. L
6. L
7. R
8. L
9. L
10. R
11. R
12. R
13. R
14. L
15. L

Page 91

1. rake
2. disagreement
3. seasoning
4. dandy
5. humanitarian
6. defect
7. incentive
8. temperance
9. consign
10. ungodliness
11. ambiguous
12. reprisal
13. vibration
14. vigilance
15. fiber
16. descendants
17. souvenir
18. obsequious
19. agreement
20. concealed
21. belittle
22. truth
23. persistence
24. diligent
25. howling

GEM

Nehemiah was the shortest man mentioned in the Bible if you pronounce his name knee-high-Meyer

Page 92

1.	bared	teals	8.	trail	15.	rifled	24.	insert
	beard	4. their		trial	16.	powder		inters
	bread	5. merit	9.	regard	17.	sight	25.	transpire
	debar	miter	10.	exist	18.	reign	26.	verdict
2.	spirit	mitre	11.	delay	19.	tennis	27.	screen
3.	stale	remit	12.	period	20.	player	28.	absence
	steal	timer	13.	leather	21.	appeal	29.	sensation
	taels	6. truth	14.	aline	22.	energy	30.	epithets
	tales	7. vital		anile	23.	preach		

Page 93

1. wandering
2. pondering
3. wondering
4. anchoring
    mooring
5. tethering
6. recovering
7. stammering
    stuttering
8. fluttering
9. lowering
10. buttering
11. clustering
12. watering
13. wavering
14. gathering
15. surrendering
16. harboring
17. lumbering
18. ordering
19. petering
20. bothering
21. shivering
22. clamoring
23. storing
24. staring
25. puttering

Page 94

5	8	5
7	3	1
6	9	2

5	7	3	7
3	8	5	8
1	7	3	11
5	1	12	6

9	3	7	10
3	8	5	7
5	7	3	8
7	5	8	11

9	4	4	10
12	6	6	13
7	2	2	3
13	7	3	12

7	5	8
1	2	3
8	3	8

Page 95

Adams
Cleveland
Eisenhower
Grant
Harding
Harrison
Jackson
Jefferson
Johnson
Kennedy
Lincoln
Madison
Monroe
Nixon
Polk
Roosevelt
Taft
Truman
Washington
Wilson

Page 96

1. 3
2. 4
3. 2
4. 2
5. 3
6. 4
7. 4
8. 4
9. 1
10. 1
11. 2
12. 3
13. 4
14. 2
15. 3

Page 97

1. ire
   tier
   trine
   tinder
   printed
   intrepid
2. if
   fie
   rife
   flier
   trifle
   fertile
3. pie
   ripe
   spire
   esprit
   respite
   prestige

4. as
   sap
   apse
   sepia
   praise
   traipse
   parasite

GEM Page 97

Place the point of your pencil on the dot in the center of the circle. Then fold your paper so that you can slide your pencil, without lifting it, over the edge of the paper and over to the circumference of the circle. Then continue tracing the circle.

Page 98

1. 12:35
2. 5:03
3. 5:27
4. 2:41
5. 12:10
6. 5:47
7. 1:26
8. 6:33
9. 9:58
10. 3:16
11. 10:09
12. 3:51

Page 98

GEM

1. liver
2. inane
3. vaunt
4. ennui
5. retie

Page 99

1. R b
2. G l
3. G k
4. G a
5. R i
6. G c
7. G b
8. R k
9. G d
10. R g
11. R l
12. G, R e

SCALE WISE Page 99

Weigh any 3 coins against any three others. If one set is heavier, weigh any 2 of these coins against each other; either one of them is the heavier, or the odd one is the heavier. If the two sets of 3 coins balance, weigh any 2 of the other set of 3 against each other; either one of them is the heavier, or the odd one is the heavier.

13. R a
14. R h
15. G f
16. R c
17. G g
18. R j
19. G i
20. G j
21. R d
22. R f
23. G h

1.	brute		mean		brad		fears		lacks		leader	18.	direst
	rebut		name		drab		safer		slack		redeal		driest
	tuber	4.	dame	7.	kale	10.	dater	13.	below	16.	canter		stride
2.	aril		made		lake		rated		bowel		nectar	19.	incest
	lair		mead		leak		trade		elbow		recant		insect
	liar	5.	lien	8.	aids		tread	14.	paled		trance		nicest
	rail		line		dais	11.	views		pedal	17.	adders	20.	begin
3.	amen		nile		said		wives		plead		dreads		being
	mane	6.	bard	9.	fares	12.	calks	15.	dealer		sadder		binge

21. panel — 24. procured
penal — producer
plane — 25. stiller
22. detour — tillers
routed — trellis
toured
23. hatters
shatter
threats

1. Move 2 sticks from A or C or G or I to make squares at B and E.
2. Move outside stick from D or F (or bottom stick of H) to make square at E.
3. Move outside sticks from any two of D, F, or H to form squares at B and E.
4. Five ways

---

5. Move three sticks from H to B, E, J.
6. Move two sticks from A to make squares at B and E; or 2 from C to B and E or J; etc.
7. Six ways
8. Move three sticks from C to make squares at L and E or J; or from K to D and B or E.

---

9. Remove right stick from F.
10. Remove three sticks from I to make squares at B and D; or three sticks from A to B and H.
11. Move bottom stick from E and two vertical sticks from F to make squares at B and D.
12. Move right stick from F to top of B.

A B C
D E F
G H I

A B C D
E F G H
I J K L

A B C
D E F
G H I

---

1. danger
2. dash
3. deception
   duplicity
4. domestic
5. dull
6. disfavor
   deride
7. durable
8. decide
9. disburse
10. dead
11. delicate
12. divide
13. definite
14. diligent
15. debit
16. dauntless
17. discover
18. deep
19. depressed
20. disobey
    defy
21. dawdle
22. discontinue
23. diversity
24. disconcert
25. defective
26. dandy
27. doubtful
    dubious
28. deny
29. decrease
30. descend

1. a
2. d
3. j
4. g
5. k
6. k
7. b
8. h
9. k
10. e
11. c
12. e
13. c
14. i
15. e
16. f
17. m
18. l
19. i
20. e

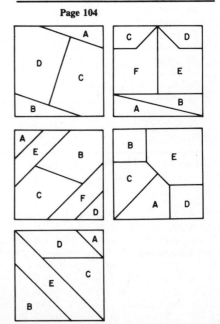

GEM Page 103
Draw a horozontal line from A to D. Draw a vertical line from the midpoint of line BC to E. From the point where this vertical line crosses line AD, draw lines to B and C. You will now have 6 triangles each containing 2 cabins.

Page 105
1. belle
2. gene
3. rob
4. flora
5. will
6. louis
7. ruby
8. olive
9. sybil
10. art
11. terry
12. homer
13. jean
14. molly
15. patty
16. basil
17. jasper
18. crystal
19. dolly
20. hyacinth
21. hank
22. phoebe
23. pearl
24. franklin
25. myrtle

Page 106
1. fleet street
2. cute Ute
3. green bean
4. lone cone
5. heavy levy
6. better letter
7. nickel pickle
8. finer liner
9. other brother
10. miniature caricature
11. clear tear
12. lame dame
13. later waiter
14. yellow fellow
15. fair hair
16. meat treat
17. tidy didy
18. lazy daisy
19. frantic antic
20. gayer player
21. greater crater
22. richer pitcher
23. stable table
24. bleak peak
25. single tingle

Page 107
1. a) $1/36$
   b) $2/36$
   c) $3/36$
   d) $4/36$
   e) $5/36$
   f) $6/36$
   g) $5/36$
   h) $4/36$
   i) $3/36$
   j) $2/36$
   k) $1/36$
2. a) 1 to 35
   b) 1 to 17 (2 to 34)
   c) 1 to 11 (3 to 33)
   d) 1 to 8 (4 to 32)
   e) 5 to 31
   f) 1 to 5 (6 to 30)
   g) 5 to 31
   h) 1 to 8 (4 to 32)
   i) 1 to 11 (3 to 33)
   j) 1 to 17 (2 to 34)
   k) 1 to 35
3. $10/36$
4. $5/36$; $7/12$ $(21/36)$
5. $2/9$ $(8/36)$
6. a) $11/12$ $(33/36)$
   b) $5/6$ $(30/36)$
   c) $13/18$ $(26/36)$
   d) $7/12$ $(21/36)$
   e) $5/12$ $(15/36)$
   f) $5/18$ $(10/36)$
   g) $1/6$ $(6/36)$
   h) $1/12$ $(3/36)$
7. a) $1/18$ $(2/36)$
   b) $1/12$ $(3/36)$
   c) $1/9$ $(4/36)$
   d) $5/36$
   e) $5/36$
   f) $5/9$ $(20/36)$
   g) $1/12$ $(3/36)$

Page 108
1. rejoicing
2. talkative
3. reproach
4. gaunt
5. bubble
6. peculiarity
7. constant
8. distorted
9. unrelated
10. criminal
11. resonant
12. origin
13. transitory
14. petty officer
15. furnish
16. intrepid
17. hardy
18. incite
19. devotee
20. workable
21. ordinary
22. expatriate
23. tease
24. austere
25. marriageable

GEM

Socrates before 400 B.C.

Page 109
Reading the reflections for each figure as 1, 2, 3 from left to right, the answers are:

1. 1	4. 1	7. 3
2. 1	5. 2	8. 3
3. 2	6. 3	

Page 110
1. real
2. reject
3. request
4. rational
5. remote
6. regard
7. rabble
8. rabid
9. riot
10. racy
11. radiant
12. radiate
13. rage
14. rob
15. raiment
16. raise
17. ramble
18. random
19. reach
20. reasonable
21. ramshackle
22. riddle, rebus
23. rift
24. rigid
25. romantic
26. revolve, rotate
27. relentless
28. rumor
29. route
30. rough

Page 111
1. swimming
2. Pierce Arrow
3. Taft
4. gazelle
5. rich
6. Antarctica
7. timetable
8. Wilson
9. moon
10. Westinghouse
11. forsythia
12. barbecue
13. Mercedes
14. thirty
15. shawl
16. nickel
17. play
18. weaken
19. acknowledge
20. anteroom
21. floor
22. bas relief
23. knitting
24. check
25. coyote

Page 112
1. bison
2. gorilla
3. badger
4. monkey
5. kangaroo
6. oyster
7. partridge
8. leopard
9. cougar
10. peacock
11. reindeer
12. gazelle
13. marmoset
14. pheasant
15. baboon
16. antelope
17. chimpanzee
18. caribou
19. pigeon
20. rhinoceros
21. greyhound
22. nightingale
23. ocelot
24. hippopotamus
25. elephant

Page 113

SECRETIVE		MODERNIZES			ENUMERATE	
cite	civet	deer	node	sore	amen	tare
ever	crest	dime	norm	zein	earn	tram
icer	cries	dine	omer	diner	mane	tree
rest	eerie	dire	reed	dozen	mare	true
rice	ester	doer	rein	drove	mart	tune
rise	reset	dome	rend	emend	mate	eaten
rite	rivet	dorm	ride	erode	mean	emeer
rive	terse	dose	rime	mined	meat	enate
sear	trice	dove	rise	miser	meet	enter
seer	tries	iron	rose	nosed	mere	enure
sere	serve	maze	seed	resin	mete	meant
sire	sieve	mend	seem	rosin	name	mature
site	steer	mere	seen	seize	near	nature
tier	stere	mien	seer	modern	neat	neater
tire	recite	mine	send		rant	neuter
tree	secret	mire	sere		rate	retune
veer	strive	mode	side		ream	tenure
vest	restive	more	sire		rent	tureen
vice	secrete	morn	size		rune	
vise	service	need	some		tame	

Page 114

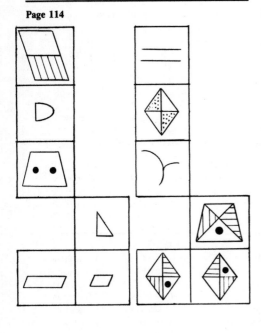

Page 115

1. foreign
2. algebra
3. germinate
4. treasured
5. intercede
6. inanimate
7. gardenia
8. tearful
9. breathing
10. teamsters
11. dilemma
12. insider
13. decreases
14. gasolines
15. yearned
16. gnostical
    nostalgic
17. miniature
18. glimpse
19. organic
20. senatorial
21. ascertain
22. overwhelm
23. insurgent
24. unheard
25. languid
26. cholera
    chorale
27. traceable
28. countries
29. mutilates
    stimulate
30. heartened

Pages 116–117

1. c-25
2. r-26
3. w-6
4. f-23
5. i-21
6. z-9
7. d-11
8. a-15
9. x-13
10. n-20
11. q−2
12. t-8
13. j-10
14. B-22
15. o-16
16. e-1
17. p-19
18. k-27
19. v-14
20. m-7
21. b-18
22. l-12
23. h-17
24. g-24
25. y-4
26. u-15
27. A-5
28. s-3

Page 118

1. manage
2. marriage
3. forage
4. carnage
5. passage
6. lineage
7. carriage
8. heritage
9. passage
10. barrage
11. damage
12. umbrage
13. postage
14. average
15. garbage
16. savage
17. package
18. advantage
19. image
20. anchorage
21. beverage
22. courage
23. visage
24. plumage
25. voyage

Page 119
1. mad
2. magnify
3. maltreat
4. meager
5. meanness
6. moderate
7. massive
8. mourn
9. mate(d)
10. miserly
11. more
12. manly
    masculine
13. mortal
14. most
15. merry
16. make, mend
17. meek
18. manifest
19. mask
20. mature
21. miss
22. modern
23. malediction
24. muscle
25. muster
26. many
27. merciful
28. mundane
29. menial
30. make-believe

Page 120
1. it
   tie
   rite
   inter
   retain
   terrain
   anterior
2. rag
   gear
   anger
   gander
   reading
   gardenia
3. pie
   ripe
   piers
   simper
   promise
   improves
   improvise
4. la
   ale
   lace
   scale
   places
   scalper
   calipers

Page 121
1. r
2. h
3. s
4. s
5. a
6. c
7. f
8. o
9. d
10. e
11. j
12. l
13. h
14. l
15. s
16. r
17. o
18. q
19. h
20. j

Page 122
1. 18
2. 48
3. 56
4. 70
5. 18
6. 41
7. 38
8. 58

PAPER WORK Page 123

The relation of the number of folds and holes is

Folds	Holes
1	1
2	2
3	4
4	8
5	16
6	32

The mathematician would make up a formula: the number of holes equals 2^{n-1} where n is the number of folds. For 6 folds that would be 2^{6-1} or 2^5, which equals 32.

Page 123
1. 37, 50
2. 49, 67
3. 16, 17
4. 24, 20
5. $^7/_8$, $^6/_7$
6. 5, 30
7. 13, 11
8. 8, 1
9. 126, 217
10. 31, 29
11. 8, 16
12. 9, 7
13. 41, 55
14. 16, 64
15. 64, 9

Page 124
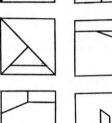

Page 125
1. brag
   garb
   grab
2. baker
   brake
   break
3. coins
   icons
   scion
   sonic
4. elver
   lever
   revel
5. bust
   buts
   stub
   tubs
6. barest
   baster
   breast
7. bedlam
   beldam
   blamed
8. carven
   cavern
   craven
9. crocus
   occurs
   succor
10. cups
    cusp
    scup
11. carps
    craps
    scarp
    scrap
12. detail
    dilate
    tailed
13. finest
    infest
14. dates
    sated
    stead
15. aspired
    despair
    diapers
    praised
16. garret
    garter
    grater
17. bolster
    bolters
    lobster
18. dowry
    rowdy
    wordy
19. cinders
    discern
    rescind
20. counter
    recount
    trounce
21. deposit
    posited
    topside
22. dueling
    eluding
    indulge
23. heeding
    neighed
24. letters
    settler
    trestle
25. parings
    parsing
    rapings
    rasping
    sparing

Page 126
1. calling
2. camouflage
3. candor
4. chagrin
5. change
6. cite
7. claw
8. confederate
9. calamity
10. clap
11. compliment
12. cajole
13. consequence
14. clash
    crash
15. crime
16. caustic
    cynical
17. close
18. cunning
    craftiness
19. count
20. compute
21. clamor
22. calm(ness)
23. characteristic
24. classify
25. conceit

Page 127

1. Folger's Coffee
2. Wheaties cereal
3. Alka-seltzer
4. Crest toothpaste
5. Lifebuoy soap
6. Chevrolet
7. Zest
8. Scope mouthwash
9. Aqua Velva lotion
10. Big Wally cleaner
11. Geritol tonic
12. Stretch n' Seal
13. Olds-Cutlass
14. Phillips' Milk of Magnesia Laxative
15. Sir Walter Raleigh tobacco
16. Quaker State Oil
17. United Air Lines
18. Folger's Coffee
19. Hertz auto rental
20. Midas mufflers
21. Alka-seltzer
22. Vicks cough syrup
23. General tires
24. Miller High Life
25. Lifebuoy Soap

Page 128

1. pine
2. broadsword
3. lute
4. orange
5. yard
6. pheasant
7. aurora
8. meter
9. zinnia
10. stroke
11. Mary
12. senator
13. degree
14. galaxy
15. Norma
16. property
17. highway
18. judgment
19. tomato
20. mohair
21. cube
22. faithful
23. Der Freischutz
24. governor
25. pansy

Page 129

1. Move one stick from the VII to the right side of the equation to form $VI - V = \sqrt{I}$.
2. Very simple. Eighty minutes and one hour twenty minutes are the same! Many people think of the latter as 120 minutes.
3. In case you missed the point, the victim is paying $1.50 for $1.00 since one of the two dollars is his.
4. Move a match from the VIII to the left side to form $IV + III = VII$.
5. Any hybrid e.g. jackass
6. A chair, a bed and a toothbrush.

Page 130

DEFENSELESS

dele	
feed	
feel	
fend	
fess	
flee	
lend	
lens	
less	
need	
ness	
seed	
seen	
self	
send	
sled	
dense	
sense	
flense	
needle	
defense	
endless	
lessened	

DISCERNMENT

cede	mind	tern	miner	direct
cent	mine	tide	miser	entire
cite	mire	time	miter	incest
deem	mist	trim	mitre	indent
deer	mite	cider	niece	insect
dent	need	creed	remit	insert
dice	nest	crest	reset	intern
diet	nice	cried	rinse	recite
dime	nine	crime	since	remind
dine	reed	deist	stein	remise
dint	rein	denim	stern	resent
dire	rend	deter	timer	reside
dirt	rent	edict	trice	tennis
disc	rest	eider	trine	centime
edit	rice	enter	cement	centner
emir	ride	inert	censer	cistern
emit	rife	inter	center	descent
ides	rind	inset	credit	discern
meed	rise	medic	cretin	endemic
meet	rite	merit	decent	metrics
mend	seed	meter	dement	increment
mere	send	midst	desert	
mien	side	mince	dinner	

FRATERNIZATION

earn	rent	orate
fain	rife	razor
fair	rift	taint
fare	rite	train
fate	rote	treat
fear	tare	trine
feat	tarn	fatten
fern	tart	fatter
fine	tear	fitter
font	tent	ionize
fort	tern	nation
into	time	ornate
naif	tint	ration
near	zein	retain
neat	zone	fritter
note	after	
raft	attar	
rain	faint	
rant	feint	
rare	front	
rate	inert	
raze	inter	
rear	niter	

Page 131

1. tulip
2. verbena
3. daisy
4. hyacinth
5. oleander
6. sweetpea
7. nasturtium
8. hollyhock
9. peony
10. gladiolus
11. chrysanthemum
12. carnation
13. hibiscus
14. jasmine
15. lantana
16. petunia
17. begonia
18. gardenia
19. camellia
20. amaryllis
21. orchid
22. hydrangea
23. violet
24. daffodil
25. magnolia

Page 132

1. sympathy
2. rule
3. suppose
4. serenity
5. risk
6. swiftly
7. degrade
8. forgetfulness
9. scent
10. ruin
11. shyness
12. maze
13. shelter
14. malleable
15. whip
16. acquit
17. epicure
18. aptitude
19. remain
20. thwart
21. perception
22. frugality
23. obituary
24. towage
25. flounder

Page 133

Row 1. 70, 50
Row 2. 130, 100
Row 3. 50, 30
Row 4. 100, 90
Row 5. 80, 60, 40
Row 6. 130, 120, 50
Row 7. 80, 100, 30, 70, 40, 70, 80
Row 8. 70, 110, 80
Row 9. 140, 70, 50, 50
Row 10. 40, 100, 130, 100
Row 11. 110, 120, 130, 20

Row 12. 100, 110
Col. 1. 130, 40, 60, 30, 60
Col. 2. 70, 60, 170, 150, 120, 70, 110
Col. 3. 110, 80, 60, 20
Col. 4. 140, 120, 80, 30
Col. 5. 30, 120, 90, 70, 70, 80
Col. 6. 90, 90, 110
Col. 7. 60, 50, 100, 30, 50, 110, 50, 80, 60
Col. 8. 130, 60, 80, 50
Col. 9. 50, 90, 50, 40, 70, 50
Col. 10. 80, 60, 100, 80, 140, 120, 70, 60, 80

SPLIT LINKS Page 133

Cut one link that is the third from either end and remove that link. You then have a single link, a double link and four links together. The one link can be used to pay for the first night. The second night the first link would be taken back and replaced by the double link to pay for the first two nights. The third night the single link would be added. The fourth night the first three links would be taken back and replaced by the four-link chain; etc.

Page 134

1. 20
2. 42
3. 66
4. 62
5. 18
6. 50
7. 63
8. 100

Page 135

1. M Adrienne
2. M Andrea
3. F Anthony
4. M Bernadette Bernadine
5. F M Carroll
6. M Cecile
7. F Nicolas
8. M Cornelia
9. F M Dale
10. F Dennis
11. F
12. M Frances
13. F M Gale
14. M Henrietta
15. F M Hilary
16. M Jeanne Jeanette
17. M Jessie
18. F M
19. F M
20. M Louise
21. F M Marian
22. F M
23. F M Rae
24. F M
25. F M
26. F M
27. F M
28. F M

Page 136

1. score
2. paddles
3. strapless
4. failure
5. written
6. actress
   casters
   recast
7. angered
   derange
   grandee
   grenade
8. rescind
9. elevations
10. regally
11. grinned
12. conjure
13. desertion
14. reactions
15. regular
16. crusade
17. tanager
18. chronicle
19. spearmint
20. garment
21. introduced
22. whereas
23. clarinet
24. gunfire
25. spanked
26. animation
27. sublime
28. construe
29. inhaled
30. blameless

Page 137

1. Move 2 sticks from any one of D, F, K, or L to form squares at C and H.
2. four
3. Move top stick from B or right stick from G to C; or top stick from G to H.
4. Move 2 sticks from A to E and 2 from G to J.
5. Move 3 sticks from A to C and J or H and J; or 3 sticks from L to E and C or J and C.
6. Four

7. Move top stick from B to F or G; or bottom stick from E to F or G; or right stick from G to F.
8. Move 2 sticks from A or C or I or J or K to F and G.
9. Move 2 sticks from B to L, or top stick from B and left one from H to L.
10. Move 2 sticks from A or D or I to L, or 2 sticks from B to F and G.
11. Remove 2 sticks from A or D or K.

12. Move the left stick from K or right stick from G to B.
13. Move 3 sticks from A, one to B and two to H or P; or three sticks from C, one to J and two to P.
14. Move 2 sticks from L or N to P.
15. Remove right stick from G or left stick from K.
16. Remove 2 sticks from N.

267

Page 138
1. expensive
2. divisive
3. massive
4. expansive
5. impressive
6. excessive
7. abusive
8. submissive
9. delusive
10. aggressive
11. evasive
12. retrogressive
    regressive
13. offensive
14. comprehensive
15. possessive
16. impassive
17. exclusive
18. elusive
19. incisive
20. successive
21. derisive
22. decisive
23. pensive
24. responsive
25. aggressive

Page 139
1. proper stopper
2. long song
3. cross boss
4. spare hair
5. flagrant vagrant
6. fussy hussy
7. solemn column
8. mellow cello
9. foxy proxy
10. loose goose
11. hairy fairy
12. stranger manger
13. ample sample
14. meeker speaker
15. pleasant pheasant
16. mock sock
17. witty ditty
18. jolly polly
19. floral coral
20. fainter painter
21. bigger digger
22. higher flyer
23. bloody buddy
24. partisan artisan
25. benign design

GEM Page 139
San Marino, an enclave in Italy, has an army of 11 men.

Page 140
1. 21, 28
2. 9, 14
3. 37, 60
4. 31, 43
5. 27, 5
6. 14, 10
7. 17, 8
8. $5 \frac{1}{6}$, $8\frac{1}{3}$
9. 65, 105
10. 23, 25
11. 3, $\frac{1}{2}$
12. 5, 28
13. 5, 6
14. 37, 214
15. 9, 15

Page 141

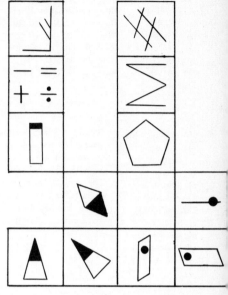

Page 137 (cont.)

A	B	C	D
E	F	G	H
I	J	K	L

A	B	C
D	E	F
G	H	I
J	K	L

A	B	C	D
E	F	G	H
I	J	K	L
M	N	O	P

Page 142
1. 2
2. 4
3. 3
4. 2
5. 4
6. 1
7. 3
8. 1
9. 3
10. 3
11. 4
12. 1
13. 4
14. 2
15. 2

Page 143
1. pain
2. poor
3. perfect
4. peril
5. prudent
6. pastoral
7. perpetuate
   prolong
8. physical
9. permissible
   pardonable
10. poise
11. passive
12. perennial
13. practical
14. peaceful
15. probable
16. penurious
17. plagiarized
18. partial
19. palatable
20. puerile
21. pleasing
22. polite
23. pertinent
24. pleasure
25. pitiless
26. petty
27. post-haste
28. pretty
29. pardon
30. positive

Page 144
1. exit
2. negligent
3. folklore
4. courage
5. abrupt
6. unruly
7. hobby
8. reticent
9. condemnation
10. defame
11. theme
12. authorization
13. wrongdoing
14. abundant
15. decorate
16. indispensable
17. defect
18. trite
19. wicked
20. attach
21. belief
22. usage
23. blameless
24. long
25. ardent

GEM Page 144
Hugo's doodle is a scrubwoman scrubbing a floor.

268

Page 145

ASSESSMENT	REVOLUTION		FACETIOUS	
amen seam	etui	note true	cafe	oust
ease seat	evil	onto tune	case	safe
east seen	into	over unto	cast	sate
mane tame	iron	rent vent	cite	seat
mass team	lent	rile vile	coat	sect
mast asset	line	riot vine	cost	sift
mate semen	lint	rite viol	cute	site
mean sense	lire	roil vole	east	soft
meat steam	live	role volt	face	coast
mesa taste	lion	root novel	fact	facet
mess tense	lone	rout olive	fast	feast
name terse	loon	rule route	fate	foist
neat ascent	loot	rune trove	feat	sauce
ness assess	lore	tine voile	fiat	factious
nest mantes	lout	toil lotion	fist	
same seamen	love	tone revolt	foci	
sane stamen	lune	tool volute	fuse	
sate	lute	tour outline	otic	
		outlive		

Page 146

1. 3
2. 5
3. 2
4. 4
5. 1
6. 4
7. 5
8. 3
9. 3
10. 2

Page 147

1. handy	14. hazard
2. harmony	15. horrible
3. headlong	16. harness
4. hoist	17. harsh
5. habitual	18. harbinger
6. hilarity	19. hoard
7. hoax	20. haggle
8. hearsay	21. homogeneity
9. honor	22. heathen
hostage	23. hideous
10. humble	24. hearty
11. hoarse	25. humbleness
12. harmless	homage
13. hybrid	

GEM Page 147

Page one of the first volume is at the right of that volume. The last page of the last volume is at the left of that one. So the bookworm goes through the right cover of the first volume, the covers and pages of the next four volumes and the left cover of the last volume—a total of $9^{1}/_{4}$ inches. (Either the bookworm just stopped because he was tired; or he must have known how to read.)

Page 148

1. 2
2. 1
3. 2
4. 3
5. 3
6. 1
7. 1
8. 2

Page 149

1. eat	stare	detracts
tear	breast	scattered
heart	barters	4. ma
reheat	arbiters	tam
earthen	barrister	meat
adherent	3. as	mated
heartened	sea	teamed
threatened	sate	mediate
2. re	dates	decimate
era	treads	
rate	started	

Page 150

1. dale	7. cedars	14. filter	22. ignores
deal	sacred	lifter	regions
lade	scared	trifle	23. notices
lead	8. bores	15. belated	section
2. bared	robes	bleated	24. palters
beard	sober	16. clients	plaster
bread	9. alined	stencil	psalter
debar	denial	17. dries	stapler
3. gears	nailed	rides	25. swelter
rages	10. decree	sired	welters
sager	recede	18. courses	wrestle
4. glare	11. douser	sources	
lager	roused	sucrose	
large	soured	19. derives	
regal	12. badger	diverse	
5. cider	barged	revised	
cried	garbed	20. deuces	
dicer	13. deist	educes	
riced	diets	seduce	
6. dare	edits	21. earnest	
dear	sited	eastern	
read	tides	nearest	

Page 151

Reading vertically:
1. 25
2. 25
3. 62
4. 71
5. 18
6. 45
7. 58
8. 64

Page 152

1. Cal	10. wash
2. me	11. d c
3. del	12. va
4. calif	13. no car
5. Ala	14. ark
6. conn	15. p r
7. mont	16. hi
8. ga	
9. miss	

Page 152

GEM

1. assesses
2. fluff
3. added

Page 153

1. Move 2 sticks from C to G and J or L; or 2 from D to G, J or L, or 2 from E to G, J or L; etc.
2. Move 2 sticks from A or C or D to B.
3. Move 2 sticks from D to G and L, and 2 from I to J and F.
4. Remove 2 sticks from D and 1 from O.
5. Remove 2 sticks from each of three of A, D, I, L.
6. Remove 1 from each of B, H, K, E or C, H, K, E, or B, H, J, E, etc.
7. Move 1 stick from B and 2 from L to form a new square outside C, H, K, J, or E; etc.
8. Remove 2 sticks from each of two of A, D, I, and L.
9. Move 1 stick from M to N.
10. Move 1 stick from B, C or I to the middle of G and H.
11. Move 2 sticks from A or D or F or J or L or O to G and N.
12. Remove 1 stick from B or C and 2 from F or J or L or M; etc.
13. Remove 2 sticks from A or D or F or J or L or M.
14. Remove 2 sticks each from A and D, or A and J, or A and L, etc.

269

Page 154

1. 6:30 P.M. Denver MDT. Half hour early
2. 7:30 P.M. Half hour late
3. No
4. between 11:15 and 11:45 EDT
5. 12:30 P.M.
6. 8 P.M.

Page 157

Read horizontally:

1. L	6. L	11. R
2. R	7. R	12. L
3. R	8. L	13. L
4. R	9. L	14. L
5. L	10. R	15. R

Page 158

1. The chances of throwing one six in a throw of five dice are $5(^1/_{16} \times ^5/_6 \times ^5/_6 \times ^5/_6 \times ^5/_6)$, or $55/6^5$, which equals $^{3125}/_{7776}$ or about 2 out of 5. In other words in $^2/_5$ of many throws a single 6 will appear. In the other throws no 6's or two or more will appear. The odds in favor of throwing only one 6 are 2 to 3; against are 3 to 2.
2. 1 to 6
3. 1 to 7776 for either
4. 151 out of 1296
5. 91 out of 216
6. 5 out of 72

Page 153 (continued)

A	B	C	D
E	F	G	H
I	J	K	L

A	B	C	D	E
F	G	H	I	J
K	L	M	N	O

A	B	C	D
E	F	G	H
I	J	K	L
M	N	O	P

Page 155

1. e		11. e	
2. l		12. h	
3. a		13. f	
4. n		14. b	
5. b		15. p	
6. o		16. l	
7. c		17. f	
8. a		18. b	
9. f		19. j	
10. b		20. a	

Page 156

1. oar	13. outcome	24. overthrow
2. observation	14. oath	overturn
3. occur	15. optional	25. occupied
4. often	16. overage	26. ordinance
5. omit	17. opinion	27. outdo
6. object(ion)	18. onset	overcome
7. oppose	19. obsolete	overtake
8. overjoyed	old	28. offensive
9. ordeal	20. origin	29. ostracize
10. onus	21. obdurate	30. oppress
11. odious	22. outlook	
12. ointment	23. offhand	

Page 159

EXTRANEOUS

axes	rest	tare	enter	steer
earn	rote	tarn	exert	stern
ease	route	tear	extra	stone
near	sane	tern	nexus	store
neat	sear	tone	rouse	taxes
next	seat	torn	route	tease
note	seer	tour	snare	extern
onus	sere	tree	sneer	nature
oust	sore	tune	snore	resent
oxen	sort	unto	snort	sexton
rant	sour	aster	snout	
rate	sure	eaten	stare	

COMPREHENSIVE

chin	mere	seer	chive	rinse	empire
chip	mice	sere	choir	riven	prince
chop	mine	ship	cover	scope	recipe
come	mope	some	creep	serve	repine
cone	move	sore	crimp	seven	revise
cope	peer	spin	crone	sheen	screen
crop	pier	veer	croup	sheep	shiver
emir	rice	vice	hence	shine	shrive
hemp	rich	vine	mince	shire	simper
here	rime	vise	never	spire	sleeve
hire	ripe	cheep	niche	viper	speech
hive	rive	cheer	pinch	cheese	precise
hove	rove	chimp	price	chrome	premise
mein	seen	chirp	prime	cipher	promise
					comprise
					converse

INTERRUPTION

into	rite	turn	route	eruption
nine	rope	unto	tenon	petition
norn	rote	upon	trine	interrupt
note	rout	erupt	tripe	
noun	runt	inert	trite	
open	tent	input	urine	
pent	tern	inter	utter	
pert	tine	enure	intone	
pier	tint	nitre	nutter	
pine	tire	otter	pinion	
pint	tone	outer	potter	
port	tort	phone	putter	
pure	tout	pinto	rotten	
rent	tree	point	turnip	
ripe	trip	prime	printer	

Page 160

1. humbler	10. forgets	triangles	23. squalid
2. plateau	11. parties	16. measles	24. despoil
3. godfather	pastier	17. caliper	spoiled
4. teaches	pirates	replica	25. centaur
5. relations	traipse	18. reveals	uncrate
6. cluster	12. tangerine	several	26. precision
7. crediting	13. arcades	19. adventure	27. drugstore
directing	14. pasters	20. admired	28. wonderful
8. technical	repasts	21. coolest	29. restraint
9. harpist	15. relatings	22. barrister	30. interlude

1. hockey
2. elm
3. bedroom
4. wool
5. tomatoes
6. Salton
7. Indian
8. coral
9. bean
10. salesclerk
11. cherish
12. rose
13. Monte Carlo
14. poinsettia
15. Oklahoma
16. New Orleans
17. New Yorker
18. Farragut
19. boots
20. psychiatrist
21. typewriter
22. Iceland
23. tobacco
24. gene
25. radio

1. captious
2. garrulous
3. salubrious
4. malicious
5. barbarous
6. analogous
7. penurious
8. unanimous
9. magnaminous
10. boisterous
11. extraneous
12. tenuous
13. heinous
14. anxious
15. innocuous
16. querulous
17. obsequious
18. chivalrous
19. fortuitous
20. precipitous
21. judicious
22. nebulous
23. rapacious
24. dexterous
25. melodious

GEM Page 164

1 oz; 2 oz;
4 oz; 8 oz;
16 oz; 32 oz;
64 oz

1. disk
   kids
   skid
2. caret
   cater
   crate
   react
   trace
3. ether
   there
   three
4. bruise
   buries
   busier
   rubies
5. capers
   crapes
   pacers
   scrape
   spacer
6. ergo
   goer
   gore
   ogre
7. cinema
   iceman
8. depart
   parted
   prated
9. clods
   colds
   scold
10. ethics
    itches
11. bluster
    butlers
    subtler
12. caliper
    replica

13. coder
    cored
    decor
14. citadel
    deltaic
    dialect
15. earns
    nares
    nears
    saner
    snare
16. detains
    instead
    sainted
    stained
17. derail
    laired
    railed
18. abridge
    brigade
19. granite
    ingrate
    tearing
20. leopard
    paroled
21. realist
    retails
    saltier
22. decimate
    medicate
23. estrange
    grantees
    greatens
24. painters
    pantries
    repaints
25. alarming
    marginal

Horizontal:
lived, devil
laid, dial
live, evil
madam
mad, dam
tubed, debut
lever, revel
level
tide, edit
got, tog
tam, mat
refer
noon
serif, fires
Vertical:
repel, leper
sloop, pools
loops, spool
loop, pool
stun, nuts

tun, nut
lager, regal
now, won
emir, rime
tuber, rebut
tub, but
kayak
tram, mart
ram, mar
leek, keel
meet, teem
ten, net
tab, bat
Diagonal:
avid, diva
remit, timer
eta, ate
part, trap
par, rap
tom, mot
straw, warts

gab, bag
mood, doom
edit, tide
rats, star
rat, tar
ban, nab
moor, room

1. Number the stacks. Take one coin from the first stack, two from the second stack, three from the third stack, and so on. Then weigh all these 36 coins together at one time. If they are one ounce less than they should be, only one coin is counterfeit, and the first stack is a bad one. If they are two ounces underweight, two coins are counterfeit and the second stack is the bad one; etc. The number of ounces underweight tells you the number of the counterfeit stack.

2. Since they got home 20 minutes before their usual time, the wife took that much less time to go toward the station and back home. Therefore she took 10 minutes less time each way. She met him 10 minutes earlier than the usual time, or at 5:20. Therefore he had been walking 50 minutes.

3. Four dollar bills, one half dollar, one quarter, two dimes, and four pennies.

4.
2	9	4
7	5	3
6	1	8

5.
17	24	1	8	15
23	5	7	14	16
4	6	13	20	22
10	12	19	21	3
11	18	25	2	9

6. Since you are the taxi driver, the taxi driver is your age!

1. truth
2. tame
3. tardy
4. tear
5. thaw
6. tall
7. tenant
8. thickness
9. thankful
10. transparent
    translucent
11. then
12. theoretic(al)
13. teacher
14. tragic
15. temerity
16. tender
17. tactless
18. tranquil
19. temporary
20. touchy
21. thinness
22. testator
23. tense
24. taciturn
25. thorough
26. torrid
27. treason
28. tentative
29. tractable
30. terrestrial

CRACK THE CULPRIT

The clue to the solution is that only one statement for each man can be false. The statements are referred to here as S1, S2, S3, S4; B1, B2, etc. If S3 is true both R1 and R4 must be false. That can't be. Therefore S3 is false. Then S1, S2 and S4 must be true. Since S1 is true T3 is true. Since S2 is true, Shorty is not guilty. Since S4 is true, J3 is false. Then J1, J2 and J4 are true. Following this line of reasoning reveals that Ben is the guilty one.

Page 170

1. You must remember which volunteer is No. 1, which No. 2, and which No. 3. There are six different ways in which the three objects can be chosen, as shown by the table. Either No. 1 can take **S**, No. 2 **M**, and No. 3 **L**; or No. 1 can take **M**, No. 2 **S**, and No. 3 **L**; and so on. There are six possible combinations. The number in the last column tells you which one it is. If only one match is left on the table, No. 1 has the Small object, No. 2 the Medium one, and No. 3 the Large one. Note there is no combination that leaves four matches, and none that leaves more than seven. To help you remember this set of combinations, you might try a mnemonic device such as: (Oh) Sole Mio, Sings My Little Lady. (You shouldn't have much trouble thinking up a more sensible one.)

No. 1	No. 2	No. 3	No. of Matches Left
S	M	L	1
M	S	L	2
S	L	M	3
M	L	S	5
L	S	M	6
L	M	S	7

2. The paler of the two hands is the one that was on the volunteer's head because the circulation of blood in that hand had decreased during the moments it had to be pumped upward. Therefore, the nickel will always be beneath the paler hand.

Page 197

The four suites of rooms are shown here, with (in that order) the name of the suite, the state from which the family came, the kind of dog they have, the day on which they arrived, and their destination.

Ohio	Florida	Arizona	Idaho
New Jersey	(Indiana)	Kansas	Maine
(cocker)	beagle	poodle	terrier
Tuesday	Friday	(Wednesday)	Saturday
Mesa Verde	Yosemite	Canada	(Yellowstone)

1. The second family (in the Florida suite) came from Indiana.
2. The third family (in the Arizona suite) arrived on Wednesday.
3. The fourth family (in the Idaho suite) was heading for Yellowstone.
4. The first family (in the Ohio suite) had the cocker spaniel.

Pages 220–221

1. Four: a sister and brother, both married, the daughter of one, and the son of the other.
2. 9, 15, 4, 36.
3. A haircut.
4. (a) Remove e, f, h, m, o, p; then q, t.
   (b) Remove f, m, o, p, q, t; then e, h.
   (c) Remove h, i, m, o, s, t, then f, j.
   (d) Remove e, f, j, l, p, q; then o, s.
5. Four moves: move the two pennies from positions 8 and 9 to 1 and 2; then two nickels from 5 and 6 to 8 and 9; move the penny and nickel from 2 and 3 to 5 and 6; move the nickel and penny from 9 and 10 to 2 and 3.
6. Each of the first nine storekeepers should chip in ten cents, paying the last one a total of ninety cents. Each of the ten storekeepers then makes fifteen cents profit on the transaction!
7. You may not cross any line more than once, but you may draw over one of the sides of a section of the figure.

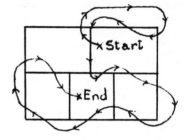

8. $1,342,177.26
9. $7.50
10. Eight boys, six girls.

Page 247

1. One marble! Start by drawing one marble from the box labeled WB. Let us assume the marble is white. Since the box is mislabeled, the other marble must also be white. Now you know the contents of the box labeled BB — since it is labeled wrong, it can't be BB, and WW has already been identified. Therefore it must be BW. The third box must then be the box with the two blue marbles. If the marble drawn from the WB box happened to be blue instead of white, you would arrive at the solution by the same reasoning process.
2. Although the Bronx and Brooklyn trains arrive equally often (every fifteen minutes), the Brooklyn train always arrives three minutes after the Bronx train. The Brooklyn train will come first if our young man arrives during that three-minute interval. He arrives at any time. Therefore, the chances are four out of five that he will take a Bronx train.
3. Forty-two trees.
4. Neither. The yolk of an egg is yellow.

Page 171

1. beach
2. chape cheap peach
3. bugle bulge
4. cream macer
5. infuse
6. cypher
7. filler refill
8. canoes oceans
9. untrod
10. bather breath
11. modest
12. mirage
13. incest insect nicest
14. etches
15. phrase seraph shaper
16. suggest
17. reveals several
18. steward
19. stewing twinges westing
20. granule
21. patters spatter tapster
22. hornets shorten thrones
23. dynamic
24. clients stencil
25. catering reacting
26. aspirate parasite
27. ingratiate
28. arguable
29. importance
30. deluding indulged

Page 205

1. fight
2. spasm
3. small
4. slash
5. hearts
6. arrive
7. garlic
8. carped redcap
9. instep
10. saliva salvia
11. exodus
12. fresco forces
13. timber
14. ethics itches
15. dearth hatred
16. erratic
17. ponders respond
18. premium
19. inflate
20. lumbago
21. pianist
22. ignores regions
23. diverts strived
24. oxidate
25. mattress smartest smatters
26. original
27. splintered
28. guidance
29. bleached
30. outspread

Page 216

1. baled blade
2. caned dance
3. swarm warms
4. lasso
5. orange
6. occult
7. soften
8. flight
9. agrees grease
10. artist strait traits
11. heater hereat reheat
12. absurd
13. elates teasel
14. syntax
15. ripsaw
16. arching chagrin
17. nastier retains stainer
18. hitless
19. minaret raiment
20. patrons tarpons
21. cleanse
22. unearth
23. bravely
24. viscera
25. thimbles
26. registrar
27. monsignor
28. indigent
29. novelist
30. doorsills

Page 229

1. aides aside ideas
2. sugar
3. peaks spake speak
4. yield
5. minuet minute
6. mantis matins
7. corset escort sector
8. editor
9. loader ordeal reload
10. fangle flange
11. alcove
12. ascend dances
13. battle tablet
14. silver
15. scenic
16. scholar
17. storage
18. oversea
19. hustler hurtles
20. bastile bestial
21. refusal
22. bastion obtains
23. console
24. engines
25. ruthless
26. sandstorm
27. erectness
28. coiffeur coiffure
29. ignorance
30. deviants

Page 173

1. e
2. A
3. g
4. i
5. a
6. j
7. b
8. j
9. d
10. f
11. k
12. n
13. e
14. s
15. u
16. v
17. r
18. h
19. x
20. i
21. p
22. l
23. z
24. t
25. c
26. y
27. m
28. w
29. q
30. o

Page 174

TELEGRAMS

agee	gram	marl	rage	sale	slag	team	agree	elate	lager	regal	stale	tease	reglet
alms	lame	mart	rale	same	slam	tela	alert	erase	large	regma	stare	armlet	relate
earl	last	mast	rate	sate	slat	tear	alter	ester	later	remit	steal	egesta	remise
ease	late	mate	real	seal	stag	teem	aster	glare	lease	reset	steam	eaglet	resale
east	leer	meal	ream	seam	tael	term	eager	gleam	least	slate	steel	grease	reseat
else	lest	meat	reel	sear	tale	tram	eagle	grate	merge	smart	steer	master	starve
game	male	meet	rete	seat	tame	tree	egest	great	ratel	smelt	stele	meager	teasel
gate	malt	melt	rest	seem	tare	aglet	egret	greet	realm	stage	stere	regale	largest
gear	mare	mere	sage	seer	teal								

ABSOLVENT

abet	bean	bone	lent	noes	sane	slob	tole	veto	besot	novel	slant	stone	ablest
able	beat	east	lest	nose	sate	sloe	tone	vole	blase	oaten	slate	stove	absent
aloe	belt	ebon	loan	note	save	slot	vale	volt	bleat	onset	slave	tabes	avoset
also	bent	etna	lobe	nova	seal	sole	vane	vote	bloat	ovate	solve	table	lanose
alto	best	lane	lone	oast	seat	stab	vase	above	boast	sable	stale	talon	nelson
ante	blot	last	love	oval	sent	stoa	vast	alone	leant	salon	stave	tonal	sloven
bale	boat	late	lost	oven	seta	tael	veal	atone	least	salve	steal	valet	stable
bane	bole	lean	nave	sale	slab	tale	vent	baste	navel	salvo	stela	venal	vestal
base	bolt	lens	neat	salt	slat	teal	vest	beast	noble	seton	stole	vesta	absolve
													solvent

HYPOCHONDRIAC

acid	chap	coon	dory	heap	odor	poor	yard	capon	dairy	heard	panic	rondo	racoon
airy	char	coop	dray	hear	paid	pray	yarn	chain	diary	hoary	parch	candor	rancho
apod	chid	cord	drip	hoar	pain	prod	yond	chair	dinar	hoard	piano	canopy	rancid
arch	chin	corn	drop	hood	pair	raid	acorn	chard	drain	honor	pinch	condor	picador
arid	chip	crap	hair	hoop	pica	racy	acrid	chary	hairy	hydra	pooch	droopy	poniard
aril	chop	crop	hand	icon	piny	rand	adorn	china	handy	inapt	radio	indoor	
arty	coda	darn	hard	inch	pond	rich	apron	choir	hardy	irony	rainy	inroad	
card	coin	door	harp	iron	pony	rind	cairn	chord	harpy	iodin	rhino	phonic	
cart	cony	dorp	head	nard	pooh	rood	candy	crony	heady	nadir	roach	poncho	

EVALUATIONS

aunt	isle	lava	lint	lute	oval	seat	tail	tone	vain	vent	anise	inset	salve	solve	stile	unlit	aviate
east	lain	lave	list	nave	sail	silt	tale	tuna	vale	vest	anvil	least	satin	stain	stole	until	vestal
etui	lane	lent	live	neat	sale	slat	teal	tune	vase	vial	avast	navel	slant	stale	stone	value	elation
evil	last	lest	lune	nest	salt	sole	tile	ulna	vast	aisle	avian	ovule	slate	steal	talon	vault	salvation
into	late	line	lust	oast	seal	tael	tine	unto	veal	alate	istle	saint	slave	stein	tonal	vaunt	valuation

DETERIORATE

arid	dear	dirt	idea	rate	ride	rote	tide	tree	ardor	drier	order	trait	tried	rotate	torrid
dare	deer	dote	ired	read	riot	tare	toad	trot	dater	erode	otter	tread	aerate	rotter	iterate
dart	diet	drat	raid	rear	road	tart	tore	trod	deter	irate	tired	treat	editor	tarred	retread
Jate	dire	edit	rare	reed	roar	tear	tort	aired	direr	orate	trade	treed	retire	tirade	traitor

SCINTILLATE

acne	case	clan	lain	lilt	neat	salt	sine	tall	tile	alien	cleat	least	scent	stile	taint	little
alit	cast	east	last	line	nest	sate	tact	teal	tilt	aline	eclat	saint	since	still	taste	talent
call	cell	etna	late	lint	nice	scat	tael	tell	tine	anile	inset	satin	stale	stilt	encase	install
cane	celt	isle	lent	list	sail	seat	tail	test	tint	anise	islet	scale	stall	stint	latent	instill
cant	cent	lace	lest	nail	sale	sill	tale	till	aisle	cilia	istle	scant	stein	tacit	lineal

ALTERNATIVE

alit	even	lean	lint	rain	tale	tile	veer	alter	elver	laver	nerve	rival	invert	native	varlet
ante	evil	lent	nail	rate	tare	tilt	veil	altar	event	learn	ratel	tiara	latter	nettle	eternal
aril	lair	leer	nave	rave	tarn	tint	vein	attar	evert	leave	ravel	trail	leaven	relate	latrine
aver	late	liar	near	real	tear	vain	vent	avert	inert	liner	reave	train	letter	relent	tertial
earn	lava	line	neat	reel	tent	vale	alert	eaten	inter	liter	revel	trial	linear	rental	tertian
eave	lave	live	rail	rein	tern	vane	alive	elite	later	natal	riata	valet	litter	travel	veteran

EXTRAVAGANCE

acre	cane	earn	gave	next	rave	tern	carve	eager	event	grant	greet	taxer	cavern	nectar	trance
agar	cant	eave	gear	race	tang	veer	cater	eaten	evert	grate	never	trace	cravat	ravage	vacant
agee	care	even	gent	rage	tare	anger	crane	eater	exact	grave	raven	avenge	craven	recant	vagrant
aver	cart	ever	nave	rant	tam	avert	crate	egret	extra	great	react	canter	garnet	recent	average
cage	cave	gate	near	rate	tear	caret	crave	enter	grace	green	reave	carven	graven	tavern	tanager

EMPIRICAL

acre	cape	earl	lair	limp	meal	pail	pear	race	ream	ample	clime	malic	calmer	parcel	reclaim
aper	care	emir	lame	mace	mica	pair	pica	rail	reap	caper	crape	maple	carpel	placer	replica
aril	carp	epic	lamp	male	mice	pale	pier	rale	rice	camel	cream	pearl	epical	plaice	
calm	clam	eral	liar	mail	mile	palm	pile	ramp	rile	carel	crime	place	lacier	primal	
came	clap	ilia	lice	mare	mire	pare	plea	rape	rime	claim	crimp	price	limper	caliper	
camp	clip	lace	lime	marl	pace	peal	prim	real	ripe	clear	iliac	prime	palmer	miracle	

BACKGROUND

back	bard	brad	bung	cord	curb	darn	drag	garb	rack	rock	argon	broad	gourd	orang	around
band	bark	brag	bunk	cork	curd	dock	drub	grab	rang	rung	board	cargo	grand	organ	dragon
bang	barn	buck	burg	crab	dank	dour	drug	grub	rank	undo	bound	crank	groan	round	ground
bank	bond	bund	card	crag	dark	drab	dung	nard	road	acorn	brand	croak	guard	abound	aground

DISCONSOLATE

acid	anti	coal	cool	date	diet	east	into	lass	lest	load	lose	nice	sail	seat	soon	teal
acne	cant	coat	coon	deal	dint	edit	isle	late	lien	loan	lost	node	sale	side	soot	tend
adit	celt	coin	coot	dean	disc	icon	laid	lead	line	lode	nail	note	sane	site	tael	tide
alit	cent	cola	cote	dent	dole	ides	lain	lean	lint	lone	neat	once	sate	sled	tail	tile
also	clad	cold	dais	dial	done	idle	land	lend	lion	loon	nest	onto	scan	slot	talc	tine
ante	clod	colt	dale	dice	dote	idol	lane	less	list	loot	ness	said	seal	sole	tale	toad

told	aisle	cleat	laden	onset	scant	slain	snail	stain	stein	tidal	dilate	silent	dissent
tole	alone	inset	least	saint	scent	slant	snide	stale	stole	tonic	lotion	solace	isolate
tone	anise	islet	loess	satin	scion	slate	snood	stead	stone	action	nation	session	
tool	class	istle	loose	scale	sidle	slide	staid	steal	stool	deacon	notion	console	

EARNESTLY

alar	lean	nest	salt	seta	tarn	yarn	ester	leery	slant	steer	leaner	resent	nearest
earn	leer	rale	sane	slay	teal	year	later	nares	slate	stere	neatly	slayer	
ease	lent	rate	sate	stay	tear	alert	layer	ratel	sleet	tease	nestle	earnest	
east	lest	real	seal	tael	tern	alter	learn	relay	snare	yeam	realty	eastern	
lane	near	reel	seat	tale	tray	aster	lease	renal	sneer	yeast	relent	eternal	
late	neat	sale	sent	tare	tree	early	least	saner	stare	antler	rental	leanest	

Page 175

1. Yes.
2. 99980001
3. $10^2 + 11^2 + 12^2 = 365$; or $13^2 + 14^2 = 365$.
4. The first: if you multiply 142857×3, you get 428571.
5. By 2: any even number; by 3: if the sum of the digits is divisible by 3; by 4: if the number formed by the last 2 digits is divisible by 4; by 5: any number ending in 5 or 0; by 6: any even number divisible by 3; by 8: if the number formed by the last 3 digits is divisible by 8; by 9: if the sum of the digits is divisible by 9.
6. When x is 1 more than y. For example, if $x = 7$ and $y = 6$, then $x + y = 13$ and $x - y = 1$; and $(x + y)(x - y) = 13 \times 1 = 13 = (x + y)$.
7. These are the initials of the digits; add a Z for zero at the start.
8. 957 436 6542
   528 564 2456
9. Four acres; it does not say the other end of the rope is tied to a stake.
10. None; the shot scared them and they all flew away.

Page 208

1. 9024; 4225; 3009; 2016; 7224
2. 990024; 983060

Page 230

1. The coin is not aware of what happened the first nine times! The chances are still fifty-fifty.
2. Starting with two digits, x and y, multiply one digit by 5; you now have 5x to which you add 7 and multiply the sum by 2, which gives you $2(5x + 7)$ or $10x + 14$. Add the other digit and subtract 14 and you end up with $10x + y$, which is the algebraic way of writing a two-digit number whose digits are x and y.
3. Yes. The circumference of a circle equals $2\pi r$, or a little more than 6¼ times the radius. In other words, the radius is about 1/6 of the circumference. Increasing the circumference by 12 inches would mean increasing the radius by almost 2 inches — plenty of space for the mouse to crawl through.
4. Call one fraction x/y. Then the other must be $(y - x)/y$. The difference between the two fractions is $x/y - (y - x)/y$, which equals $(2x - y)/y$. The difference between the squares of the two fractions is $x^2/y^2 - (y^2 - 2xy + x^2)/y^2$, which also equals $(2x - y)/y$.
5. A pound of feathers. A pound of feathers is measured in avoirdupois weight, which has 16 ounces to the pound. Gold is measured in troy weight, and a pound of troy weight equals .823 pound avoirdupois.
6. She wasn't overcharged. She bought 2 pounds of cake. She got 2 pounds whether or not there was a hole in the cake.

Page 176

1. enough stuff
2. sound hound
3. malign design
4. septic skeptic
5. funny honey
6. sooty booty
7. frisky whisky
8. iron lion
9. thorough furrow
10. able sable
11. better sweater
12. damp stamp
13. bigger digger
14. good wood
15. shyer flyer
16. sweet treat
17. tender lender
18. rosy posey
19. Flemish blemish
20. nimble thimble
21. athletic aesthetic
22. regal beagle
23. funny money
24. glossy bossy
25. slender lender
26. last blast
27. smart heart
28. loose moose
29. meaty sweetie
30. green screen

Page 215

1. Roman showman
2. slender fender
3. sweeter greeter
4. nice slice
5. late mate
6. quaint saint
7. double trouble
8. pliant giant
9. dumber plumber
10. staid maid
11. bored lord
12. faint paint
13. real seal
14. great date
15. wide slide
16. slower blower
17. drowned sound
18. saline praline
19. lighter fighter
20. missed list
21. spry fly
22. sore boar
23. loose noose
24. dizzy Lizzy
25. groovy movie
26. snug bug
27. wide slide
28. classy lassie
29. middle fiddle
30. oily doily

Page 177

1. angel, angle, glean
2. nest, nets, sent, tens
3. past, pats, spat, taps
4. abet, bate, beat, beta
5. stew, west, wets
6. dorp, drop, prod
7. darn, nard, rand
8. aimed, media
9. death, hated
10. bares, baser, bears, saber
11. pelts, slept, spelt
12. abler, baler, blare, blear
13. dirge, ridge
14. afield, failed
15. anoint, nation
16. circle, cleric
17. cartel, claret, rectal
18. binder, brined, inbred, rebind
19. misled, slimed, smiled
20. asleep, elapse, please
21. fretful, truffle
22. disport, tripods
23. grained, reading
24. lameness, maleness, nameless, salesmen
25. agnostic, coasting, coatings
26. altitude, latitude
27. auctioned, cautioned
28. bounders, rebounds, suborned
29. claviers, visceral
30. restrain, retrains, strainer, terrains, trainers

Page 200

1. rite, tier, tire
2. gash, hags, shag
3. abut, tabu, tuba
4. nips, pins, snip, spin
5. calk, lack
6. oafs, sofa
7. diver, drive, rived
8. cited, edict
9. outer, outre, route
10. defer, freed
11. adder, dared, dread
12. false, fleas, leafs
13. chore, ocher, ochre
14. rialto, tailor
15. heater, hereat, reheat
16. whiter, wither, writhe
17. resort, roster, sorter, storer
18. livens, snivel
19. stover, strove, troves, voters
20. gadget, tagged
21. deepest, steeped
22. carting, crating, tracing
23. ceramist, scimetar, matrices
24. filters, stifler, trifles
25. ancients, instance
26. sunders, undress
27. corselet, electors, selector
28. royalist, solitary
29. patroness, transpose
30. cognition, incognito

Page 224

1. lion, loin, noil
2. chin, inch
3. part, rapt, trap
4. acme, came, mace
5. hoes, hose, shoe
6. naps, pans, snap, span
7. marts, smart, trams
8. egret, greet
9. adept, pated, taped
10. palsy, plays, splay
11. civet, evict
12. loops, pools, sloop, spool
13. roost, roots, torso
14. poster, presto, topers, tropes
15. brides, debris
16. feasts, safest
17. forces, fresco
18. median, maiden
19. darter, retard, tarred, trader
20. leaser, resale, reseal, sealer
21. canister, scantier
22. bestead, debates
23. grantee, greaten, reagent
24. caterer, recrate, retrace, terrace
25. cheaters, hectares, teachers
26. rattles, starlet, startle
27. parties, pastier, pirates, traipse
28. arrested, serrated
29. decorate, recoated
30. bleating, tangible

Page 246

1. lose, sloe, sole
2. lame, male, meal
3. acts, cast, cats, scat
4. nags, sang, snag
5. dies, ides, side
6. opts, post, pots, spot, stop, tops
7. cadre, cared, cedar, raced
8. alert, alter, later, ratel
9. pores, poser, prose, ropes, spore
10. dense, needs
11. pesos, poses, posse
12. mares, reams, smear
13. apses, passe
14. wander, warden, warned
15. plains, spinal
16. lowest, towels
17. unions, unison
18. insure, inures, urines, ursine
19. palest, palets, petals, pleats
20. sorted, stored, strode
21. missile, similes
22. conferer, confrere, enforcer
23. molders, remolds, smolder
24. bedroom, boredom, broomed
25. bothering, nightrobe
26. actress, casters, recasts
27. allergy, gallery, largely, regally
28. altered, related, treadle
29. aspirate, parasite
30. coteries, esoteric

Page 178

1. laud
2. lease, let
3. liability
4. limp
5. lazy
6. literal
7. laborious
8. lineament
9. loafer
10. legend
11. lofty
12. liberality
13. lone
14. lasting
15. lot
16. linger, loaf
17. lenient
18. location
19. logical
20. let
license
21. lair
22. loyal
23. lie
24. level
25. liquid
26. luminous
27. languid
28. lucid
29. litigant
30. lubrication

Page 202

1. debate
2. deserve
3. diabolic
4. defer, delay
5. dainty
6. dig
7. devoid
8. decoration
9. drab
10. dogma
11. destination
12. dauntless
13. deceit
14. dregs
15. dubious
16. dagger
17. defeat
18. deviate, digress
19. decay
20. dynamic
21. delectable
22. dodge
23. dally
24. dominate
25. delete
26. duplicity
27. declaim
28. duration
29. detach
30. dilemma

Page 225

1. unaided
2. unbiased
3. upbraid
4. unabashed
5. useless
6. uncongenial
7. uncivilized
8. upshot
9. ultimate
   utmost
10. urbane
11. undisguised
12. upper
13. uncanny
14. upheaval
15. utterly
16. uniform
17. unarmed
18. uproar
19. uncouth
20. urban
21. upright
22. undue
23. umbrage
24. under
25. uphold
26. urgent
27. undergo
28. upset
29. undecided
30. usurper

Page 180

1. 22, 28
2. 36, 30
3. 37, 43
4. 33, 41
5. 3, ½
6. 18, 18
7. 1, 2
8. 9, 8
9. 32, 64
10. 13, 10
11. 15, 7½
12. 8, 6
13. 9, 8
14. 5, 5
15. 16, 64
16. 13, 15
17. 945, 236¼
18. 11, 18
19. 40, 16
20. 214, 341

Page 214

1. 32, 64
2. 97, 116
3. 10, 11
4. 125, 216
5. 243, 729
6. 5/7, 6/8
7. 10, 3 1/3
8. 4, 16
9. 720, 5040
10. 26, 37
11. 600, 3600
12. 2, 1
13. 42, 48
14. 15, 16
15. 126, 217
16. 17, 15
17. 216, 49
18. 5, 20
19. 1, 27
20. 39, 50

Page 179

a
h
b
i
c
j
d
k
e
l
f
m
g
n

Page 181

1. effect
2. effeminate
3. erratic
   eccentric
4. elastic
5. easygoing
6. elevation
7. educated
8. eligible
9. early
10. eliminate
11. emerge
12. effective
    efficient
13. emit
14. earthly
15. employ
16. elder
17. economy
18. endless
19. egress
20. emancipate
21. equality
22. each
    every
23. expansion
24. enhance
    enlarge
    expand
25. elegance
26. eminent
27. evict
    eject
28. elucidate
29. excessive
30. eclipse

Page 211

1. quite
2. quaint
3. quarrel
4. qualm
5. quack
6. quaver
7. quotient
8. quake
9. querulous
10. quibble
11. quaff
12. query
    question
13. quisling
14. queer
15. quiet
    quiescent
16. quick
17. quit
18. quarantine
19. quivering
20. quip
21. quotation
22. quandary
23. quarry
24. quash
25. quixotic
26. quagmire
27. quell
28. quiz
29. qualified
30. quasi

Page 228

1. jaded
2. jeer
3. jaunty
4. jazz
5. jejune
6. jabber
7. jell
8. jeopardy
9. jeremiad
10. jagged
11. jesting
12. jet
13. jetsam
14. jack-of-all-trades
15. jingoist
16. jinx
17. jailer
18. justice
19. jealous
20. jargon
21. junior
22. juicy
23. just
24. jammed
25. jumble
26. junction
    joining
27. jolly
    joyous
28. jangle
29. journeyman
30. juvenile

Page 206

Page 182

1. $2 \times 3 = 4 + 5 - 3$
2. $(2 + 3) \times 4 = 25 - 5$
   $25 - (4 \times 5) = 2 + 3$
3. $8 - 5 = 24 \div 8$
4. $(4 \times 5) - 6 = (2 \times 4) + 6$
5. $3 + 4 + 4 + 5 = 8 \times 2$
6. $3^2 - (2 \times 2) = 10 \div 2$
7. $(17 - 5) \div 3 = 8 \div 2$
8. $2^3 = (2 + 3) \times 3 - 7$
9. $(2 \times 3) \times 3 = 4^2 + 2$
10. $(6 \times 2) - (2 + 3) = 3 + 4$
11. $5 + (3 \times 2) = 2^3 + 3$
12. $4 + (3 \times 5) = 3^3 - 8$
13. $3^2 + 2^3 = (4 \times 3) + 5$
14. $\sqrt{9} + (2 \times 5) = 2^2 + 9$
15. $5(2 + 3) - (5 \times 4) = 10 \div 2$

Page 209

1. $3 + (2 \times 5) = 8 + 5$
2. $12 \div 3 = (3 \times 3) - 5$
3. $3^2 - 2^2 = 4 + 1$
4. $(2 + 1) \times (2 + 2) = 8 + 2^2$
5. $(15 \div 3) + 1 = 2 \times 3$
6. $(6 \times 3) - 9 = (2 \times 3) + 3$
7. $(6 \times 5) - 12 = 9 \times 2$
8. $20 - 3 = 3^2 + (4 \times 2)$
9. $3^3 - 4^2 = 5 + 6$
10. $(19 - 5) \div 7 = 6 \div 3$
11. $\sqrt{16} + 1 = 3^2 - 4$
12. $5(2 + 3) - 10 = 30 \div 2$
13. $3^3 - (2 \times 10) = \sqrt{9} + 4$
14. $(3 \times 3) + (4 \times 2) = 2^4 + 1$
15. $(20 - 4) \div 8 = 10 \div 5$

Page 184

1. Minute hand.
2. Leg.
3. One earpiece.
4. One finger.
5. OK.
6. Slot.
7. Chains and weight.
8. Blade.
9. Handle.
10. Strings.
11. One flower.
12. OK.
13. One shadow.
14. Clapper.
15. Holes.
16. OK.
17. Reflection of left candlestick.
18. STOP in place of YIELD.

Page 227

1. Pages.
2. One support.
3. Headlight.
4. Handle on pitcher.
5. OK.
6. Tuning dials.
7. One pip.
8. Eyebrow.
9. Phone dial.
10. OK.
11. Drawer handle.
12. Pocket and buttonhole.
13. OK.
14. Incorrect spelling.
15. Arrow reversed.
16. One ear.
17. State.
18. Antennae.

Page 183

1. asphalt
2. pentagon
3. television
4. watergate
5. furnace claimed
6. decimal declaim medical
7. domestic
8. escapade
9. sideboard
10. insolence
11. maltreat
12. multilates stimulate ultimates
13. empirical
14. teaspoon
15. incarnate
16. immediately
17. periscope
18. transformed
19. navigates
20. geraniums
21. diabolic
22. instigated
23. monologues
24. wonderfully
25. interferences
26. abnormal
27. telephones
28. decimation medication
29. despicable
30. emergencies

Page 234

1. banned
2. imposter
3. household
4. insertion
5. heirloom
6. jaundice
7. gabardine
8. limerick
9. pinnacle
10. fusillade
11. carpenter
12. laughter
13. guerrilla
14. agnostic coasting
15. permeate
16. pharmacy
17. sackcloth
18. underscores
19. shattering
20. idealism
21. janitor
22. transpose
23. toreador
24. freshman
25. nectarines
26. auctioned cautioned education
27. earnestly
28. instigate
29. machinery
30. inelegant

Page 185

1. Athena
2. Gauguin
3. Washington
4. Afghanistan
5. navy
6. furious
7. corn
8. Mammon
9. Melbourne
10. triangle
11. Colonial
12. biography
13. Taft
14. tomato
15. Christianity
16. payment
17. druggist
18. recapitulate
19. premonition
20. O. W. Holmes
21. Tokyo
22. harp
23. gyration
24. quince
25. Switzerland
26. lemming
27. carrot
28. Du Maurier
29. Chevalier
30. Stevenson

Page 210

1. Victor Hugo
2. Johnson
3. Georgia
4. Ketchel
5. notch
6. reflect
7. bookkeeping
8. matchless
9. linoleum
10. Austria
11. respite
12. height
13. Pontiac
14. Turkey
15. indubitable
16. Christie
17. hound
18. October 21
19. tower
20. Tanzania
21. volleyball
22. Estonia
23. perpetual
24. saxophone
25. nihilism
26. Steinbeck
27. badminton
28. Saudi Arabia
29. The Hague
30. dugong

Page 233

1. Aldebaran
2. messenger
3. Ellsberg
4. Peter Pan
5. Galápagos
6. posthumous
7. Disraeli
8. Joshua Tree
9. foot
10. beauty
11. sausage
12. Gaynor
13. Opel
14. chance
15. Persian
16. Guinea
17. Yukon
18. kitten
19. guilt
20. dividers
21. Washington
22. henna
23. decay
24. rhyme
25. telephone
26. Somalia
27. repudiate
28. Jupiter
29. simulate
30. Black

Page 186

1. speculate
2. accumulate
3. capitulate
4. interpolate
5. desolate
6. manipulate
7. escalate
8. coagulate
9. immaculate
10. percolate
11. mutilate
12. annihilate
13. expostulate
14. undulate
15. assimilate
16. isolate
17. stipulate
18. disconsolate
19. articulate
20. inflate
21. recapitulate
22. contemplate
23. translate
24. formulate
25. simulate
26. circulate
27. ventilate
28. emulate
29. stimulate
30. oscillate

Page 203
1. delusion
2. vision
3. collusion
4. passion
5. tension
6. exclusion
7. accession
8. depression
9. lesion
10. succession
11. compassion
12. possession
13. erosion
14. aggression
15. submission
16. mansion
17. version
18. impression
19. occasion
20. aversion
21. propulsion
22. dissuasion
23. seclusion
24. extension
25. concession
26. incursion
27. remission
28. regression
29. diversion
30. recession

Page 226
1. arrogance
2. fragrance
3. pittance
4. intolerance
5. hindrance
6. abundance
7. instance
8. reluctance
9. balance
10. resistance
11. radiance
12. annoyance
13. variance
14. finance
15. temperance
16. glance
17. sustenance
18. dance
19. ordinance
20. cognizance
21. romance
22. stance
23. importance
24. nuisance
25. countenance
26. prance
27. nonchalance
28. perseverance
29. distance
30. severance

Page 243
1. baldness
2. fickleness
3. humbleness
4. witness
5. selfishness
6. dizziness
7. vividness
8. artlessness
9. shallowness
10. holiness
11. forgiveness
12. ugliness
13. conciseness
14. numbness
15. hopelessnes
16. lawlessness
17. bluntness
18. eagerness
19. roughness
20. silliness
    foolishness
21. darkness
    dimness
22. rashness
23. liveliness
24. business
25. plainness
26. emptiness
27. harness
28. mildness
29. sharpness
30. likeness
    sameness

Page 188
1. 4
2. 1
3. 1
4. 2
5. 3
6. 4
7. 2
8. 3
9. 3
10. 2
11. 1
12. 4
13. 3
14. 4
15. 2

Page 204
1. 4
2. 1
3. 3
4. 2
5. 2
6. 4
7. 4
8. 3
9. 1
10. 1
11. 3
12. 4
13. 3
14. 2
15. 2

Page 187
1. Shoe.
2. Screw.
3. Wood.
4. Man's hat.
5. Crochet hook.
6. Adult.
7. Circle.
8. Pencil.
9. Adult.
10. Ping-Pong paddle.

Page 213
1. Sculpture.
2. Pool.
3. Motor, or sidewheel.
4. Adult.
5. Steering wheel.
6. Ear.
7. Napkin.
8. Fork.
9. Wrist watch.
10. Motor.

Page 189
1. flighty
2. profuse
3. irascible
4. hissing
5. deceptive
6. mournful
7. clown
8. antagonism
9. ruined
10. cloudy
11. fraud
12. suave
13. professed
14. encourage
15. revengeful
16. desolate
17. unworldly
18. front
19. thin
20. gloomy
21. complain
22. soothing
23. cheerful
24. notched
25. mutual
26. explain
27. turn
28. attest
29. calm
30. compose

Page 207
1. distort
2. lessen
3. meager
4. messenger
5. repair
6. belief
7. farthest
8. harmful
9. peculiar
10. forerunner
11. exemption
12. loving
13. stormy
14. conciliatory
15. sycophant
16. release
17. tangle
18. obligation
19. meditate
20. sharpen
21. impudent
22. profuse
23. flabby
24. refund
25. impair
26. young
27. decline
28. discernment
29. moral
30. correctness

Page 219
1. jeer
2. slave
3. gloomy
4. pacify
5. unsophisticated
6. sink
7. fall back
8. drink
9. bizarre
10. wheedle
11. forgo
12. submission
13. law
14. freak
15. support
16. profess
17. journeying
18. stint
19. relation
20. elicit
21. encroach
22. half
23. mangle
24. rashness
25. circuitous
26. oblique line
27. oily
28. wander
29. teachable
30. lamb

Page 241
1. tomboy
2. faint
3. feed
4. refuse
5. east
6. dark
7. shrewd
8. infected
9. privilege
10. slander
11. suggest
12. evade
13. voracious
14. estimate
15. minority
16. tenancy
17. acrid
18. whim
19. complaining
20. gaseous
21. bad-tempered
22. wild
23. unworldly
24. rope
25. omnipresence
26. wriggle
27. hearty
28. weariness
29. picture
30. deceptive

Page 190

1. kimono
2. nephew
3. outrage
4. fragile
5. default
   faulted
6. hearing
7. personal
8. whimper
9. butcher
10. somehow
11. hindrance
12. disgrace
13. capsize
14. teethes
15. stratagem
16. avarice
17. denials
18. squadron
19. magnolia
20. manifest
21. extirpate
22. revelation
23. gauntlet
24. contagious
25. lassitude
26. dismantle
27. dialects
28. skeptical
29. versatile
30. enterprise

Page 236

1. league
2. hackles
   shackle
3. scholar
4. meridian
5. powerful
6. magenta
7. lavender
8. ellipse
9. lacerate
10. glacier
11. congested
12. forbade
13. rowboat
14. semaphore
15. ominous
16. sediment
17. overalls
18. ingratiate
19. careful
20. perfidy
21. germinate
22. symbols
23. theorist
24. obscene
25. clarionet
26. petunia
27. cauldron
28. hospital
29. heartache
30. metropolis

Page 192

1. Picnic grounds, or in the country, or in the park.
2. No shadows; therefore, no sun.
3. Six.
4. Two.
5. Four.
6. Refreshment stand.
7. Five
8. Nothing.
9. One.
10. A pair of slacks.
11. No.
12. Don't Litter (on the garbage can).
13. No, because they are fastened to the tables.
14. Picnic basket, thermos, cup.
15. Refreshment stand.
16. None.
17. Grandpa is fishing; mother and father are rowing.
18. Playing ball, asking a question, watching little brother.
19. None.
20. Garbage can.
21. None.
22. Man (father).
23. Big sister.
24. Three.
25. One.

Page 218

1. Eight.
2. Tailor, beauty parlor, pet shop, laundromat, dentist, lawyer, sales, and dressmaker.
3. Space for Rent.
4. Standing inside his door.
5. Nine.
6. Seven.
7. Two.
8. Laundromat.
9. Sidewalk.
10. Yes.
11. Laundromat.
12. None.
13. Two.

14. Tailor shop.
15. Pet shop.
16. One.
17. Nobody.
18. One is in a dress, two are in pants.
19. Two are, one isn't.
20. Nothing.
21. Sales.
22. Man's suit.
23. Reading.
24. Neither (it's a shoulder purse).
25. None.
26. Four.
27. Dentist, lawyer, sales, dressmaker.

Page 193

VEGETABLES
artichoke
asparagus
bean
beet
broccoli
cabbage
carrot
cauliflour
celery
corn
cucumber
dandelion greens
endive

COLORS
aquamarine
black
blue
brown
cerise
claret
dun
ecru
emerald

COUNTRIES
Albania
Argentina
Australia
Belgium
Bolivia
Brazil
Bulgaria
Canada
Chile
China
Colombia
Denmark
Dominican Republic
Ecuador
Egypt
Ethiopia

PAINTERS
Audubon
Bonheur
Botticelli
Cézanne
Corot
David
Degas
Eastlake
Eakins

SCHOOL SUBJECTS
arithmetic
art
biology
botany
calculus
chemistry
drawing
English

MUSICAL INSTRUMENTS
accordion
bassoon
bass viol
bugle
cello
clarinet
drum
English horn

TREES
alder
ash
aspen
balsam
boxwood
beech
birch
catalpa
cedar
chestnut

dogwood
elm

U.S. PRESIDENTS
Adams, John
Adams, John Quincy
Arthur
Buchanan
Cleveland
Coolidge
x
Eisenhower

FLOWERS
aster
azalea
begonia
calendula
camelia
chrysanthemum
daffodil
dahlia
daisy
dandelion
Easter lily

OCCUPATIONS
accountant
artist
aviator
baker
banker
bookkeeper
carpenter
chemist
clerk
dentist
doctor
draftsman
druggist
embalmer
engineer

Page 239

RIVERS					
Fraser	Howard	Grieg	Harte	Firebird	field hockey
Ganges	Lafayette	Grofe	Hawthorne	Gremlin	football
Garsune	Lehigh	Handel	Hearn	Grand Prix	gymnastics
Green	Loyola	Haydn	Hemingway	Hudson	hockey
Hudson	Manhattan	Hindemith	Lardner	Impala	lacrosse
Housatonic	Miami	Lalo	Lewis	Lincoln	x
Lena	Michigan	Lehar	Lewison	LeMans	
Loire	Middlebury	Liszt	Marquand	Maverick	STATE CAPITALS
Marne		Leoncavallo	Melville	Monte Carlo	Frankfort
Missouri	STATES	MacDowell	Mitchell	Mustang	x
Mississippi	Florida	Massenet		Mercury	Harrisburg
	Georgia	Mendelsohn	FRUITS		Hartford
	Hawaii	Mozart	fig	HOUSEHOLD	Helena
COLLEGES	Louisiana	Meyerbeer	grape	FURNISHINGS	Honolulu
Fisk	Maine		grapefruit	footstool	Little Rock
Florida	Maryland	AUTHORS (U.S.)	huckleberry	garbage can	Lansing
Fordham	Massachusetts	Faulkner	lemon	hassock	Lincoln
Georgetown		Ferber	lime	highboy	Montgomery
Georgia	COMPOSERS	Fisher	mango	lamp	Montpelier
Goucher	Franck	Gale		mat	Madison
Hamilton	Flotow	Glasgow	AUTOMOBILES		
Harvard	Gounod	Grey	Ford	SPORTS	
Haverford	Grainger	Gunther	Fury	fencing	

Page 194	Page 195	Page 198	Page 237	Page 201	Page 235
1. peter	1. d	1. re	1. do	1. C	1. H
2. valentine	2. h	ear	sod	2. F	2. X
3. dawn	3. b	rate	rods	3. X (hidden)	3. I
4. patience	4. j	trace	doers	4. F	4. A
5. sally	5. l	carter	droves	5. X	5. X
6. benedict	6. n	refract	voiders	6. X	6. C
7. ray	7. c	craftier	divorces	7. C	7. X
8. miles	8. q	2. rue	discovery	8. I	8. X
9. van	9. p	user	2. ran	9. X	9. I
10. pansy	10. f	rouse	near	10. D	10. H
11. mike	11. g	sourer	range	11. A	11. D
12. fanny	12. a	courser	garnet	12. G	12. E
13. alma	13. o	resource	granite	13. H	13. F
14. bill	14. s	3. arc	alerting	14. E	14. G
15. daisy	15. v	scar	triangles	15. G	15. E
16. lizzie	16. r	cares	3. it	16. E	16. G
17. oscar	17. e	cranes	tie	17. H	17. D
18. ted	18. m	ranches	site		
19. nick	19. z	changers	tines	1. C	1. C
20. marshall	20. i	searching	insert	2. F	2. E
21. angelica	21. w	4. pa	stainer	3. X	3. X
22. polly	22. k	ape	granites	4. X	4. C
23. hector	23. C	pear	asserting	5. G	5. E
24. chuck	24. u	drape	signatures	6. X	6. X
25. emery	25. A	paired	4. rid	7. A	7. X
26. morris	26. D	aspired	dire	8. D	8. H
27. dexter	27. t	paradise	cried	9. H	9. X
28. kit	28. B	disparage	priced	10. I	10. A
29. sandy	29. x		pierced	11. E	11. D
30. ward	30. y		decrepit	12. H	12. F
			receipted	13. E	13. I
				14. D	14. G
				15. F	15. G
				16. C	16. F
				17. X	17. I

Page 212

1. bob
2. peep
3. gag
4. tot
5. sees
6. mum
7. sis
   mom
   dad
8. noon
9. did
10. madam
11. ewe
12. tat
13. deed
14. gig
15. toot
16. dad
    pop
17. refer
18. pap
19. sis
20. boob
21. eve
22. pup
23. deified
24. poop
25. level
26. pip
27. radar
28. dewed
29. sexes
30. deled

Page 232

Alabama	Montgomery
Alaska	Juneau
Arizona	Phoenix
Arkansas	Little Rock
California	Sacramento
Colorado	Denver
Connecticut	Hartford
Delaware	Dover
Florida	Tallahassee
Georgia	Atlanta
Hawaii	Honolulu
Idaho	Boise
Illinois	Springfield
Indiana	Indianapolis
Iowa	Des Moines
Kansas	Topeka
Kentucky	Frankfort
Louisiana	Baton Rouge
Maine	Augusta
Maryland	Annapolis
Massachusetts	Boston
Michigan	Lansing
Minnesota	St. Paul
Mississippi	Jackson
Missouri	Jefferson City

Montana	Helena
Nebraska	Lincoln
Nevada	Carson City
New Hampshire	Concord
New Jersey	Trenton
New Mexico	Santa Fe
New York	Albany
North Carolina	Raleigh
North Dakota	Bismark
Ohio	Columbus
Oklahoma	Oklahoma City
Oregon	Salem
Pennsylvania	Harrisburg
Rhode Island	Providence
South Carolina	Columbia
South Dakota	Pierre
Tennessee	Nashville
Texas	Austin
Utah	Salt Lake City
Vermont	Montpelier
Virginia	Richmond
Washington	Olympia
West Virginia	Charleston
Wisconsin	Madison
Wyoming	Cheyenne

Page 80

Afghanistan	Kabul
Bahrain	Manama
Bangladesh	Dacca
Bhutan	Thumphu
Burma	Rangoon
Cambodia	Phnom Penh
Ceylon	Colombo
India	New Delhi
Indonesia	Jakarta
Iran	Teheran
Iraq	Baghdad
Israel	Jerusalem
Japan	Tokyo
Jordan	Amman
Kuwait	Kuwait City
Laos	Vientiane
Lebanon	Beirut
Malaysia	Kuala Lumpur
Mongolia	Ulan Bator
Nepal	Katmandu
North Korea	Pyongyang

North Vietnam	Hanoi
Oman	Muscat
Pakistan	Islamabad
Philippines	Quezon City
Qatar	Al Dewhah
Saudi Arabia	Riyadh
Siberia	Moscow
Singapore	Singapore
South Korea	Seoul
South Vietnam	Saigon
Syria	Damascus
Taiwan	Taipei
Thailand	Bangkok
Turkey	Ankara
United Arab Emirates	Dhabi
Yemen (People's Democratic Republic of)	Aden
Yemen Arab Republic	Sana

Page 242

1. c	7. b	13. f	19. x	25. s
2. h	8. d	14. t	20. A	26. B
3. l	9. r	15. g	21. q	27. w
4. a	10. o	16. y	22. u	28. C
5. i	11. e	17. j	23. m	29. z
6. p	12. n	18. k	24. D	30. v

Page 231

a

b

c

d

e

f

Page 245

1.
b	a	f
d	e	d
k	l	k

2.
a	f	b
e	f	d
l	h	k

3.
a	b	a	b
d	e	d	e
l	k	l	k
j	i	j	i

4.
i	g	j	e
k	c	l	k
g	j	i	g
a	f	f	b

5.
d	e	b	c
c	b	e	b
a	d	a	d
e	f	d	c

6.
a	f	d	c
c	e	b	c
d	c	e	b
b	a	b	a

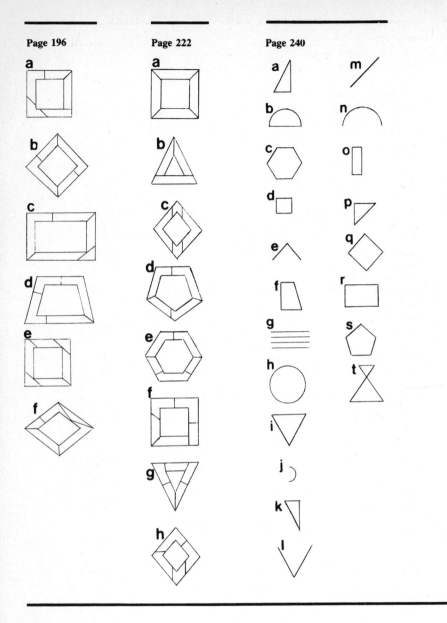

Page 196

Page 222

Page 240

Page 182

Alaska. Its most northerly point is about the 70th parallel; its most westerly point is at the International Date Line (beyond which everything is "east"); its most easterly point is the island of Amchitka, which is just beyond the International Date Line.

Page 197

At least eleven.

Page 209

Nine out of ten people will probably omit the second "the" in the first and third, and the second "a" in the middle saying.

Page 216

Why did you bring the book you know I do not want to be read to out of?